HANS URS VON BALTHASAR'S THEOLOGY OF REPRESENTATION

HANS URS VON BALTHASAR'S THEOLOGY OF REPRESENTATION

God, Drama, and Salvation

JACOB LETT

Foreword by Cyril O'Regan

University of Notre Dame Press
Notre Dame, Indiana

University of Notre Dame Press
Notre Dame, Indiana 46556
undpress.nd.edu

All Rights Reserved

Copyright © 2023 by the University of Notre Dame

Published in the United States of America

Paperback edition published in 2026

Library of Congress Control Number: 2022950310

ISBN: 978-0-268-20502-7 (Hardback)
ISBN: 978-0-268-20503-4 (Paperback)
ISBN: 978-0-268-20504-1 (WebPDF)
ISBN: 978-0-268-20501-0 (Epub3)

GPSR Compliance Inquiries:
Lightning Source France, 1 Av. Johannes Gutenberg, 78310 Maurepas, France
compliance@lightningsource.fr | Phone: +33 1 30 49 23 42

To my Grandma and Grandpa Lett

CONTENTS

	Foreword by Cyril O'Regan	ix
	Acknowledgments	xvii
	Abbreviations	xix
	Introduction	1

PART 1. Theological Foundations for Representation

CHAPTER 1	A Trinitarian Metaphysic and Representation: Divine and Creaturely Pro-Existence	17
CHAPTER 2	Balthasar's Mission Christology: The Theo-Dramatic Representative	52

PART 2. Dramatic Action: He Acts in Our Place That We Might Act in His Place

CHAPTER 3	Dramatic Representation: Recapitulation, Suffering, Tragedy, and Liberation	89
CHAPTER 4	Emplaced *theosis*: The Spirit as the Continual Representative	131
	Conclusion	165
	Notes	173
	Bibliography	223
	Index	253

FOREWORD

The swell of monographs, dissertations, and essays on Hans Urs von Balthasar continues to rise across a huge variety of languages (German, French, English, Spanish, Italian, Polish, etc.) and across continents (mainly Europe and North America, but also Central and South America and Australia). As a theologian who is captivated by the ground of reality as replete and fecund, Balthasar's work is a parable of the divine creative origin or original creativity that he would intimate rather than conceptually capture. The result is a massive volume of interpretation that seems to be the only way to capture the richness of his enormously expansive—perhaps even explosive—oeuvre of more than 100 books and more than 500 essays and translations produced over a sixty-year span of almost tireless literary activity. Because of the perceived novelty of this work—which novelty is entirely unintentional—a large swathe of interpretation has been expository in form, but in the case of the five-volume work by Aidan Nichols, which naturally tends toward its own redundancy, it has proven to be enduring and necessary and thereby has risen to the status of a classic. A not insignificant portion of the commentary material has focused on particular aspects of Balthasar's work, whether his particular use of analogy (Junius Johnson), truth (David C. Schindler), theological aesthetics (Anne Carpenter, Francesca Murphy), eschatology (Nicholas Healy), Christology (Marc Ouellet, G. De Schrijver, Giovani Machesi), God (Gerald O'Hanlon, Pascal Ihde), the Trinity (Rowan Williams, Christopher Hadley, Thomas Krenski, Angela Franks), theological anthropology (Thomas Dalzell, Michele Schumaker), sacramental theology (Jonathan Ciraulo), spirituality (Mark McIntosh), saints (Matthew Moser), Mary (Brendan Leahy), tradition (Oleg Bychkov), political theology (David L. Schindler), theology of religions (Anthony

Sciglitano), or ethics (Christopher Steck). In addition, there have been a number of studies of Balthasar's relations either to particular Christian thinkers, such as Irenaeus (Kevin Mongrain), Maximus the Confessor (Anne Carpenter, Cyril O'Regan), Aquinas (Matthew Levering, Aidan Nichols, James Buckley, Joshua Brotheron), Luther (Rodney Howsare), Ignatius of Loyola (Jacques Sevrais), Barth (Stephen D. Long), Hegel (Matthew Levering, Cyril O'Regan), Bulgakov (Katy Leamy), Charles Taylor (Carolyn Chau), Sobrino (Todd Walatka), and Ferdinand Ulrich (David C. Schindler), or to some broader-based studies on Balthasar's relation to Protestantism (Rodney Howsare), modern Russian religious thought (Jennifer Martin), liberation theology (Todd Walatka), literature (Christopher Denny, Francesca Murphy, Michael P. Murphy), and modernity (Graham Ward, Carolyn Chau, and Cyril O'Regan). With the rise of Balthasar's reputation, recent years have seen a sharp rise in criticism, from a traditional Thomistic perspective (Guy Mansini, Joshua Brotheron), a revisionary Thomistic perspective (Fergus Kerr), a Barthian perspective (Ben Quash), a Rahnerian perspective (Karen Kilby), and finally a feminist perspective (Tina Beattie, Michelle Gonzales). As it goes with the reading of Balthasar, so it goes with the reception of Balthasar in thinkers such as Jean-Luc Marion, Jean-Yves Lacoste, and Jean Louis Chrétien, who, all inspired by Balthasar, continue his thinking either by clarifying and developing his philosophical commitments in a postmodern register (Marion, Lacoste) or by broadening Balthasar's reflection on prayer (Chrétien, Prevot) and liturgy (Lacoste), and deepening his reflection on figures such as Augustine and St. John of the Cross, with respect to which his interpretation regrettably fell somewhat short.

Now, it would be tempting to force these different kinds of interpretation of Balthasar into a temporal-developmental scheme moving from exposition, through studies of particular aspects of his thought and comparative analysis limited to a particular thinker, to large-scale analysis that either involves complex comparative analysis or places Balthasar in a broader thematic of his complex critical engagement with modernity and postmodernity. Yet, this would be illusory. The interpretative output resists being reduced to a simple chronological scheme. Even if there is some discernible shift to the wider-angle view, more criticism, exposition, interpretation of a topic and/or of a particular band of his texts continue apace, as does more local comparative analysis. Indeed, many of these studies are truly splendid, and a number irreplaceable.

How then to place Jacob Lett's *Hans Urs von Balthasar's Theology of Representation: God, Drama, and Salvation* in our general mapping? In one respect the answer is easy: we are dealing with the study of a particular concept, that is, "representation" (*Stellvertretung*), which enjoys pride of place in Balthasar's soteriology and constitutes a decision with regard to the available soteriological options, even if it is not intended to be exclusive of them. However, it is not an exaggeration to say that this study is not simply one particular study among others. Representation is not only a key concept in Balthasar's articulation of theo-drama, but, with due deference to the achievements of his theological aesthetics, it is responsible for one of his more original—even constitutive—theological contributions. *Balthasar's Theology of Representation* is a book that is long overdue.

In another and more important sense, the answer is not so easy. Lett's ambitions seem to go well beyond a local study of Balthasar and do so for precisely Balthasarian reasons. That is, if representation is at the center of Balthasar's soteriology, by the same token it informs and is supported by Balthasar's post-Chalcedonian Christology of Christ's two wills and is similarly supported by Balthasar's articulation of the Trinity. Moreover, for Lett, when we are talking about how representation both informs and is supported by the doctrine of the Trinity, we are not simply talking about the economic Trinity in which Christ is the incarnate or enfleshed Son who bears a filial relation to the Father and whose saving earthly activity is made possible by the Holy Spirit, who is also sent. On the basis of the immanent Trinity being the ground of the economic Trinity, and more particularly that the creative, redemptive, sanctifying activity of the triune God expresses the persons of the Trinity and their relations, Lett concludes that a proper account of representation necessarily involves a discussion of the shape and dynamism of self-giving and self-receiving in Balthasar's articulation of the immanent Trinity. Aware that Balthasar's depiction of the trinitarian tradition has been critiqued as being florid and baroque when it has not been criticized for its failure to stick to the limits of creaturely knowledge, Lett suggests that when speaking of the relations between divine persons, Balthasar is always aware of the analogical nature of his discourse while, nonetheless, insisting that the activity of the persons as sent is expressive of what the divine is *in se*.

In his deeply probing and enormously informed book, Lett is suggesting nothing less than that representation is both a theological keynote and a theological lever in Balthasar's theology, which, if not systematic in a modern sense, nonetheless is always faithful to the matrix of doctrines and the interconnection of the excessive reality they intend. Lett draws attention to the capacity of representation to function as a theological lever when it comes to presenting the Christian understanding of the person as irradicably other, rather than self-centered, indeed, when not incapacitated by sin, grounded in a *pro nobis* that finds its archetype and empowering cause in Christ and its basic pattern in the radical giving and receiving that characterizes the divine life. For the same reason, representation is carried forward into the church as the exemplary—if always imperfect—site of the prolongation of Christ in the mode of representation and the Trinity in the mode of the ultimate condition of its possibility, with the consequence that the church is to be judged with how well it performs its mission of giving and receiving and self-emptying rather than by its use of and access to power.

From the above it is obvious that Lett considers his textual responsibilities to extend far beyond *Theo-Drama* 3 and 4, which is the main textual site for Balthasar's reflection on Christ and how his representative activity involves going into the extremes of identification with our sin and alienation and solidarity with a lost humanity. *Theo-Drama* 1 is in play in that it is there that Balthasar articulates the basic dimensions of drama that the ponderings in *Theo-Drama* 2 of infinite and finite freedom and the prospect of attunement or lack of attunement theologically specify, which in turn gives way to reflections on Christ as our "representative" and the church *en Christo* as the historical site in which representation is present in history in human beings' prayers, liturgies, and works of justice and mercy. And given the trinitarian framing of Christ's representation, Balthasar's trinitarian theology, presented in outline in *Theo-Drama* 5 and clarified and expanded in *Theo-Logic* 2 and 3, becomes relevant for a full account of representation.

In short, both textually and in terms of topics covered, Lett's book is far more ambitious than it at first appears. It most certainly is the best and most focused study of Balthasar's soteriology that has yet appeared. At the same time, it is comprehensive in unexpected ways and throws light on Balthasar's Christology, trinitarian theology, anthropology, ecclesiology, and perhaps to a somewhat lesser extent even his eschatology. Yet this is not all. If with respect to *Balthasar's Theology of Representation* we are speaking of a text of significant theological range, we are equally speaking of a text of significant comparative range. Throughout his tightly woven text, important discussion partners for Balthasar, such as Przywara and Maximus, come in for illuminating treatments that go well beyond the *ipsissima verba* of Balthasar and throw light on such pivotal supporting beams as analogy, with its commitment to similitude qualified by an even greater dissimilitude and a doctrine of two wills that is not only a desideratum for a dramatic account of Christ's saving act, but also a requirement for a full acknowledgment of the humanity of Christ. Nor does Lett avoid the more uncomfortable comparative discussions—oftentimes critical in nature—on the relation between Balthasar and Aquinas and Balthasar and Rahner, both on the level of theological method and with respect to their specific alternatives to Balthasar's dramatic Christology, and in Rahner's case a different account of representation itself. The concerns of Thomists and Rahnerians—particularly the epistemological concerns—are treated with the seriousness they deserve, even as Lett makes the case that if Balthasar's speculative ventures could be trimmed somewhat, nonetheless they have the virtue of rendering a God who truly discloses himself in the world and history. Moreover, Lett allows the discussion between Balthasar and major figures in the theological tradition to expand beyond what we find in Balthasar's texts. To Maximus is added John of Damascus; to Gregory of Nyssa is added Gregory Nazianzen, Basil, and Cyril of Alexandria. This enlarging of the patristic base in Lett's interpretation of Balthasar clearly suggests the ecumenical intent of a text that seems to be equally aimed at Orthodox, Protestant, and Catholic readers.

Finally, however, it should be said that *Balthasar's Theology of Representation* is the work of a real theologian. Lett is a real admirer of Balthasar and throughout is respectful of his theological achievements, in general, and supportive of his dramatic theology of representation, which, for him, is nothing short of a *Grundkategorie*, in particular. He manages to walk the fine line between critical and ironic distance. Lett does all that is possible to articulate representation in the immediate context of soteriology, while indicating the need to look beyond the immediate context, but in uplifting some conversations of Balthasar and adding others, he does so with a view not solely toward a recommendation and defense of what Balthasar has said, but with regard to *die Sache*, that is, what is intended by Balthasar's theological discourse. Because Balthasar is faithful to *die Sache*, it is not sufficient to repeat him. One must supplement him, in some cases complete this thinking, bring out the unthought thought or at least develop a thought that was merely inchoate. Thus, Lett has fully engaged the theological literature on representation and not simply with that of Balthasar and the thinkers whom he evokes or on whom he depends. In addition, Lett is also willing to entertain criticisms of Balthasar, some judged to be fair, others judged to be unfair, and although he does not signal criteria of distinction between them, Lett operatively tends to focus far more on the former than the latter. The openness to criticism of Balthasar is a feature of the entire text and is evident not only in Lett's discussion of representation in the narrow soteriological sense, but as it bears on and is supported by would-be independent areas of theological inquiry, such as theological anthropology, the Trinity, and ecclesiology. Of particular note is Lett's surprisingly detailed discussion of Balthasar's articulation of the immanent Trinity, which has alarmed Thomists, Rahnerians, and feminists alike. Overall, Lett defends Balthasar while granting that the Swiss theologian may not be careful enough in indicating the analogical and merely symbolic nature of his discourse. In particular, Lett's discussion of the status of Balthasar's placial and spatial metaphors is as good as can be found in all the commentary literature on Balthasar.

In sum, *Balthasar's Theology of Representation* is the best book yet on the crucially important topic of representation as it functions in Balthasar's distinctive soteriology, one of the best books on Balthasar's Christology, and one that has important things to say regarding Balthasar's articulation of the Trinity, both with respect to how it connects with Christology and how the symbols and hyperboles adduced regarding the immanent Trinity can be justified. Most importantly—and it bears emphasizing—it is a book of deep theological thinking, thinking both with Balthasar and with those who think like him but also thinking with those who are indifferent to him or belong to entirely different theological dispensations. This is the latest offering on Balthasar offered by the University of Notre Dame Press. It will take a seat at the roundtable of the extraordinary and fine books on the great Swiss theologian and will shine with others, such as Anne Carpenter's *Theo-Poetics: Hans Urs von Balthasar and the Risk of Art and Being* (2014), Jennifer Martin's *Hans Urs von Balthasar and the Critical Appropriation of Russian Religious Thought* (2014), and Jonathan Ciraulo's *The Eucharistic Form of Theology: Hans Urs von Balthasar's Sacramental Theology* (2022).

Cyril O'Regan
Huisking Professor of Theology
University of Notre Dame

ACKNOWLEDGMENTS

Appreciation is owed to many people and communities who have contributed to this research. The faculty and students of Nazarene Theological College, partner institution of the University of Manchester, have enriched my life and research. Special thanks go to the two supervisors of this project when it was in the form of a PhD dissertation. Thomas A. Noble's historical and theological insight and insistence on clear, ordered writing kept my work grounded. Likewise, the overall contribution of my research would be much different without Stephen John Wright's reading recommendations and consistent challenge to be more critical and constructive.

Various scholars helped to reshape this work into its present form. David Law's German suggestions prompted me to clarify my translations. Brandon Gallaher directed me to the works of Ferdinand Ulrich, whose influence on Balthasar is often underexplored, and Martin Bieler provided me documents of Ulrich's and helped me to make a crucial connection between Ulrich's metaphysics and the concept of *Stellvertretung*. In addition, the recommendations offered by the scholars who reviewed this work for the University of Notre Dame Press led to a much improved manuscript. I am incredibly appreciative of the time they dedicated to reading the manuscript and thinking about how I might reshape it. Finally, I'm beyond honored that Cyril O'Regan engaged my theology and wrote the foreword.

The majority of this research was completed while I was a faculty member at MidAmerica Nazarene University. I am indebted to the ministry faculty for offering me my first place to teach theology and for extending grace to me: I had to decline numerous requests and work outside of the office to focus on my research. Additionally, I'm grateful to the library staff for tirelessly searching for the books and journal articles I requested.

Special thanks to the staff of the Balthasar Archives in Basel for sending me a vital document that is no longer published.

The friendship and encouragement of three people pushed my research forward at various stages. Junius Johnson's yearly meetings with me at the American Academy of Religion provided me the encouragement to continue when I was doubting the validity of my project. Jonathan Platter's reading accountability, regular Skype conversations, and writing feedback have significantly shaped my theology, writing, and research interests. Dean Flemming modeled for me what it means to pursue scholarship with faithfulness and humility.

Thanks also to my many family members, whose decades of support, love, and competition molded me into the person I am. My mom and dad have always displayed pride in my abilities and work ethic, leaving me with an insatiable desire to continue my education.

I thank my wife, Whitney. I will fondly remember the hours we spent discussing my research over walks, the freedom she extended to me when I studied beyond the expected time, the patience she had with me when I misplaced various items or pretended to listen while I was lost in a thought, and the atmosphere of rest she cultivated when I put pressure on myself to push my way through fatigue. Also, my children, Rowan and Beatrice, have cultivated laughter and love that would otherwise be unknown to me. The joy they bring to our home is always a welcome break from research.

An impossible debt is owed to my grandparents. The educational endeavors that made this book and my vocation a possibility would not have been feasible without my grandparents' generosity. Furthermore, they have been exemplary witnesses to the kind of faithfulness, continued growth, and sacrificial dedication that I strive for. In a sense, the central argument of this book is made concrete in the way they have consistently "acted in my place" and have done so in such a manner that my own capacity, freedom, and responsibility were heightened by their action. I dedicate this book to them.

ABBREVIATIONS

Works by Hans Urs von Balthasar

CA	*The Christian and Anxiety*
CL	*Cosmic Liturgy: The Universe according to Maximus the Confessor*
Credo	*Credo: Meditations on the Apostles' Creed*
DJ	*Does Jesus Know Us? Do We Know Him?*
EP	*Epilogue*
ET	*Explorations in Theology* I–V
GL	*The Glory of the Lord: A Theological Aesthetics* I–VII
H	*Herrlichkeit: Eine theologische Ästhetik* I–III
HMR	*To the Heart of the Mystery of Redemption*
HW	*Heart of the World*
LA	*Love Alone Is Credible*
MP	*Mysterium Paschale: The Mystery of Easter*
MW	*My Work: In Retrospect*
PT	*Presence and Thought: An Essay on the Religious Philosophy of Gregory of Nyssa*
TD	*Theo-Drama: Theological Dramatic Theory* I–V
TDg	*Theodramatik* I–IV
TH	*A Theology of History*
TL	*Theo-Logic: Theological Logical Theory* I–III
TLg	*Theologik* I–III
TKB	*The Theology of Karl Barth*
YC	*You Crown the Year with Your Goodness: Sermons through the Liturgical Year*

Other Works

CD	Karl Barth, *Church Dogmatics* I–IV
DS	*Enchiridion Symbolorum: A Compendium of Creeds, Definitions, and Declarations of the Catholic Church*
HA	Ferdinand Ulrich, *Homo Abyssus: The Drama of the Question of Being*
ST	Thomas Aquinas, *Summa Theologiae* (Blackfriars edition)

Full reference information can be found in the bibliography.

INTRODUCTION

Hans Urs von Balthasar (1905–88), a Swiss Catholic theologian whom Henri de Lubac called "the most cultured man of Europe," reflected deeply on the relationship between God, drama, and salvation.[1] Balthasar's prodigious fifteen-volume trilogy reflects on the transcendentals—beauty, goodness, and truth—and imports art, drama, and philosophy to a degree uncommon in other major theological projects. The second part of the trilogy, *Theo-Drama: Theological Dramatic Theory* (1973–83), reimagines the goodness of God revealed in Jesus Christ in dramatic terms.[2] "I regard the last three volumes of the Theodramatics as the culmination and capstone of his work, where all the themes of his theology converge and are fused into a synthesis of remarkable creativity and originality, an achievement which makes him one of the great theological minds of the twentieth century," says Edward T. Oakes.[3] Of fundamental significance to these three volumes is Balthasar's "dramatic soteriology,"[4] which narrates the "dramatic action" of God's entry onto the world stage in Christ.[5] "God's entire world drama is concentrated on and hinges on this scene," says Balthasar. "This is the theo-drama into which the world *and* God have their ultimate input; here absolute freedom enters into created freedom, interacts with created freedom and acts *as* created freedom."[6]

Yet, contemporary atonement theology in general, and, therefore, Balthasar's dramatic soteriology, stands in contentious territory. In 1979, British philosopher A. J. Ayer declared, "Of all religions, a strong case can be made against Christianity as the worst, because it rests on the allied doctrines of original sin and vicarious atonement, which are intellectually contemptible and morally outrageous."[7] As the Enlightenment disabused society of the mythological[8] and feminists critique the tacit and grotesque abuse underlying traditional understandings of the cross,[9] the church finds itself in a quagmire, turning its proclamation of the cross into a stammering question: *Did God kill Jesus?*[10] Recognizing this abject quandary, Peter Schmiechen states, "It is difficult to have confidence if one does not know what to proclaim regarding Christ. Thus at the heart of the church's struggle to find their identity and mission are the christological questions posed by the life, death, and resurrection of Jesus. When ordained and lay leaders are not clear about atonement, there can be no confidence regarding vocation, ministry, or the future of the church."[11] A host of contemporary atonement literature has sought to reposition God's people on firm ground,[12] and an "egalitarian approach" to atonement has ensued, with no atonement model superseding the others.[13]

Dorothee Sölle's *Christ the Representative* (1965), a work Rowan Williams says is "important, difficult, and (in the English-speaking world) largely neglected,"[14] recommends that the term "representative" (*Stellvertreter*) be reconsidered in a "post-theistic" age: "Its linguistic advantage is that it is more abstract than titles like King and Lord, that it is not already appropriated and filled out with images. It seemed easier therefore to take up this term again and to test the weight of meaning it will bear in an age very different in outlook."[15] Similarly, as developed in his doctoral dissertation-turned-book *Sanctorum Communio*, and culminating in his crown work, *Ethics*, representation stands at the heart of Dietrich Bonhoeffer's Christology, ecclesiology, and personal ethics.[16] In fact, many major German theologians employ the term positively, including Barth, Kasper, Moltmann, Pannenberg, Ratzinger.[17]

Balthasar also seeks to rehabilitate the category of representation within a broad and textured theological schema. In an article published in *Communio* the year he passed away, Balthasar states, "The one word that most centrally characterizes the existence of Jesus Christ is representation."[18] In fact, the journal *Communio* itself is the fruition of Balthasar, Henri de Lubac, and Joseph Ratzinger's enduring companionship and is guided by the idea of communion with God and others—communion not simply defined by life together, but by "an active life for each other, and, thus, as an act of 'representation.'"[19] Representation is anything but another theological category, neatly set alongside a list of others. Reflected in the trinitarian life of God, representation is integral to Balthasar's metaphysics, Christology, dramatic soteriology, ecclesiology, and theological methodology. An account of how all of this is so is in order.

Stellvertretung, Theo-Drama, and Dramatic Soteriology

Balthasar and Sölle both seek to define *Stellvertretung*.[20] *Stellvertretung* is a combination of the German *vertreten*, meaning to "stand in for," and *Stelle*, which means "place." According to Williams, "*Stellvertretung* is acting in or from the place of another, 'standing in' for the other, being actively there on behalf of the other, negotiating for the other."[21] It is often translated as "representation" or "substitution" in English, but neither term fully captures "the resonance and concreteness of the German."[22] Daniel P. Bailey believes the most exact English equivalent is "place-taking,"[23] but Sölle distinguishes *Stellvertretung* from "substitution," noting that the word "substitution" (*Ersatzmann*) is more exclusive and is related to "replacement."[24] Therefore, "place-taking" may not be the best translation. According to Morna D. Hooker, there can be both *exkludierende Stellvertretung* ("exclusive place-taking") and *inkludierende Stellvertretung* ("inclusive place-taking"). Exclusive place-taking can refer to a substitutionary act, such as someone suffering in place of another. Inclusive place-taking involves an action with others (such as parenting) and comes closer to what is usually meant by representation in English.[25] Karl Rahner was very critical of soteriologies of *exkludierende Stellvertretung* because they depict Christ's action as a replacement for human freedom and participation. Rahner preferred the term *Repräsentation*, but he was willing to use *Stellvertretung* in his mature theology so long as it was a soteriology of *inkludierende Stellvertretung*.[26]

Therefore, it is clear, as Stephan Schaede notes, that it is difficult to comprehend the precise meaning and relevance of *Stellvertretung* in German because its meaning is contextual to how it is used soteriologically.[27]

The thoroughness of Schaede's research, alongside three other large German works specifically on *Stellvertretung*, demonstrates the complexity and relevance of the *Grundkategorie*. Karl-Heinz Menke's is the most comprehensive, showing how the linguistic, biblical, historical, and theological aspects of the term function in various thinkers.[28] This brief review of the various issues at stake in the definition, function, and translation of *Stellvertretung* demonstrates the need to define and qualify the term by analyzing its development in Balthasar's theology.

The translation of *Stellvertretung* in Balthasar's translated works includes "representation" (*TD3*, *TD4*), "substitution" (*EP*, *TL2*, *TD5*), and "vicarious representation" (*EP*). Although there are places in his dramatic soteriology where Christ's work is exclusive and substitutionary, Balthasar is chiefly concerned to portray the Christ–creation relationship in participatory and inclusive terms. Therefore, I employ the term "representation" from here forward and will argue that it depicts Balthasar's theology of *Stellvertretung* more accurately than "substitution."

Representation is used sparingly in Balthasar's early works. Yet, Andrew Louth argues that it is foreshadowed in and essential to *The Heart of the World* (1945), a book inspired by Adrienne von Speyr's mystical experience of Holy Saturday,[29] but it is not explicitly present because Balthasar does not use technical language.[30] Given that representation is a key Barthian soteriological theme, one can find it in Balthasar's *The Theology of Karl Barth* (1951),[31] even though Barth's full account of representation in *Church Dogmatics* IV.1 was not yet published (1953). The editor of this volume notes the difficulty of translating *Stellvertretung* to English without losing some of its meaning.[32] In volume 3 of *The Glory of the Lord* (1962), Balthasar describes Charles Péguy as a unique Christ figure who simultaneously represents the world and the church. The term Balthasar uses here is *Repräsentation*, which he defines as standing in "solidarity" (*Solidarität*) with the other.[33] Solidarity is the primary theme Balthasar uses to describe Christ's action for humanity in the final volume of *The Glory of the Lord* (1969).[34] Furthermore, although Veronica Donnelly says that *Stellvertretung* holds an "important and central place" in *Theologie der drei Tage* (1970; English edition, *Mysterium Paschale*),[35] Balthasar notes that *Mysterium Paschale* focused on "solidarity with the dead," which he will later say was a "compromise" and is replaced by *Stellvertretung* in volume 2 of the *Theo-Logic* (1985).[36] "Solidarity," Balthasar notes, "is much too weak to express the whole depth of the identification taken on by Jesus."[37]

To whatever extent *Stellvertretung* is an underlying theme of Balthasar's early theology, it manifests itself as one of the central themes of Balthasar's theology in the mid-1970s and throughout the 1980s.[38] In 1973, Balthasar directly addressed representation in an article titled "Über Stellvertretung."[39] Three years later, he published a booklet titled "Stellvertretung: Schlüsselwort christlichen Lebens."[40] It is in this booklet that representation overtly moves to the center of Balthasar's theology: "The idea of representation . . . stands at the heart of Christian dogma."[41] Also, in 1977 he defended the significance of representation at the priestly association Lumen Gentium. This defense was later published in *To the Heart of the Mystery of Redemption*.[42] In 1980, when *TD4* was published, Balthasar delivered an acceptance speech for an honorary doctorate at the Catholic University of America where he states that the entire Christian faith hangs on the notion of representation.[43]

Although representation shows up in the *Theo-Logic*, the third part of the trilogy, and is a vital concept in the *Epilogue* of the trilogy,[44] the most mature theology of representation is developed in the *Theo-Drama*. In *TD3* (1978), Balthasar quoted Joseph Ratzinger's article on representation in the *Handbuch Theologischer GrundBegriffe*.[45] Ratzinger states, "*Stellvertretung* is one of the fundamental categories of biblical revelation; however, arguably due to the lack of a suitable philosophical model, the concept's development in theology has been stunted and has ultimately been largely relegated to purely devotional literature."[46] Likewise, Sölle claims, "The term 'representation' may still retain its meaning in law, sociology, and psychology, but in theology it has become colorless."[47] Ratzinger's charge, and perhaps Balthasar's concerns with Rahner's soteriology,[48] prompted Balthasar to provide a theological foundation for representation in his Christology in *TD3* and in his doctrine of the Trinity in *TD4* (1980). In the preface to *TD4*, Balthasar states, "One of the chief concerns of this volume is the exact elaboration [*Herausarbeitung*] of the term representation, which after a period of neglect suddenly enters newly into the light."⁴⁹ The English edition of *TD4* translates *Herausarbeitung* as "precise definition,"⁵⁰ which is misleading since Balthasar never provides one, nor would a precise definition be expected given his dramatic conception of the theological language,⁵¹ which is often displayed in his elliptical, analogical, and idiosyncratic style.⁵²

To move toward a theology of representation, we need to understand how it fits within Balthasar's dramatic theory generally and his doctrine of atonement specifically. Balthasar's theological dramatic theory assimilates the language of theater into his theological vision.⁵³ Drama is about characters, action, and roles, the collaboration and conflict of which perform a narrative.⁵⁴ Such dramatic terms inexorably appeal to humanity's social existence:

> As human beings, we already have a preliminary grasp of what drama is; we are acquainted with it from the complications, tensions, catastrophes, and reconciliations which characterize our lives as individuals and in interaction with others . . . nowhere is the character of existence demonstrated more clearly than in stage drama . . . probably nowhere else but in this interplay of relationships (which is the essence of the theater) can we see so clearly the questionable nature and ambiguity not only of theatre but also of existence itself, which the theatre illuminates.⁵⁵

Where else better to grasp God's action than on the stage of existence itself, a stage that God freely inhabits as the chief actor, signaling the move from drama to *theo-drama*. *Theo-Drama* is the elliptical portrayal of the interplay of divine and human freedom (*TD2* and *TD3: The Dramatis Personae*), the dramatic action of the triune God on the stage of creation (*TD4: The Action*), and the final movement of created freedom into the Infinite (*TD5: The Final Act*).

Representation stands in unimpeded relation to drama in both Sölle and Balthasar. How does the role of one actor affect the roles and places of the others? What is the relationship between existents (*Wesen*) and places (*Stellen*)? "Our agency is also conditioned by the related fact of being ineluctably *social* (it involves entanglement with the things experienced by other people)," says Ben Quash. "In this way, drama raises with a particular, authoritative agency the key question of what it is not only to be free, but (more than that) to be free in the company of others."[56] For Sölle, the reason why one person's role cannot replace another person's is because the world stage takes place in the *theatrum Dei*. Each person is assigned a role, a part in the great play of creation, and is thus irreplaceable. It is only in the *theatrum mundi* that one's identity can be replaced through the substitution of another.[57] Such concerns present Balthasar with a tantalizing *aporia* in the face of God's universal action for humanity in Christ: How does the sphere of Christ's action extend to the ambit of others without replacing or consuming it? The answer to the question lies at the heart of Balthasar's doctrine of atonement, his dramatic soteriology, in *TD4*.[58]

Following a lengthy review of historical and contemporary atonement models,[59] Balthasar asks, "Are the systems hitherto attempted sufficiently dramatic? Or have they always failed to include or to give enough weight to one element or another that is essential to the complete dramatic plot? For no element may be excluded here: God's entire world drama is concentrated on and hinges on this scene."[60] Several theses lie behind Balthasar's "dramatic" judgment: a recognition of the various movements and countermovements needed to interpret properly the roles of characters involved in the scene of the cross and its meaning (hermeneutics), the transformative interaction that occurs between the actions on the stage and the audience (ecclesiology), and the relation between the cross and the final act (eschatology).[61] In response to the problems associated with the history of atonement theology, Balthasar opens up the curtain and proposes five scriptural motifs to represent his dramatic soteriology, which if given equal attention he believes will encompass the full meaning of the work of salvation in Christ:

> (1) The Son gives himself, through God the Father, for the world's salvation. (2) The Sinless One "changes places" with sinners. While, in principle, the Church Fathers understand this in a radical sense, it is only in the modern variations of the theories of representation that the consequences are fully drawn out. (3) Man is thus set free (ransomed, redeemed, released). (4) More than this, however, he is initiated into the divine life of the Trinity. (5) Consequently, the whole process is shown to be the result of an initiative on the part of divine love.[62]

Since drama is opposed to the factuality and systematization of epics and since the "cross explodes all systems,"[63] Balthasar does not proceed with a detailed examination and precise integration of the five motifs, but rather avers that one must ascend from the surface meaning to the essential theological meaning, or, to put it more prosaically, from the cross to the Trinity,[64] which, as in Aquinas, always concludes with mystery.[65] Balthasar's theological movement up the "analogical ladder"[66] and back down to the dramatic *communio sanctorum* is the key to his soteriology. This comes to expression in motif 2: the patristic exchange formula interpreted through the lens of representation. "For von Balthasar, only the notion of Christ 'vicariously representing' sinful mankind before God can capture the essential meaning of the mystery of the Cross," states Robert Pesarchick.[67] Aidan Nichols also perceives this, noting that the other four motifs are "held together—coherently united—by the *Stellvertretung* idea."[68] The self-giving of God for humanity (motif 1) reveals God's triune life of generative activity for the other (motif 5), providing the exchange of places a theological foundation (motif 2), which results in humanity's liberation from sin (motif 3) and participation in the triune life (motif 4). Chapter 1 unravels this summary in detail.

From this brief excursus, we can observe a dramatic definition of "representation" as "place acting" or "action in, with, and for the other"—the definitions operative throughout this book—and the inauguration of what I entitle a "dramatic exchange formula" interpreted through a theology of representation: Christ acted in humanity's place that humanity might act in his place.

The Muddled State of Balthasar's Theology of *Stellvertretung*

Numerous studies on Balthasar note the significance of representation in his theology.[69] Ellero Babini calls Balthasar's theology of representation his "essential contribution" to contemporary theology.[70] To whatever extent this may be true, its place in contemporary theology is dubious, for several reasons. To the massive scope of Balthasar's corpus in number and topic, Junius Johnson adds that Balthasar "often speaks in an incomplete or non-precise way about topics that seem by their very nature to require utmost precision."⁷¹ When Balthasar says in *TD*4 that one of the primary aims of the volume is to provide an exact elaboration of the concept of "representation" and later acknowledges in the *Epilogue* to his trilogy that the term "representation" is useless if one does not "see the sense of it,"⁷² one would foresee an adroit and ordered exposition—a reasonable expectation that is further heightened by Balthasar's grand claims regarding the term's integral place in doctrine. But such a detailed elaboration is not offered. Donnelly confirms this concern, remarking that Balthasar's theological intention in using the term *Stellvertretung* "is not easy to grasp due to his style of writing which is cyclical and synthetic rather than systematic."⁷³ At best, Balthasar gestures toward theological foundations for representation and criticizes inept interpretations.

We can further see how Balthasar's formulation of representation is incipient by looking at how secondary works are at odds over how to best conceptualize his use of representation. The translation of the term *Stellvertretung* is contested: Louth argues "substitution" theologically depicts Balthasar's account,⁷⁴ yet Steffen Lösel labels it "christological representation" as conceptually distinct from "substitution" or "biblical sacrifice."⁷⁵ Aidan Nichols more accurately asserts a nondivaricated translation that it is "at once representation and vicarious substitution."⁷⁶ Others attempt to interpret Balthasar through a particular atonement model: David Brown, David Coffey, and Alyssa Lyra Pitstick claim Balthasar aligns with the framework of penal substitution,⁷⁷ while Gerald F. O'Hanlon contends that he works with a nonpenal approach to atonement.⁷⁸ Antione Birot agrees with O'Hanlon, calling it an "authentic vicarious atonement."⁷⁹ John R. Cihak believes an integration of Anselm's and Luther's theories of atonement is at the heart of Balthasar's soteriology,⁸⁰ but Pesarchick translates *Stellvertretung* as "vicarious representation"⁸¹ to differentiate Balthasar from Luther's "vicarious substitution."⁸¹ *Stauro*-monistic readings (interpretations that are exclusively preoccupied with Balthasar's theology of the cross) of Balthasar's theology of representation further complicate this onerous conundrum. For example, Michele Schumacher asserts,

> The concept of representation in Balthasar's theology is obscured, in my judgment, by a subtle reversal of the Creator–creature relationship so that the creature rather than the Creator becomes the primary referent. In this

understanding, Christ is conceived as the representative of the human race, not because he is the eternal prototype in whose image creation is fashioned, but because and insofar as he responds in time to the human race's needs by taking humanity's place in the jaws of death and even beyond the gates of hell.[82]

We shall see in chapters 2 and 4 that a broader reading of Balthasar's theology of representation would recount his trinitarian and christological structure and the role representation tacitly plays in *theosis*, depriving Schumacher's judgment of warrant and, at the very minimum, complicating a reductive vision of Balthasar's soteriology as penal substitution. An example of this type of reductive reading can be seen in David Coffey's interpretation of Balthasar's theology of the cross. He labels it a version of penal substitution, but in his account he primarily uses *Mysterium Paschale*, which is not a mature presentation of Balthasar's theology of the cross.[83]

Considering all that we have raised thus far, it is disappointing that more time has not been given to analyzing the nuances of Balthasar's usage of representation, establishing its place within his larger theological oeuvre, and developing the category further with various interlocutors. Balthasar's theology of representation is given exclusive attention in two unpublished dissertations, Schumacher's article, and two book chapters.[84] None of these provides an extensive theological description, analysis, or development of representation. Additionally, most of what has been said about Balthasar's conception of *Stellvertretung* was published prior to a current wave of Balthasarian books and articles (Jennifer Newsome Martin, Cyril O'Regan, Todd Walatka, Anne Carpenter, etc.) that constructively reexamines his theology in light of the way that he creatively "remembers" the tradition by dramatically retrieving its theologians, saints, and artists.[85] Therefore, this book addresses this lacuna in the scholarship.

Moving Forward

In this book, I analyze and develop the relationship between God, drama, and salvation in Hans Urs von Balthasar's *Theo-Drama* by constructing a theology of representation. With "*theology* of representation" in the main title, I show how representation is a *Grundkategorie* of Balthasar's doctrine of the Trinity, Christology, and dramatic soteriology. Representation is grounded in the generative activity of the triune processions, inherent to created being, depicted in the Christ–creation metaphysic, universalized in Christ's dramatic action for humanity, and rendered essential to the theotic activity of the *communio sanctorum*. Thus I fulfill my objectives in this book by (1) exploring relevant aspects of Balthasar's trinitarian theology and Christology in order to lay a foundation for a metaphysic of representation and a dramatic reading of the patristic exchange formula, (2) presenting a systematic analysis of how representation functions in Balthasar's dramatic soteriology, (3) analyzing the relationship between tragedy, the cross, and the Trinity in Balthasar's dramatic depiction of the cross, and (4) constructing proposals for the underdeveloped features of Balthasar's theology of representation.

Furthermore, to help achieve these four aims, I argue how representation—acting in the place of the other—not only shapes doctrine but also the nature of theological knowledge and the theological task. To understand Balthasar's theology, one must first understand that Balthasar perceives his theotic mission as theologian is to act in the place of the tradition. In his series on the church fathers, Balthasar explicitly connects his dramatic way of reading the tradition to representation and acknowledges that it is the method that he will use to write the series.[86] His "action in the place of" the tradition does not consist of a repetition of past data, but is a dramatic reenactment of its theological and spiritual spirit for his own place and time. The tradition, in the words of Cyril O'Regan, is something that can be "given back to"; it is "an open-ended process of continual excavation, perpetual quarrying of what has not been said, what has not been said adequately about the exigent reality of love and forgiveness which governs all Christian response and makes it possible."[87] Seeking to "rehabilitate a sense of the suppleness and fluidity of tradition," Balthasar creatively retrieves the tradition by considering its relation to the present cultural, spiritual, and political stage.[88] His method of retrieval, according to Martin and Walatka, is less systematic and logical and more contemplative, spiritual, and experimental, like that of

Origen, making Balthasar's theology "adventurous" but "difficult to pin down and classify."[89] I argue that this way of representing the tradition is deeply embedded in Balthasar's reconsideration of the dramatic relation between Christ and those he represents, a relation that is mediated by the Holy Spirit. Balthasar makes the connection between his theological task and representation, but I go further and show how language itself is a form of action for the other, a connection made by Balthasar's friend Ferdinand Ulrich, who was one of Balthasar's most significant interlocutors when writing the *Theo-Drama*.

Therefore, by developing Balthasar's theology of representation and its relation to his theological task, my book joins a growing list of scholarly works that offer sympathetic and constructive, and in some places critical, interpretations of Balthasar. In particular, I focus on aspects of Balthasar's doctrine of the Trinity, Christology, and dramatic soteriology that are relevant to representation, yet are often criticized by scholars. I argue that critics may fail to discern the panoply of hidden voices involved in key texts,[90] and it is these voices that constitute Balthasar's dramatic portrayal of the divine life and human salvation. Regarding Balthasar's theology broadly, I seek to draw out the presence of three of Balthasar's most significant mentors and friends: Erich Przywara, Henri de Lubac, and Ferdinand Ulrich. Balthasar acknowledges that he would be incapable of communicating theology without them,[91] yet he often leaves the work of discerning their tacit voices to the reader. Regarding Balthasar's theology of representation specifically, I focus on the particular voice of Norbert Hoffmann. Balthasar commends Hoffmann's understanding of representation after the critical sections of *TD*4 on representation are completed.[92] I reexamine parts of the *Theo-Drama* by educing these general and specific voices in Balthasar's reenactment of the tradition and develop Balthasar further by considering their key ideas. In addition, as with Walatka's book on Balthasar, I also situate Balthasar in "dialogical encounter" with other voices in order to move Balthasar's theology of representation forward in a manner that is faithful to his own way of theologizing.[93] My chosen interlocutors are Dietrich Bonhoeffer, Dorothee Sölle, and Rowan Williams.[94] I choose these theologians because they also desire to rehabilitate the concept of *Stellvertretung* and their practical and theological concerns about how the term should function are similar to Balthasar's.⁹⁵

Overall, this book is a careful and sympathetic exposition of Balthasar, like Johnson's *Christ and Analogy*; it reinterprets aspects of Balthasar's doctrine by elucidating his dramatic way of representing the tradition, like Martin's *Hans Urs Von Balthasar and the Critical Appropriation of Russian Religious Thought*; and it develops underrealized "theo-dramatic" features of Balthasar's thought by "extending and correcting" his vision, like Walatka's *Von Balthasar and the Option for the Poor*.⁹⁶ I hope to move Balthasar's theology of representation forward—an inevitable outcome of a dramatic understanding of theological language⁹⁷—elucidating, judging, amending, and developing his theology. As in Anne Carpenter's book on Balthasar's theo-poetics, I am not seeking to give a final "endpoint" to Balthasar's theology of representation, which would contradict Balthasar's own mode of theologizing, but rather to offer a "road map" that brings to light the variety of voices, logics, and dramatic movements at play.⁹⁸

To develop the argument of this book, I employ a two-part structure, with the motifs of Balthasar's dramatic soteriology forming the outline of the chapters. Part 1, "Theological Foundations for Representation," answers the question, How does Christian doctrine provide a foundation for and distinction between divine and human representation? I establish the definition, shape, and possibility of representation (Balthasar's motif 2) by critically sketching some of the most basic theological commitments in Balthasar's doctrine of the Trinity (motif 5) in chapter 1 and Christology (motif 1) in chapter 2. The aim of the two chapters in part 1 is to show how representation is mutually involved with Balthasar's doctrine and, by showing how that is the case, to produce further theological foundations for the category and to reinterpret certain aspects of Balthasar's doctrine. Part 2, "Dramatic Action: He Acts in Our Place That We Might Act in His Place," seeks to define Balthasar's theology of representation through the explication of the soteriological themes of redemption (motif 3) and *theosis* (motif 4). Chapter 3 defines how representation functions in Balthasar's dramatic theology of redemption. Chapter 4 shows how representation is essential to understanding humanity's participation in the triune life and is related to ecclesiology and ethics. Part 2 builds on the theological components of part 1, which will allow us to amend Balthasar's dramatic depiction of the cross and further construct the relationship between representation and *theosis*. The cumulative result is a systematic treatment of how representation functions in Balthasar's theology and a robust understanding of how it is a central category of his dramatic soteriology.

PART I
THEOLOGICAL FOUNDATIONS FOR REPRESENTATION

CHAPTER ONE

A TRINITARIAN METAPHYSIC AND REPRESENTATION

Divine and Creaturely Pro-Existence

The ontic possibility for God's self-emptying in the Incarnation and death of Jesus lies in God's eternal self-emptying in the mutual self-surrender of the Persons of the Trinity . . . the possibility of Jesus's expiatory "pro-existence" [lies in] the "pro" of the Persons within the Godhead: their reciprocal action on behalf of each other.
—Hans Urs von Balthasar, *TD5*, 243–44

The inextricable integration of Balthasar's dramatic soteriology with his doctrine of the Trinity is one of the prime features of the *Theo-Drama*.[1] The relationship between the "guilty and the Lamb," the Representative and the represented, is metaphysically situated in the Trinity, which to Balthasar is the "ever-present, inner presupposition of the doctrine of the Cross."[2] Thus, to explicate *The Action* (*TD4*) and *The Last Act* (*TD5*), which is the subject of the second half of this book, we must consider Balthasar's trinitarian metaphysic and grammar. Interpreting Balthasar with the help of his mentor Erich Przywara, we can say that "metaphysic" here means "a 'going behind' into the 'back-grounds' of being." Przywara states, "What is at issue, then, is the formal question of this 'ground and end and definition in itself,' which poses itself here from the question of being as being."[3] For Balthasar, the immanent Trinity is the "ground and end and definition" of all being, hence the chapter title, "A Trinitarian Metaphysic." The central aim of the chapter, then, is to answer the question: How does the trinitarian background of being shape and provide a foundation for a theology of representation? In short, I hope to demonstrate how Jesus can "act-for-the-other" (pro-existence) because acting-for-the-other is already part of triune and creaturely being.

Balthasar's theology of representation is grounded in the soteriological movement from the economic to the immanent Trinity, an analogical apprehending he believes is essential to understanding representation and the patristic exchange formula.[4] Given the terseness of his account and its narrow focus on trinitarian distance, I hope to develop Balthasar's metaphysic of representation further. To do so, I first offer a sympathetic reinterpretation of Balthasar's spatialization of the triune life in the *Theo-Drama* by considering further developments in the *Theo-Logic*, the influence of his key interlocutors, and a musical understanding of space. This may seem like a detour from the primary goal of this book, but Balthasar's spatial analogies are so pivotal to his theology of representation that a failure to engage the critical concerns that they have raised would jeopardize this project. After doing this, I then interpret the Trinity through the category of "pro-existence," which shows how representation is an essential aspect of triune processions. In the last section, I extend the trinitarian metaphysic to creaturely being, which will set the foundation for and definition of christological *pro nobis*, representation, and a dramatic exchange formula. The resultant framework situates redemption and *theosis* in a trinitarian theology of representation and displays the unity of Balthasar's five soteriological motifs.

Representation, Trinitarian Spatial Analogies, and the *analogia entis*

In the preface to *TD*4, Balthasar notes that one of the primary intentions of the volume is to provide an exact elaboration of his theology of representation.[5] He offers this elaboration in a short section entitled "On the Nature of 'Representation.'" Balthasar's account of representation is driven by questions about the rationality of representation: "How can someone 'represent' sinners?"[6] How can a person *act in the place of* another person? He is still wrestling with these questions when he writes the *Epilogue* of the trilogy: "One speaks constantly of 'vicarious representation.' But please, this is valid only if I see the sense of it. But just think of what this really is supposed to mean: First, I find myself declared guilty of I know not what, like some character out of a Kafka novel, and then I am told that someone has just taken my place in prison. And I am supposed to believe both of these assertions!"[7] The reason these concerns arise for Balthasar is because he believes that both representation and the patristic exchange formula lack the theological and metaphysical development necessary to make them coherent and relevant, a concern that Sölle shares.[8] To move representation from a "devotional category" to a *Grundkategorie*,[9] Balthasar develops it on two "theological foundations": the doctrine of the Trinity and his mission Christology.[10] I will discuss the former now and the latter in chapter 2.

Representation and the patristic exchange formula are "ultimately grounded in" two of Balthasar's specific trinitarian categories: distance and place. In the economy of redemption, Christ represents humanity—he acts in humanity's place. The place of Christ's representative action is included in Balthasar's triune framework of distance. Creation is ultimately located within the distance or difference of the three divine Persons, and, consequently, creation's unholy distance of sin is also located in the "place" (*Stelle*) of intradivine distance or difference.[11] Therefore, when Christ acts in the place of (*Stellvertretung*) creation's unholy distance, he does not need to alter his place. "He can do this on the basis of his place within the absolute, divine difference from the bestowing Father," states Balthasar.[12] In *TD*5, Christ's descent from divine place/distance to humanity's place/distance reverses so that humanity's place/distance ascends into Christ's place/distance. Ultimately, in eschatological fulfillment of the created order, the Spirit will welcome humanity into the roominess of the triune life, the infinite and ever-greater place Christ has prepared for humanity (John 14:2–3).[13] We can see here how the relationship between representation and Balthasar's trinitarian theology are mutually involved: if Christ is to *act in the place of* humanity and *make a place* for humanity in the triune life, then there must already be distance, roominess, and place-acting in the triune life.[14]

Phrases such as "making room for the other" or "the movement of love" express the otherness and freedom of the divine Persons. These types of expressions have become common since the inception of the "trinitarian revival" of the twentieth century, which seeks to imagine divine oneness within the context of the mutual love of the Father, Son, and Spirit. In recent days though, theologians have critiqued spatial imagery for being too "object-related" to apply to the divine life, because it disintegrates divine oneness and simplicity by depicting "ontologically distinct entities" in God.[15] God is inherently nonspatial, because divine being is not composite or bounded. In contrast to the pro-Nicene focus on the inseparability of divine operations, modern trinitarian theology's emphasis on divine otherness and freedom within the Trinity and its elaboration via spatial analogies seem to negate divine simplicity by splitting God into parts. In particular, the spatialized grammar of Balthasar's trinitarian theology has attracted much criticism (Kilby, Levering, Tonstad, etc.), raising the question: Can we apply spatial language to God at all or is it always doomed to be too object-centered? If we completely dismiss any use of spatial analogies, as Linn Marie Tonstad recommends in her critique of their use across the spectrum in modern trinitarian theology, then the kind of foundation of representation pursued by Balthasar crumbles.

Therefore, since the spatialized grammar of Balthasar's trinitarian theology is pivotal to his theology of the Trinity and representation, I aim to offer a sympathetic reinterpretation of Balthasar's spatial analogies that shows how they can be compatible with a dramatic view of the tradition, such as that proposed by O'Regan, Martin, and Walatka, which I develop further in relationship to representation in chapter 4. In this first section, I provide the framework for my reinterpretation by introducing Balthasar's doctrine of the Trinity and by analyzing the relationship between divine distance, the doctrine of simplicity, and the *analogia entis*. In the next section, I review the main critiques of Balthasar's spatialization of the triune life and attune divine spatial analogies and the doctrine of simplicity by reinterpreting Balthasar's doctrine of the Trinity through the *analogia entis* and a musical understanding of space. This account of Balthasar's divine spatial analogies will allow us to move forward with more assurance to a more direct development of trinitarian representation in the second and third sections of this chapter.

The Primal Drama: Distance, the analogia entis, and Simplicity

Let me introduce Balthasar's doctrine of the Trinity, particularly through a critical examination of his understanding of divine and creaturely distance in relation to the doctrine of simplicity and the *analogia entis*. Because Erich Przywara and Ferdinand Ulrich influenced Balthasar and developed more systematic accounts of the *analogia entis*, Balthasar's own use of these categories needs to be interpreted through dialogue with them. This account will enable us to understand how trinitarian distance and spatial analogies in general may be problematic. At the same time, I suggest that is precisely the relationship between distance and the *analogia entis* that can offer an alternative way of reading Balthasar's spatial analogies, which I explore in the following subsection.

Balthasar uses Karl Rahner and Jürgen Moltmann to represent two extremes before proffering his alternative explanation of the Trinity. He describes his doctrine of the Trinity as an attempt to "walk on a knife edge" between these two theologians.[16] "Rahner's Rule" (*Grundaxiom*) may have initially shaped the "trinitarian revival" of the twentieth century,[17] but Balthasar ultimately believes Rahner's theology of the *immanent* Trinity is "strangely formal," because Rahner limits authentic self-communication between the triune Person to the *economic* Trinity.[18] For example, Rahner states, "Within the Trinity there is no reciprocal 'Thou.'"[19] In another place he says that there is "no *mutual* love between the Father and Son, for this would suppose two acts."[20] If, for Balthasar, Rahner did not integrate the economic and immanent Trinity enough, Moltmann represents the opposite extreme of overidentifying the economic and immanent Trinity. Starting with Rahner's Rule, Moltmann develops his doctrine of the Trinity from the center of the Christian faith, the cross. The economy of the cross reveals the history of God, a history that is not without the pain, death, and suffering of the cross. Moltmann notes, "If one describes the life of God within the Trinity as the 'history of God' (Hegel), this history of God contains within itself the whole abyss of godforsakenness, absolute death, and the non-God."[21] According to Balthasar (and others), Moltmann has so identified the immanent Trinity with the economic Trinity that the latter does not simply reveal the immanent Trinity, but becomes the "locus of the Trinity's authentic actualization."²² Though Balthasar does acknowledge that Moltmann seeks to clarify the distinction in *The Trinity and the Kingdom of God*, a "Hegelian ambivalence" remains.²³

Building on Moltmann and Rahner, Balthasar believes that "a way must be found to see the immanent Trinity as the ground of the world process (including the crucifixion) in such a way that it is neither a formal process of self-communication in God, as in Rahner, nor entangled in the world process, as in Moltmann."²⁴ From Balthasar's critiques of Rahner and Moltmann, we learn the intent of his trinitarian theology: to offer a depiction of the divine life that is defined by the economy of Christ without collapsing the primordial difference between God and creation.

At the heart of his alternative understanding of the Trinity lies a "primal drama" that "contains and surpasses all possible drama between God and man."²⁵ This primal drama does not hover above time and creation self-enclosed, abstract, and static. Rather, it is dynamic and concrete, containing all possible drama between God and the world. What is this drama? "It is the drama of the 'emptying' of the Father's heart, in the generation of the Son," responds Balthasar.²⁶ In this divine emptying, Balthasar introduces his controversial concept of trinitarian distance, which contains all other types of economic distances.

Balthasar's notion of trinitarian distance is explicitly present as early as 1954 in *Heart of the World* and is described in the most vivid and detailed terms in his more mature works, such as the *Theo-Drama*.²⁷ Yet, the broader concept of distance had certainly been on his mind as early as the 1930s through his relationship with his theological teacher, mentor, and friend, Erich Przywara, whom Balthasar labeled an "unforgettable guide and master" and one of the two most important theological influences on his life. Balthasar also acknowledges that "none of [his] own books should hide what it owes to him."²⁸ However, I suggest in the next subsection that a conscious reading of triune distance through Przywara's concept of the *analogia entis* is imperative for affirming divine simplicity in Balthasar's thought and clarifying the concept of divine distance in light of the critiques Balthasar has received. Balthasar signals the underlying relation between the *analogia entis* and his trinitarian theology when he briefly refers to it and negative theology as a way of differentiating himself from Moltmann.²⁹ I discuss various aspects of the analogy of being throughout this book. For now, I review how the analogy of being provides the possibility and honors the limits of human knowledge of God, how it defines the relationship between infinite and finite being, and how it relates to distance.

Though the principle of an analogical way of speaking of "being" does not receive technical formulation until the Middle Ages by Thomas Aquinas, Przywara believes that the *analogia entis* is an implicit "biblical doctrine" that is "commended by tradition."[30] The Fourth Lateran Council (1215) formulates what it means to speak of God analogically: "For between creator and creature there can be noted no similarity so great that a greater dissimilarity cannot be seen between them."[31] There are two types of analogies used in this statement: analogy of attribution and analogy of proportion. Theological analogies draw out similarities (*analogia attributionis*) between God and creation, but in Thomas and Przywara, the Catholic accent always lies in the ever-greater dissimilarities (*analogia proportionalitatis*).[32] The *Deus semper maior* (ever-greater God) infinitely transcends any attribution predicated by creatures. God is "in-and-beyond" predication ("in-and-beyond" is an often-repeated phrase in Przywara).[33] Therefore, Przywara speaks of the distance between human knowledge and God in terms of darkness and mystery: "God, in whom knowledge of this order is grounded, comes to be known only insofar as he is 'not known'. . . . The word that best captures the essence of Augustinianism is therefore 'night.'"[34] The fundamental linguistic principle of analogy is held to be a central strategy employed by pro-Nicene trinitarian grammar in the fourth century.[35]

For Przywara, the analogy of being is not simply a linguistic tool, providing the rules of predication. The *analogia entis* is a metaphysic, as the "utterly fundamental principle of Catholicism, because analogy is the utterly fundamental principle obtaining between God and creature."[36] In other words, analogy defines the relationship between infinite being and finite being. For Przywara, interpreting Thomistic metaphysics, finite existence is distinct from its essence and, consequently, finds its essence in-and-beyond itself—being-in-itself (*In-sich-sein*) and being-beyond-itself (*Über-sich-hinaus-sein*)—whereas infinite being, God, is the ineffable unity of existence and essence. Thus, Przywara states, "God is 'being by his essence' (*ens per essentiam*), whereas the creature is being only 'by participation' (*per participationem*)."³⁷ God is utterly simple. The central claims of simplicity are that God is not composed of parts and God's essence is his existence.³⁸ God's simplicity is paramount to the theology of the church fathers. Divine simplicity is one of the three primary claims of pro-Nicene trinitarian theology,³⁹ and it is later comprehensively used and synthesized by Aquinas.⁴⁰

The more traditional usage of distance finds its place here in the difference between divine and creaturely being. There is an infinite distance, not of spatiality but of quality, between infinite being and finite being. Finite being finds its source and essence beyond itself—being by participation—whereas infinite being is simple in itself. God simply is, whereas, according to Augustine, creaturely being is "a nothing-something" and "an is-that-is not" (*est non est*).⁴¹ We can also find this teaching in Gregory of Nyssa's *The Great Catechism*: "For every *created* being is distant, by an equal degree of inferiority, from that which is the Highest."⁴² This "concept of spacing" lies at the heart of Balthasar's early patristic study on Gregory of Nyssa (1939).⁴³ Therefore, distance understood through the *analogia entis* shows that the relationship between God and creation is one of participatory distance, which maintains the untraversable interval from finite knowledge to God's being that the *analogia entis* sets out to affirm.

This metaphysic and its effect on finite knowledge can be further explained by looking at Ferdinand Ulrich's *Homo Abyssus: The Drama of the Question of Being*. Ulrich's influence on Balthasar cannot be underestimated. Balthasar acknowledges his influence on the crucially important section on the "fourfold difference" in *GL5* and in the whole of the *Theo-Drama*.⁴⁴ "There can be no doubt that Ulrich was Balthasar's most important interlocutor, especially after Siewerth's death and during the period when the Theodrama was being conceived," says Wiercinski.⁴⁵ To further substantiate the importance of Ulrich for Balthasar, Bieler notes that Ulrich's way of conceiving the *analogia entis* "is of great help for spelling out the concrete relevance of the *analogia entis* Balthasar had in mind."⁴⁶

Ulrich considers the analogy of being "from the perspective of being's movement of finitization," which is the fundamental form of creaturely being. Since creaturely being arises from divine being, it only exists as it "descends from the primary being."⁴⁷ In different words, Ulrich states, "The reception of being already means participating in an absolute originating ground [*Urground*] 'through' the abyss [*Ab-grund*] of being."[48] Thus, any analogy predicated to God "occurs only through the entity's descent," through its "being-given" character.[49] What enables analogical predication is God's presence in the gift of being. Bieler states of Ulrich's use of the *analogia entis*, "The giver is really *present* in his gift."[50] Ulrich calls this "thinking as thanking" (a common phrase in *Homo Abyssus*), which is the "properly enacted movement of being's finitization." In the act of gratitude, which is the concrete form of creaturely thinking, the creature receives itself as gift—the basic form of its existence.[51] In summary, analogy always takes place within the ever-present gift of being's movement of finitization, within its ontological distance from God. The metaphysic determines how analogical knowledge functions. In the words of Ulrich, analogy is not the "golden middle way" or the "absolute metaphysical weapon . . . because being's movement of finitization never permits itself to be objectified as a speculative instrumentarium."[52]

These metaphysical and noetic principles set forth by Przywara and Ulrich set the stage for understanding how Balthasar employs the concept of distance throughout his dramatic soteriology. Using the work of Russian Orthodox theologian Sergius Bulgakov, Balthasar suggests that there must be an "initial kenosis" within the Godhead that establishes all "subsequent kenosis."[53] In Bulgakov, the self-emptying of God in his creation of the world and in the Son's incarnation have their foundation both in the Father's primordial kenosis of begetting the Son and in the Son's "self-depletion" in being begotten. To Bulgakov, this eternal kenosis reveals that sacrifice, self-emptying, and self-renunciation already occur for God in the generation of the Son.[54]

Constructing from Bulgakov's theology of kenosis, Balthasar uses a variety of terms to describe this initial kenosis: "self-surrender," "self-giving," "renunciation," "selflessness." The eternal generation of the Son by the Father is a paradoxical act of power and powerlessness. Balthasar entitles this initial and eternal kenosis the "action" and the "primal drama." The "super-death" in God that makes possible all other types of death is the "unconditional self-surrender of each divine hypostasis to the others." Holding true to his Thomistic heritage and denying any form of Arianism, Balthasar believes this action is not simply something that God *does*. God *is* the event of self-giving generative activity, and such self-giving is elliptically portrayed in terms that are common to the Christian narrative of the cross: letting go, surrender, risk, and sacrifice.[55]

The Father's generation of the Son reveals an "absolute, infinite distance" (*Abstand* can mean "interval," "space," "distance," or "difference") between the Father and the Son, a "place" of otherness and freedom.[56] The Father does not merely lend his divinity to the Son, but he gives it to the Son in such a way that the Son is "equally substantial." To Balthasar, this suggests "an incomprehensible and unique 'separation' [*Trennung*] of God from himself."[57] Therefore, the trinitarian life includes a positive notion of separation, distance, and forsakenness. This positive, primordial distance "can contain and embrace all other distances that are possible within the world of finitude, including the distance of sin."[58]

Balthasar uses several German words that connote different interpretations of trinitarian distance and difference. Thomas Schumacher and Peter Henrici argue that *Abstand* should be translated as "distance" because it stresses the interpersonal nature of Balthasar's trinitarian theology over the abstract *Differenz*,[59] whereas Rowan Williams translates *Abstand* as "difference."[60] The ambiguity is further intensified by the variety of terms Balthasar uses in the *Theo-Drama* to describe the difference/distance resulting from the Son's generation: *Trennung, Distanz, innergöttliche absolute Differenz, Raum*, and *Gottferne*,[61] whereas in the *Theo-Logic* Balthasar primarily uses *Distanz* and *Differenz*.[62] I shall argue below that, although unstated by Balthasar, there is modification of terms from the dramatic portrayal of distance in the *Theo-Drama* to a more analogical description in *Theo-Logic*, and that this change is essential to recognizing the relations between distance and simplicity and the economic and the immanent Trinity.

What can we observe from this excursus is multiple forms of distance in Balthasar's theology. Robyn Horner develops one way of interpreting these forms and how they relate to one another.[63] According to Horner, there are two human and two divine dimensions of distance. The *first human dimension* is the natural distance between God and humanity, which we have seen in Przywara and Gregory of Nyssa. Balthasar affirms this view: "The basis of the biblical religion is the *diastasis*, the distance between God and the creature that is the elementary presupposition that makes it possible for man to understand and appreciate the unity that grace brings about."[64] This natural form of distance is the basis for a more tragic distance, *the second human dimension*, which is the result of sin. I call this "sinful distance," and it will be described in detail in chapter 3. The *first divine distance* is the interpersonal distance between the Father and Son, which provides a basis for the first human dimension. The *second divine distance*, according to Horner, is that which is created between the Father and the Son from the triune work on the cross through his assumption of the second human dimension.[65]

Elements of the *two divine distances* are what become so problematic for Balthasar interpreters. Divine distances may compromise some aspect of the *analogia entis* or the doctrine of simplicity by stretching analogical language to the breaking point and collapsing God into creation. Consequently, if a distance taxonomy is to be employed, it must be entirely clear how these types of distance relate to one another, especially in relation to our discussion of the economic and immanent Trinity, the analogy of being, and the doctrine of simplicity.

Reinterpreting Balthasar's Spatial Analogies

Balthasar applies spatial grammar to the triune life precisely because it emphasizes the "the personal distinctness of each Person both in being and acting."[66] The persons of God "make space" for one another by giving one another freedom.[67] However, a fully developed pro-Nicene trinitarian theology argues that such personal appropriations always occur in the inseparability of the one divine will and operation.[68] Spatial metaphors seem to negate divine simplicity, splitting God into parts, which is why Gregory of Nyssa would not ascribe intervals between the divine persons.[69] Consequently, Balthasar's fixation on divine distance, difference, and distinction in the *Theo-Drama* has received criticism from various directions. Matthew Levering believes that Balthasar compromises divine simplicity in his attribution of spatial analogies to God: "Balthasar strains the doctrine of analogy and the biblical revelation of the Trinity to the breaking point. The spatio-temporal analogies by which Balthasar fills out the inner life of the Trinity are inadequate to their subject matter, and they can even frighten."[70] Nicholas Healy and Karen Kilby do not think Balthasar's notion of trinitarian distance maintains the proper analogy between God and creation.[71] Similarly, Kevin Vanhoozer believes Balthasar's trinitarian theology, specifically his notion of the Father's kenosis in "recklessly" begetting the Son, is purely speculative and without biblical evidence.[72] At least part of the reason these issues arise is Balthasar's elliptical style of writing that circumambulates the mystery of God's essence, so that discerning the exact meaning of distance/difference is onerous.[73] Because of this, there is room to develop a more precise understanding of Balthasar's spatial analogies. In the following, I proffer an alternative way of reading Balthasar's trinitarian theology by interpreting his spatial analogies through his underlying usage of the *analogia entis* and the more explicit correlations between distance and divine simplicity in the *Theo-Logic*. I then build on this account by considering how a musical conception of space differs from a visual or bodily conception.[74] Finally, I reconsider three issues that arise in Balthasar's trinitarian theology through this analogical and musical conception of divine space.[75] My development offers a reinterpretation of Balthasar that is simultaneously sympathetic and more precise.

Of the critiques offered of Balthasar's trinitarian grammar, Linn Marie Tonstad's is the most developed; she analyzes and dismisses the overall use of spatial analogies in modern trinitarian theology (Balthasar, Moltmann, Ward, Coakley, etc.). Tonstad maintains that spatial metaphors, such as "distance," "interpenetration," "emptying," and "filling," are inappropriately applied to God, because they are used in ways that "are projectionist and incoherent and that illuminate the unexpected ways divine difference gets gendered and sexed, grounding the ultimacy of heterosexuality in the Christian imaginary."[76] When divine Persons make room for another, which mirrors the "spatialization of the womb" when a woman makes room for the other, we project the frangibility and boundedness of human bodies onto God and tear asunder divine unity.[77] "To be given over to is to suffer, and to be given (even oneself)—as gift—is to suffer. *Givenness* joins these elements to each other, and givenness belongs to the inner-trinitarian relations of glorification, begetting, and emptying in order to be filled. This implies that *sonship* itself constitutes sacrifice. To be a son is to have one's origin outside of oneself," says Tonstad.[78] Divine relations, in this manner, would require that one sacrifice one's own space to make room for the other: "The symbolic order spatializes kenosis by thinking it as space-making in which the self must move aside to make room for the other, to be filled by the other, for self and other cannot be in the same place at the same time, as it were."[79]

If we are to continue using spatial language in relation to God—as the concept of *Stellvertretung* seems to require—then this brief analysis impels us to develop an analogical grammar of divine spatiality and representation further. Can we conceive space in God that is not object-related? The key issue with Tonstad's critique of spatial analogies—and with that of other critics of Balthasar, such as Bruce Marshall, who accuses Balthasar of tritheism—is that they seem to read Balthasar's spatialized language univocally.[80] However, Balthasar is adamant in *TD*4 that he is approaching the ineffable being of God via negative theology through a dramatic reading of scripture. Balthasar reminds his readers that this way of reading scripture is like walking on a knife edge between Rahner and Moltmann.[81] Therefore, we need to reconsider the *physical-embodied-sexual* interpretations of Balthasar's spatial grammar in light of the inherent difference between God and humans. In other words, the first human distance—the distance between God and creation based on Przywara's metaphysical doctrine of analogy and Ulrich's concept of being's movement of finitization—pervades all theological language, separating finite knowledge from the infinite.[82] With this in mind, I seek to reinterpret Balthasar's trinitarian theology by introducing Przywara's conception of divine space based on the *analogia entis*, then further develop this through an *aural* interpretation of space.

Although Przywara inextricably links space and making space to creaturely mutability, creaturely space reveals an analogous form of divine "supraspatiality."[83] There is a "relation of otherness" between creaturely space and divine supraspatiality. "Supra" does not simply mean an oppositional above, but "supra" is the in-and-beyond of the *analogia entis*—a divine "super-space" and an "un-space." Creaturely spatial dimensions—inner/outer, above/below, and such—reveal an "ultimately incomprehensible . . . divine 'ever inward, ever outward, ever above, and ever below.'" God's space is infinite, a space of "*plenum*," and creaturely space is empty, a space of "*vacuum*."⁸⁴ The *maior dissimilitudo* between divine and creaturely space is the ontological possibility of God's transcendent and immanent relation to creaturely space. Przywara states, "The essentially supraspatial and supratemporal God pervades the intraspatial and intratemporal realm of the creature so thoroughly that, in relation to space, he is the one who is 'both interior to all things, because all things are in him, and exterior to all things, because he is beyond all things.'"⁸⁵ Therefore, for Przywara, since God in Christ is the infinite space of creaturely space (Col. 1:15–18, Eph. 1:23, 1 Cor. 15:18), he can assume, redeem, and resurrect mutable space from within it, becoming the "God-of-the-All," while still remaining the transcendent God beyond all forms of the creaturely space, precisely because he is the infinite fullness of space.⁸⁶

Spatial analogies then occur within the noetic and metaphysical principles of the *analogia entis*. Divine distance and place is in-and-beyond creaturely distance and place. The basis of this argument is not clearly laid out in *TD4*, but it is in *TD5* and *TL2*, where Balthasar provides a more explicit reference to the *maior dissimilitudo* between creaturely and divine distance and even refers to the notion of "super-space."⁸⁷ Creaturely distance implies an interval between essence and existence, signifying change, potency, and nonbeing, whereas divine difference is absolutely positive, albeit ineffable because it is approached through the distance that spans divine and creaturely knowledge.⁸⁸ For this reason, Balthasar does not believe he jeopardizes the doctrine of simplicity: "But, since God is the simplicity of being itself, to say this [distance] is to affirm at the same time 'that the greatest of differences does not violate the unity and simplicity of being'; consequently, division in God can 'essentially be nothing other than absolute relation.'"⁸⁹ To whatever extent the similarities are attributed to creaturely and divine difference/distance (*analogia attributionis*) in Balthasar's dramatic portrayal of triune distance in the *Theo-Drama*, it needs to be read in light of the *maior dissimilitudo* (*analogia proportionalitatis*) asserted between creaturely and divine difference/distance in the *Theo-Logic*.⁹⁰ The *Theo-Drama* is read in light of the *Theo-Logic*, which is warranted given that the former depicts the drama between God and creation and the latter treats the governing logic of such an account.

We can further clarify how divine spatial analogies might function by interpreting them through a musical understanding of space as distinct from visual or bodily space.[91] Robert Jenson's theology provides an example of how this might be systematically developed. He believes "roominess" is an attribute of God and conceives such roominess musically by describing God as an "infinite fugue":[92] "God is a great *fugue*. There is nothing so capacious as a fugue."[93] Stephen John Wright characterizes Jenson's view: "A fugue is pure polyphony, a contrapuntal composition of harmony arising out of the interplay of distinct voices. . . . In the fugal form, voices freely and happily share and exchange lines, developing themes introduced by one another."[94] The main melody (theme or subject) remains the same throughout the fugue, but it undergoes various alterations and developments as it passes between soprano, alto, tenor, and bass. The tri-unity of God is like this. "God, we may thus say, is a melody. And as there are three singers who take each their part, a further specification suggest itself: the melody is fugued," says Jenson.[95] The three Persons in God sing the melody as a fugue, allowing for places of variation, freedom, and counterpoint. The exchange or conversation that is God is ultimately sung as a triune fugue.

Jenson points us in the right direction, but his explanations are terse. Jeremy Begbie more fully captures what I intend to say about aural space and its ability not to be object-centered. In music, sound is not bound to the location of a particular object, as it is in vision. Visually, two objects occupy mutually exclusive places. Physical objects mediated by space compete for space, which is precisely Tonstad's concern about ascribing room-making to God, especially when combined with language of emptying and filling. However, Begbie claims, "in aural experience, although a sound may have a discrete material source whose discrete location I can identify ('the trumpet is on the left, not on the right'), the sound I hear is not dependent on attention to that 'place.'"[96] Sounds can be present in the same place and time without competing to be heard. Sounds can "interpenetrate" one another without one displacing the other. Begbie continues,

> In the case of music, we find that sounds and spatial framework (and temporal framework, as we shall see) are completely intertwined. Because

music depends supremely on the interrelationship-through-attraction of sounds, it exploits the "omnipresent" and "interpenetrating" quality of sound-experience. Music directly "pulls the strings," so to speak, of the spatial framework in which it is deployed—no neat divide marks off occupant and place in musical experience. We only need think of a three-tone major chord, which we hear as three distinct, mutually enhancing (not mutually exclusive) sounds, but together occupying the same aural space. The sound is rich and enjoyable, even more so in polyphony when different melodies can interweave and enhance each other. (Contrast the confusion of three people speaking simultaneously.)[97]

When aural co-presence is musical, it can connote a kind of space that allows specific sounds to make room for one another without displacing the other—they are not objectifying. Musical sound is roomy.

With the *analogia entis* and this musical understanding of space in mind, we can now reconsider three issues that arise in Balthasar's trinitarian theology. First and foremost, we can continue to make use of Balthasar's triune spatial analogies without compromising the doctrine of divine simplicity. Reading Balthasar's theology through the *analogia entis* reveals that any form of separation, alienation, or distance in God's eternal kenosis is a positive aspect of personal relations that is ultimately incomprehensible.[98] Bieler says distance is not "separation *from* the other," but "separation *toward* the other."[99] Similarly, Balthasar himself describes distance as a function of unity in *TD*5: "In God, distance and nearness exist in a unity that exhibits their constantly intensifying relationship: 'The more the Persons in God differentiate themselves, the greater is their unity.'"[100] In *TL*2, Balthasar provides the clearest definition of trinitarian distance/difference as the "personal other," an "otherness of supreme positivity," and a "distance of relation," and he asserts the "absolute positivity of difference." Within the simplicity of God's essence, concepts such as "division," "difference," and "distance" are simply describing "absolute relation."[101]

O'Regan also proposes a positive understanding of distance through super-space and interprets it through an apocalyptic framework,[102] but this *aural* conception of space provides a more precise conceptualization of a divine spatial framework. The divine Persons can make room for one another without sacrificing their own space, because God is *supra-place*. In a trinitarian grammar of generation, the divine essence finds itself shared in different ways by the three distinct Persons. The Father can generate an other of the same nature without his place decreasing, because the same divine essence is possessed completely and yet differently by each Person. Each Person sings a distinct rendition of the original theme (the Father generates, the Son is begotten, and the Spirit proceeds). To say it differently, there is unbounded but also shared room for each Person to act. In God, space is without interval, a distance without separation; God is the shared place of mutuality, exchange, and activity. Therefore, to say God is spatial musically is to say that his supra-place can be specified by the distinction, concreteness, and particularity of the Persons of God by how they are revealed in the economy of redemption without being space-bound like embodied beings. The language of emptying and filling, which Balthasar uses to describe begetting and begottenness in the Trinity, does not need to mean the decrease or increase of a Person's space, because the divine Persons are not space-restricted, as creaturely bodies are. This account does not compromise God's oneness, but portrays divine simplicity through dramatic language in order to "be faithful to [scripture's] basic intention."[103]

The second aspect of divine spatial analogies that we need to repair is what Balthasar means by there being "realms of freedom within the Godhead."[104] When writing about trinitarian distance, Balthasar claims that the Son's economic prayers to the Father are an expression of the Son's divine nature/will, and, therefore, Balthasar speaks of the "wills" or "freedoms" of the three Persons of God.[105] Consequently, Balthasar consistently speaks of "love's element of surprise" in the trinitarian relations.[106] These claims are at odds with pro-Nicene trinitarian theology, which claims that there is one indivisible divine will and operation.[107] I will argue in the next section that Balthasar moves beyond the limits of analogical language when speaking of the divine freedoms. For now, I qualify my use of Balthasar's trinitarian grammar of divine freedom(s).

If we conceive space musically instead of bodily, the Persons remain inseparable, yet can still exercise freedom. Triune inseparability is not displayed statically and timelessly but dynamically and harmonically in the economy of redemption. As the Persons in God continue the theme of the divine fugue, each one does so in harmonic relation to the others' singing. Fugues "make room" for the adaptation of the original theme or subject. The original subject does not need to empty itself for the sake of the adaptation, but the subject is sung differently—enhanced—without increasing or decreasing. Each Person in God makes space for the freedom of the others, a freedom that is mutually shared in absolute giving and receiving. There is one divine subject, will, or freedom, but within this divine subject there is free variation.[108] For the purposes of this book, whatever personal freedom a divine Person exercises in the economy is fully received by the others in God's eternal and indivisible simplicity of being.[109] Personal freedom in God is of divine excess, love, and plenitude, not disbanding the divine essence, but is incorporated in the *semper maior*, the ineradicable fullness of God.[110] Like the dramatic interpretation of the simplicity of God's *being*, the inseparability and unity of God's interminable *activity* are displayed dramatically, rather than abstractly or statically, in a metaphysic of divine distance and receptivity.[111]

The final aspect of divine space I need to address is the relationship between divine distance and creaturely distance. According to Horner's taxonomy, God's assumption of the second human distance leads to the creation of a second divine distance.[112] If a taxonomy such as this is assumed, then the critiques of Balthasar's concept of divine distance are warranted because creaturely distance would add to the divine essence, compromising God's simplicity by disintegrating his essence and existence. As an alternative, I propose an *ascending planal distance taxonomy*, according to which the four forms of distance are like planes in an ascending hierarchy, with higher-level planes containing the lower: *immanent divine distance, economic divine distance, natural human distance,* and *sinful human distance*.

Between the escarpments of Moltmann and Rahner lies a very thin pass—a pass that Balthasar treads through the analogical attribution of distance to the divine being.[113] Because the eternal generation of the Son already reveals a positive notion of death, suffering, and forsakenness in God (immanent divine distance), the economy of the cross (economic divine distance and sinful human distance) is contained and infinitely overcome in the positivity of God's eternal self-giving.[114] The divine distance of eternal generation includes, contains, and transcends all the other distances. There is only one divine distance—God's economy does not introduce a new distance for God. Economic divine distance is contained in the distance-in-unity of God's eternal self-giving and self-receiving love. Triune love makes natural human distance possible, including its tragic and sinful distance. In order not to annihilate God's unity and simplicity, the grammar of the cross must carefully portray this ascending planal distance taxonomy (developed more fully in chapter 3).

By conceiving the distances in an ascending order, I am carrying forward an interpretation of Balthasar similar to Jennifer Newsome Martin's and Cyril O'Regan's. Martin argues that the economy of Christ's action is simply a "continuation and continuous ratification" of the primordial distance within God. By framing the economic divine distance as excess and nonnecessary, Balthasar is separated from Hegel and Moltmann.[115] Such a framing of distance requires an understanding of space that is noncompetitive and noncontrastive, like our supraspatial and musical account.

In conclusion, spatial analogies may indeed be too objectifying and annihilate divine oneness. In particular, Balthasar's depiction of the Trinity in the economy of salvation can be excessive, as we will see more fully in chapter 3. As a result, some of the critiques of his notion of trinitarian distance are warranted. At the same time, given Balthasar's conscious movement between the dangers of Moltmann and Rahner in the *Theo-Drama* and the more explicit references to distance and the doctrine of simplicity in the *Theo-Logic*, I have sought to offer a charitable reading of Balthasar by interpreting intratrinitarian spatiality through the *analogia entis* and music. When defined musically, spatiality invites new possibilities, allowing one to imagine divine oneness together with the diversity, drama, and freedom depicted in the economy of God without being exclusively centered on a particular object, place, or person. Musical space captures the capacious, interpenetrating, and polyphonic nature of divine space, uniting inward (God *in se*) and outward (God *ad extra*) activities. Ultimately, divine spatial analogies are a dramatic expansion of the tradition's analogical expression of trinitarian appropriation and intradivine relations. With this account in place, we can turn to constructing Balthasar's theology of representation.

Trinitarian Pro-Existence and Representation

We now arrive at a principal question of this book: How is representation not simply established upon a trinitarian metaphysic but realized in the immanent activity of the triune processions? Unfortunately, Balthasar's exact elaboration of representation in *TD*4 is limited to describing the relationship between divine distance and Christ's representation of the distance created by human sin, which I shall analyze in chapter 3. This narrow focus on the cross seems to fall short of Balthasar's intention of providing a metaphysical and theological foundation for representation. If the immanent Trinity is truly the foundation for explaining how representation—action in the place of the other—is a creaturely and christological possibility, then it seems Balthasar would need to address how representation functions in the triune life. To satisfy Balthasar's soteriological demands, questions such as the following should be addressed: How is acting in the place of the other reflected in trinitarian grammar? How is it that a person can act vicariously for another or assume something outside of his or her own spatial place?

This broader development of representation does occur in Norbert Hoffmann's work, which Balthasar cites in the preface of *TD*4. Balthasar notes that it is unfortunate that he was not able to take into account Hoffmann's "richly documented essay" on the immanent Trinity and representation since it was published after *TD*4.[116] Balthasar positively acknowledges Hoffmann's work again in *TD*5, where Balthasar begins using Hoffmann's term "pro-existence," noting that pro-existence is at "the very heart" of *TD*5, but he does not repeat the term for the remainder of the volume. Balthasar commends Hoffmann for showing "with ever increasing care" how the vicarious action of Christ is possible because of the original pro-existence of the triune life.[117] By "pro-existence," Balthasar means relations of "reciprocal action on behalf of each other" or "an active life for each other,"[118] which he directly relates to *Stellvertretung*.[119] Thus, with Balthasar's high approbation of Hoffmann and the fact that Hoffmann uses Balthasar's theology of the immanent Trinity to develop his own understanding of representation, I now construct Balthasar's theology of representation further by using Hoffmann's theology of pro-existence and developments of Balthasar's doctrine of the Trinity that occur after the critical section on representation in *TD*4, especially his notion of triune receptivity. By ascribing pro-existence to the Trinity, I conclude that representation is an essential aspect of triune processions.

In many ways, as Hoffmann notes, it is easy to describe one's ability to act on another's behalf in human affairs. For example, a medical doctor, lawyer, and police officer all act on behalf of someone else, but these are external representatives. Instead, Hoffmann articulates the "reality of action-for-another" at the ontological level and "as the law of the Being of God himself."[120] In other words, Hoffmann is arguing for a form of *internal*, rather than *external*, representative action.

According to Hoffmann, the trinitarian processions include three elements of internal representation or pro-existence: (1) "the active, enabling movement of the positing subject," (2) "the passive receptivity of the posited 'other,'" and (3) "the 'repercussive' effect on the former."[121] In a very similar account to Balthasar's doctrine of the Trinity, Hoffmann notes that the first element is seen when the "positing subject" begets a being that is distinct in personhood but identical in nature. Pro-existence is seen here in that the "positing principle, through its own self-investment (self-sacrifice), creates a 'place,' a locus, in which the posited 'other can express its own self.'"[122] In the generation of the Son, the Father acts for the Son by creating a place for the Son to be and act, and thus the Son is given freedom to act in unity with the Father. Pro-existence generates freedom and activity.[123]

The second and third elements can be seen together. The posited other passively receives his identity from the positing Subject; the latter receives his identity from the other. There is a repercussive effect. In other words, the Son can only be Son because of his "absolute refusal of self-dependence," and the Father can only be Father because the Son allows himself to be Son. In this way, there exists in both Persons an "orientation toward the other," a key feature of Hoffmann's and Balthasar's understanding of triune Personhood.[124] Trinitarian pro-existence essentially describes an other-oriented interpersonal ontology by which each Person exists for and constitutes the others.

At the summit of Balthasar's trinitarian thought, with the assistance of Hoffmann's conception of trinitarian pro-existence, three conclusive formulae on trinitarian representation emerge, but I still insist that these are analogical formulae that are inadequate to express the ineffability of God's triune being. First, the traditional language of generation and procession reveals a kind of action in the place of the other that is eternal in God. If God is absolute love, then there must be a genuine form of exchange, which is the gift-giving of the eternal processions of God.[125] Such action-for-the-other is without interval—a distance without a distance—as in humanity's relations. This gift-giving constitutes the ever-greater "We" of God and is both the "presupposition" and "realized union" of trinitarian love.[126] What Rowan Williams says of Augustine is also true of Balthasar's trinitarian theology: "The Father is Father, and so is concretely and actively God, by being for the Son . . . the Son is Son, and so is concretely and actually God, by being from the Father . . . the Spirit is concretely and actually God by being from or through the Father and the Son."[127] Therefore, each Person exists entirely as the action in, with, and for the other divine persons, while still not "needing" the others, as each subsists as the one divine essence. Representation, then, is a positive feature in God because it is not needed to make up for another's deficiencies, as is often the case in human representation where human bodies are finite and bounded (chapter 4).

Second, trinitarian representation is only possible if the Persons are capable of being affected by the generating other. According to Balthasar, "The divine hypostases proceed from one another and thus (including the Father, the Primal Source) are perfectly open to one another."[128] Balthasar insists that although there is no passive potentiality in God in a creaturely sense, the triune processions connote a form of triune receptivity. Extending Aquinas's notion of the Son's receptivity in his procession,[129] which is what Hoffmann bases the second element of pro-existence on, Balthasar suggests a concomitant relation between activity and receptivity in divine generation.[130] The Father and the Son both give and receive, which is what Hoffmann bases the third element of pro-existence on. How is that so? By letting himself be begotten, the Son actively participates in his procession from the Father. "Letting be" is an implicit activity in the receptivity of the Son's procession and is revealed economically in his obedience to the Father's mission for him to become incarnate. Balthasar calls this obedient reception an "infinite gratitude," an eternal *eucharistia* of self-giving, which unifies the distance between the Father and Son.[131] It is precisely at this point that Balthasar speaks of the Father's receptivity. Since divinity had to be actively received by the Son, the Father's giving is incomplete unless the Son responds to his giving in obedient reception: "Where absolute love is concerned, conceiving and letting be are just as essential as giving. In fact, without this receptive letting be and all it involves—gratitude for the gift of oneself and a turning in love toward the Giver—the giving itself is impossible."[132] Furthermore, not only is the Father's giving to the Son unfinished unless received by the Son, it is also reliant upon the Son's return gift. The Father receives in that he could not be Father without the Son, making receptivity a perfection not only of divine sonship but of divine paternity.[133] Complementing Balthasar's formulation, David L. Schindler notes, "Thus receptivity is a perfection because it is necessary for a complete concept of love."[134] Though Balthasar insists that the Father does not cease being the divine essence in his self-giving to the Son, as this would contradict the Fourth Lateran Council, he paradoxically wants to show that the Father gives himself away in such a manner that he receives something of his identity and being back from the Son.[135] God, then, is the positive and dynamic unity of wealth and poverty, a formula Balthasar explicitly borrows from Ulrich.[136]

Triune receptivity is an essential presupposition of triune representation and pro-existence. Though the Persons of the Trinity remain free within their personal differences (triune distance), "they can mutually interpenetrate in the most intimate manner possible" since they are of the one divine essence (triune receptivity).[137] Because Balthasar conceives personhood as both activity and receptivity, the Persons of God are able to act for the other without threatening the others' space or identity. Tonstad's concern that personal space-making requires that the self has to sacrifice its own space to make room for the other does not apply here, as it may in the case of bounded human bodies, because each Person's place and activity can be received and returned by the other.

As a result, the third quality of triune representation is two-sided: one Person can act in the place of another Person without the latter being absent in this activity, and the "passive" Person can become active by participating in the action and the fruits of the "active" Person.[138] Trinitarian pro-existence enables both active and participatory Subjects who act in dynamic unity. The first side can be substantiated through the Father's generation of the Son. Because the Father gave himself entirely to the Son, the Son can fully represent the Father. In the economy of redemption, this means that the Son can represent or do the Father's work since the Father dwells in him (John 14:9–10).[139] Thus, although it may be appropriate to speak of how one Person acts in the economy of redemption, each Person is inseparably involved in this activity. Triune representation is entirely "*Miteinander*."[140] A grammar of distance and receptivity taken together allows one to speak of divine appropriation in the drama of redemption, while also maintaining the doctrine of inseparable operations.[141]

Likewise, since each Person mutually indwells the others, they can also participate in the fruit and attributes of the others. Although the language of participation does not apply to each Person's relation to the essence of God, it does apply to how each Person relates to the others' personal distinctions.[142] Balthasar states, "In what Father and Son *are* 'there are essential differences . . . but in terms of what they possess, they both possess Fatherhood and Sonship.'"[143] Furthermore, to be receptive is to be open, available, and in dialogue, and therefore Balthasar consistently speaks of love's element of surprise, wonder, and fruitfulness in the trinitarian relations, but he distinguishes trinitarian process from creaturely becoming. Balthasar narrates the *semper maior* of God's ineffable being as the fructifying exchange among the divine Persons in the plenitude of God's boundless and everlasting giving and receiving.[144] This triune way of participating in the other opens up a way of speaking of how action in the place of the other occurs in God. One Person in the Trinity can act in the place of the other because the place of the other is best expressed as a shared and patulous place of mutuality, exchange, and activity. The Persons of the Trinity reciprocally represent one another, and each Person participates in the life, action, and fruit of the others.

By interpreting Balthasar's account of intratrinitarian representation with the aid of his larger corpus and in dialogue with Hoffmann, I have now expanded Balthasar's laconic account of how Christ's action in the place of humanity is possible by showing how representation is already in God. The notion of pro-existence and *Stellvertretung* take interpersonal models of the Trinity one step further by elucidating a more active and concrete relation between the triune Persons. For Balthasar, the communion or the "pro" of the triune Persons is not simply defined as "togetherness" or "mutual love," but more importantly as "an active life in place of the other," "being fruitful for the other," and "participating in the life of the other."[145] Balthasar's critique of Rahner's doctrine of the Trinity is clear now. If God is to communicate himself to the world through Jesus Christ, then there must be dynamic, not simply formal, self-communication and exchange in triune relations. Representation—action in, with, and for the other—stands at the heart of a Christian witness to a God of procession and generation. The "reality of action-for-another" exists at the very being of being. In *Elucidations*, Balthasar summarizes this well: "If there were a definition of God, then one would have to put it in the form: unity as being-for-one-another."[146]

Creaturely Pro-Existence and the Dramatic Exchange Formula

Thus far, we have attempted to go to the backgrounds of being by reflecting on Balthasar's doctrine of the Trinity, specifically the concepts of distance, receptivity, and pro-existence. Now that we have ascended the analogical ladder into the inner life of God, Balthasar instructs us to kata-logically descend back to creaturely being.[147] If representation and pro-existence apply to trinitarian relations, then they are mirrored in creaturely relations through the *imago Trinitatis*. By making this descent through the provided trinitarian metaphysic, I show how representation is reflected in creaturely being, and I set the foundation and definition of christological *pro nobis*, representation, and the dramatic exchange formula. By doing so, I display the unity of the five motifs of Balthasar's dramatic soteriology in a theology of representation.

Creaturely Being: Pro-Existence, Christological pro nobis, *and Representation*

The commonality between divine and creaturely being is ultimately established in the *imago Trinitatis*.[148] The move from the Trinity to the creature, which is the inverse of "ana-logical" predication, is what Balthasar terms his "kata-logical" approach in the *Theo-Logic*, developed on the basis of the incarnate Logos.[149] Therefore, the analogy between trinitarian pro-existence and creaturely pro-existence will reveal how representation is an essential category of creaturely existence and will be shown to be the foundation and interpretive lens of christological *pro nobis* and our definition of representation. In chapter 2, we will see how this analogy is performed concretely in the Chalcedonian Christ, which demonstrates that Christ is ultimately the basis of analogy. For now, I will enhance Balthasar's narrow foundation of representation in *TD*4 by integrating the trinitarian theology we've seen so far and material developed later in his *Theo-Logic* with christological *pro nobis* and representation.

For Balthasar, the image of the Trinity is not primarily found in the mind of an individual (Augustine), in the body/soul dichotomy, nor in the "polarity between male and female" (Barth).[150] In fact, if Christianity were to proclaim a personhood akin to modernity's image of self-consciousness (Descartes) or absolute, ethical freedom (Kant), then Balthasar believes action in the place of the other would not be conceivable.[151] For Balthasar, the trinitarian form within creaturely being is ultimately found in "two pillars" of finite freedom. These two pillars form two distinct shapes of being: every being is free "to-be-for-itself" (*für-sich-Sein*; self-possession/autonomous motion) and at the same time "to-be-for-another" (*für-ein-ander(es)-Sein*; consent).[152] Balthasar adopts the phrase "in/for/with-itself" (*an/für/bei-sich*) from German idealism;[153] Hegel explicitly uses "being for an other" and "being for itself" dialectically.[154] His distinct development of the these phrases seems remarkably similar to that of his friend Ferdinand Ulrich.[155] I will point out places of overlap and ultimately show how Balthasar and Ulrich see the concept of *Stellvertretung* functioning in these two pillars.

The drama of creaturely existence is found in the tension between its self-possession (pillar one) and its fundamental need to give to and receive from God and others (pillar two). Balthasar summarizes this in the *Epilogue* of his trilogy: "The 'to be real' that is given to every being thus hides a duality in itself that might at first seem to be contradictory: (1) it is grounded in itself (which a mere being cannot do on its own, or otherwise it would be God); and (2) it proceeds out of itself by virtue of a dynamic given to it in order to real-ise itself (its innerness) in the very act of expressing."[156] Creaturely being exists out of God's self-communicative being, and likewise it expresses its essence in self-communication to others. The way that Ulrich expresses the dynamic of creaturely being ultimately confirms how the two pillars function in Balthasar. "Liberated being-oneself and loving being-for-another [*liebendes Hinsein zum Anderen*] may therefore not be separated from each other," says Ulrich. "Each is possible *only in coincidence with the other*."[157]

The second pillar of created being highlights the inherent connectedness and exchange of created entities. "Real beings find completion in one another," states Balthasar.[158] "Receptivity signifies the power to welcome and, so to say, host another's being in one's own home."[159] For Balthasar receptivity is not part of humanity's "imperfect spirituality,"[160] but rather is a positive feature of creaturely being. The poverty of human essence "contain[s] a super-finite, super-essential aspect by which they point to their origin, their conservation, and their end in God."[161] In its positive difference from God—the creaturely is and is not—the creature realizes its essential "gift-character" and recapitulates the movement of finitization as it receives from God and others (Ulrich).

With the nature of creaturely being reflecting the grammar of triune pro-existence, representation becomes an essential category of creaturely existence.[162] Bieler believes representation is implicitly at the heart of *Homo Abyssus*,[163] but Ulrich makes the direct connection between "being" and "representation" in 1973 in *Leben in Der Einheit von Leben und Tod*,[164] which is around the same time *Stellvertretung* becomes central to Balthasar. Speaking of the nature of *esse commune* ("common being") in Aquinas and Ulrich, Adrian J. Walker says it is where "love means embodying being as 'vicarious representation.'"[165] Based on the "ontic solidarity" between all humans "on the basis of the singularity of their essence," humans are created to go out of their own "I" and stand in the place of the other, being both acted upon and acting for.[166] Representative acts of self-giving love are essential to the activity of creaturely existence. Such exchange of being can produce fruit beyond procreation. The drama of movement, surprise, and becoming are all positive parts of creaturely being.[167]

In the process of drawing analogies between the creaturely and the divine in relation to a theology of representation, the *maior dissimilitudo* must persist. Action for the other in God arises from the plenitude of the simple divine being and, thus, is a solely *inkludierende Stellvertretung* ("inclusive representation"). Any other consideration would deny the inseparability of divine activity, whereas finite action for the other is out of a deficiency of being and includes both inclusive and exclusive acts of representation. Since finite being cannot achieve the divine identity-in-difference, one cannot speak of finite acts of representation as completely inclusive.[168] Additionally, human activity for others is often needed because of the displacement of human subjects, which could never occur in God, and so exclusive acts for others are often needed when the other has no place (chapter 4).

I can now integrate divine pro-existence and its reflection in created being with christological *pro nobis* and representation. Christological *pro nobis* finds its place in the Nicene Creed (*crucifixus etiam pro nobis*) and is of central concern to the fathers' Christology.[169] "Everything in the Christian faith depends on the two little words '*pro nobis*,'" says Balthasar.[170] These two words have attracted much theological attention, and varied interpretations are available. For example, Karl Barth provides a "systematic reflection on the *pro nobis*," interpreting *pro nobis* as a fourfold forensic representation[171]: "He took our place as Judge. He took our place as the judged. He was judged in our place. And He acted justly in our place."[172] Barth's theology of representation may initially prompt Balthasar to consider the pivotal importance of the term, but Balthasar's own theology of it is developed in a much different system, however imprecise it may seem in places. For our purposes, trinitarian pro-existence, which is reflected in the drama of creaturely existence, is the foundation and interpretive lens of christological *pro nobis* and our definition of representation.[173]

First, how is divine and creaturely pro-existence the foundation for christological *pro nobis*? "What we have already said about the priority of the 'we' in the human 'I' is important at this point," answers Balthasar. "Since we share a world with others, there is in every human subject a formal *inclusion* of all the other subjects (who are materially *excluded* because each one is 'for himself'). The a priori of the 'we' is the anthropological point of departure for christological representation [in the sense of being-for-others] although the latter is something new and qualitatively different from it."[174]

In fact, Balthasar says that if the above understanding of creaturely representation is not true, then "the mystery of the Cross would have remained forever alien and inaccessible to humanity."[175] To situate Christ's work *pro nobis* in the flesh is characteristic of Nicene theology, whereas Arius, Asterius, and Eusebius made Christ's work *pro nobis* the purpose and origin of the Son's created semidivine existence. Christ was simply generated for the sake of creation.[176] For Athanasius, christological *pro nobis* is located in the economy of salvation, particularly in Christ's assumption of human flesh. At the same time, for Athanasius the *pro nobis* of Christ's work is ultimately established in the divine nature of love, "rather than through a secondary attenuated divinity."[177] Thus, *Deus in se* is both distinguished from and the foundation of *Deus pro nobis*.[178]

Balthasar's christological, trinitarian, and anthropological reflections follow a similar trajectory to Athanasius's. According to Balthasar, human nature does not only need others to exist, but it also possesses this "fluidity and transitional quality" in relation to absolute being.[179] In particular, created being already exists toward and in the "other in God," Christ, and thus rather than Christ being created for humanity, humanity was created in Christ (see chapter 2).[180] The natural fulfilment of finite freedom by infinite freedom in Christ is the "hidden background" that makes it possible for Christ to represent all of humanity.[181] As a result, the "organic" unity between Christ's divine nature and human nature is the pro-existence of divine and creaturely being, which Balthasar believes is the missing component in forensic or juridical atonement theories, such as in Anselm or in Barth's conception of *Stellvertretung*.[182] In summary, God's work *pro nobis* in the economy of redemption is the natural fulfilment of finite freedom by the infinite, a freedom that can go outside itself because it is already immanently from and toward itself (the *opera Trinitatis ad extra indivisa sunt*).

Second, by interpreting *pro nobis* through the provided trinitarian metaphysic, we come to see the background to our definition of representation. I have been describing *Stellvertretung* as "acting in, with, and for the other." The first aspect of representation in this definition is related to *action*. Clarke highlights the importance of action to self-manifestation of being: "Action is thus the final natural fruition or self-expression of any real nature, which is a unified center of natural potencies or dispositional properties for action. It follows that the final fruition of any being, its peak of self-realisation, is reached only in its *self-communication to others*, its self-sharing with others."[183] For Balthasar, Rahner's formulation of Christ's *pro nobis* "lacks the decisive dramatic element" by underestimating the gravity of Christ's dramatic action for humanity because of the consequences of human sin.[184] Similarly, Henri de Lubac believes the Reformers' focus on the work of Christ rather than the being of Christ can also often reduce the christological *pro nobis* to an attitude of God.[185] Christological and creaturely representation is not simply symbolic, an abstract for-ness, but is concrete for-ness, displayed in generative, creative, and dramatic action for others.

The second aspect of our definition of representation is that it is action *in*, *with*, and *for* the other. Based upon our trinitarian metaphysic, representation can be internal ontological action and not simply external and forensic ("for our benefit").[186] "The human being is social in its very structure," says Schindler. "Gift and receptivity—and hence relation (love, dialogue)—are given *a priori* with or in the human existent. What this means is that relation is ontological before it is voluntary."[187] The legal and juridical notions of representation do not fully capture the ontological unity of the human flesh, its disposition toward Christ, and the centrality of action to being. Balthasar states, "This osmosis [between the I and Thou in human nature] helps to make sense of the claim that men, who together form 'one dough' (Gregory of Nyssa) or 'one cake' (Luther), can be, act, and suffer much more profoundly for one another than they often think."[188] Since the place of the other is a receptive, shared, and fluid place, then representative action is in, with, and for the other.

The third and final aspect of our definition of representation is that it is action in, with, and for the *other*. Just as the Father, Son, and Spirit's unified action maintains personal distinction, so representative action must be conceived as preserving the place and space of the other. This is important even for how the term *Stellvertretung* is translated. Bailey's definition of *Stellvertretung* as "place-taking"[189] does not fully grasp the metaphysic provided by Balthasar's trinitarian ontology, because it seems to emphasize exclusive representation to the neglect of inclusive representation. By contrast, dramatic action for the other, both christological and creaturely, increases the personal freedom of the other— it is *place-acting* for the sake of *place-making*. In fact, Christ's work *pro nobis* heightens human responsibility for others. Balthasar says that

A Trinitarian Metaphysic and Representation 47

"Christ's *pro nobis* perfects his members' ability to *be* and *act* on behalf of others."[190] Therefore, for Balthasar, "the '*pro nobis*' contains the innermost core of the interplay between God and man, the center of all theodrama."[191] I examine the content of this interplay in chapters 3 and 4.

It is perplexing Balthasar did not make these connections in *TD*4. How can one human act in the place of the other? What is the foundation for christological representation? By synthesizing different pieces of Balthasar's theology, I have developed the category of representation further by defining and interpreting it through a trinitarian metaphysic. Creaturely being is naturally created in and for others. Therefore, it is normative for human persons to act for one another. Ultimately, humanity was created in and toward the other, Christ, and it is designed to be represented by him.

The Dramatic Exchange Formula

Balthasar believes that "the central feature of Jesus's mission is the 'holy' or 'wondrous exchange' so often described by the Fathers."[192] Despite the centrality of the church fathers' exchange formula (*admirabile commercium*) to Balthasar's soteriology, he does believe there are limits in the patristics' formulation of it. First, Balthasar believes the patristic exchange formula "lacked an adequate theological foundation." Although Balthasar does not explain what is lacking, he states that his theology of the immanent Trinity, specifically trinitarian distance, is what ultimately provides the foundation.[193] Second, he believes the fathers limit Christ's assumption of sin to the consequences and punishment of sin and not sin itself. This is an "unconscious limit" that Balthasar attempts to revise through the radicalism of Luther's theology of the cross and his own theology of representation and trinitarian distance.[194] In other words, we find an unstated amalgamation of the patristic exchange formula and the category of *Stellvertretung*, which together form motif 2 of Balthasar's dramatic soteriology. The most explicit integration of the two concepts in the *Theo-Drama* occurs through the phrase "exchange of places" (*Platztausch*).[195] I further articulate the relation of these two concepts in the dramatic exchange formula (Christ acted in humanity's place so that humanity might act in his place), which also displays the eclectic synthesis of the fathers and Luther in the five motifs of Balthasar's dramatic soteriology.

In the dramatic exchange formula, we can see how redemption (motif 3) and *theosis* (motif 4) are incorporated and unified in Christ's representative activity for humanity (motif 2). Furthermore, these motifs are related to the remaining two motifs: "The second motif, the *commercium*, is now firmly based on the first, *the Son's self-surrender*, insofar as the latter is the 'economic' representation of *the Father's trinitarian, loving-self surrender* (the fifth motif)."[196] That is, the Son's economic place-acting (motif 2) is based upon the Son's self-giving (motif 1) and trinitarian kenosis and distance (motif 5).

Although trinitarian distance captures the dramatic aspect of the first half of the exchange formula, it does not provide an adequate theological foundation for the unified action of redemption and *theosis*. What does provide a more comprehensive metaphysic is the eternal pro-existence—giving and receiving—between the triune Persons. The personal place of each Person in God is a participatory place without boundaries, which through the infinite and generative activity of three Persons becomes supra-place. Triune processions, interpersonal relations, and inseparable operations display the performance of an infinite exchange of places in God. Such a supra-place contains and exceeds Christ's dramatic and redemptive activity in humanity's place and invites humanity to participate in God's life. The economic exchange of places—"He acted in our place that we might act in his"—is situated in the primordial place-acting, or exchange, already in God. Since the places of the divine persons and human persons are shared, exchanged, and active places, over against individualistic, isolated, and static places, then the integration of the fathers' exchange formula with the language of representation (place, action) shows how the economic and immanent activity of God relate. As a result, we can now say that Christ's dramatic action for humanity (motif 2) is grounded in a trinitarian metaphysic (motif 5), while also seeing how such a dramatic activity unveils analogous grammar to speak of God's own life of exchange and place-acting.

To further show why this metaphysic is necessary to Balthasar's dramatic soteriology, I will now briefly look at how it is the presupposition to the particulars of redemption and *theosis*. Christ can act in humanity's place, assuming and redeeming it, because he opens up a place of otherness and difference within God for humanity to exist. Przywara states, "The eternity (of God in Christ) is, therefore, so thoroughly the 'all in all' of cosmic space that all that 'stands' in its 'place' in 'space,' and all that 'stands together' with everything creaturely as a 'universe,' ultimately 'stands' and 'stands together' only in the One Eternity (of God in Christ)."[197] God's super-space and super-time make it possible for him to enter the limited space and time of the cosmos. Thus, the in-and-beyond rhythm of the *analogia entis* makes redemption possible. God can assume the similarities between God and creation without becoming identified with created being precisely because of the ever-greater dissimilarity between creation's finite and bound place and God's infinite and immeasurable space and time.[198]

Furthermore, Christ can give himself completely to the tragic places of human existence because of the excessiveness of divine giving and receiving. The "in" of metaphysical analogy is the "in" of Christ's assumption of the emptiness of human distance, while the "beyond" of metaphysical analogy is the redemption of emptiness within the excessive fullness of divine distance. This emptiness-to-fullness movement overcomes the tragedies of human otherness without introducing any form of separation or bifurcation in God's immanent being. The provided ascending planal distance taxonomy offers a formulization of how tragedy and restoration in the drama of creation can occur within God's immutable being. The economic tragedy of the cross and Christ's forsakenness is further restored by triune receptivity. In his incomprehensible richness of being, Christ can hand over his self to the darkness of human privation, while trusting in the return of being from the Spirit. Unfortunately, Balthasar's formulation of Christ's cry of dereliction and descent into hell leaves the door open for tragedy to ascend to the highest level of distance. I provide the details and amendment to his trinitarian grammar of the cross in chapter 3.

The second half of the dramatic exchange formula is humanity's participation in the place of Christ, which is "the final form" of the *communio sanctorum*.[199] Although Balthasar makes use of Luther's radical theology of the cross, he believes Luther failed to give equal attention to *theosis*. The main purpose of the Son's indwelling of humanity is for humanity's participation in the triune life.[200] Humanity is not simply "redeemed through" Christ but is "essentially redeemed 'into' him." Given the ever-greater nature of the Trinity—the roominess of God—God's eternal communion can grow without introducing change into God's essence.[201] Just as this trinitarian exchange of life, fruit, and love is grounded in the idea of pro-existence, so too can Christ, in his representation of humanity, be seen as the "positing principle, [who] through its own self-investment (self-sacrifice), creates a 'place,' a locus, in which the posited 'other can express its own self.'"[202] As the Father actively participates in the Son and Spirit, so too can humanity participate in the Son by trinitarian "being for the other."[203] Christ's dramatic action *pro nobis* does not override human freedom, but enables humanity to be more fully itself.[204] By attributing particularity and otherness to the divine Persons, humanity's theotic participation is a dramatic one that enables particularity, otherness, and freedom.[205] Trinitarian pro-existence extends to Christ's representation of humanity, inviting humanity to participate in the triune life.

In the introduction, I considered Aidan Nichols's assertion that the motifs of Balthasar's dramatic soteriology are "held together—coherently united—by the *Stellvertretung* idea."[206] This statement seemed moribund without considering how action, place, and otherness were part of the underlying grammar of triune giving and receiving. If we define the patristic exchange formula through the lens of representation and give this dramatic exchange formula a trinitarian foundation, Nichols's observation becomes more intelligible. The self-giving of God for humanity (motif 1) reveals God's triune life of generative and receptive activity for the other (motif 5). Together, these motifs provide the patristic exchange formula and representation a theological foundation (motif 2), which results in the unified activity of Christ for the redemption of humanity (motif 3) and its initiation into the triune life (motif 4).

Conclusion

We've now seen how Balthasar's doctrine of the Trinity provides a metaphysic for a theology of representation. Balthasar's claim to give an exact elaboration and theological foundation for representation in *TD4* was shown to be incomplete, because it primarily focused on trinitarian distance and redemption from sin. Therefore, I developed Balthasar's metaphysic of representation further by analyzing how God eternally acts in the place of the other in the triune processions. This construction required that we consider Norbert Hoffmann's notion of pro-existence, developments of Balthasar's doctrine of the Trinity that occur after the critical section on representation in *TD4*, and a more explicit articulation of how the *action in the place of the other* occurs in triune and creaturely being. Furthermore, in adopting Balthasar's spatialization of the triune life, I also had to attend to the various critiques that have arisen because of it, or else the foundation for representation would crumble. By offering a more consistent analogical formulation of triune spatial analogies, combined with a musical understanding of space, I hope to have resolved many of these critiques. I now turn to the second theological foundation for representation, Christology.

CHAPTER TWO

BALTHASAR'S MISSION CHRISTOLOGY
The Theo-Dramatic Representative

Verbum caro factum est, et habitavit in nobis; illi carni adjungitur ecclesia, et fit Christus totus, caput et corpus.

The Word was made flesh, and dwelled among us. The Church is joined to that flesh, and Christ becomes the whole, head and body.
—Augustine, *Homilies on the First Epistle of John* 1.2

In chapter 1, we considered the relationship between Balthasar's doctrine of the Trinity, representation, and dramatic soteriology. In this chapter, we will explore the second theological foundation of Balthasar's theology of representation, Christology. Christ is not simply another actor in the *theatrum mundi*, but he transforms the drama into a theo-drama, into the *theatrum Dei*. A theology of representation—a metaphysic that considers the relationship between actors, places, action, and responsibility—is weighted toward Christ. "The Christian faith radicalized the idea of representation in an unprecedented way: it made representation the effective and potent basic event of existence," says Sölle. "It elevated the representative as the decisive figure of world history who bears all things—namely, the sin of the world. It removed the temporal and local limitations of the representation he carried out, and thus made it universal."¹ Yet, the *universal* nature of Christ's action for humanity presents Balthasar with a tantalizing *aporia*: How does the sphere of Christ's action extend to the ambit of another without replacing or consuming it? Summarizing Balthasar's concern, Jennifer Newsome Martin states that "any system that privileges the universal at the expense of the personal and particular, flattening out individual freedom, 'signals the abdication of drama in favor of a narrative philosophy of history, an epic story of the Spirit or of mankind.'"² God's universal relationship to the stage of creaturely existence in Christ is concrete, dynamic, and personal. In this vein, Anne M. Carpenter argues that Balthasar synthesizes the theological tradition and the personalism of modernity in his christological aesthetic, calling this synthesis a "christological metaphysic of personality."³ Her analysis focuses primarily on his christological metaphysic's relationship to personal "expression" in the *Glory of the Lord*.⁴ I am continuing the work of Balthasar scholars who note the unique configuration of the universal and the dramatic (historical, concrete, and personal), but I focus on Balthasar's mission Christology in the *Theo-Drama*, where he is chiefly concerned about the theo-dramatic relationship between Christ's two natures.

It is in this conversation about the universal and the dramatic in Balthasar's mission Christology where the originality of Balthasar's theology of representation tacitly emerges. Generally, interpreters' definitions of Balthasar's theology of *Stellvertretung* focus on its *soteriological* account in *TD*4. These frequently *stauro*-monistic interpretations do not discern the theological foundations of Balthasar's theology of the cross and lead to underdeveloped understandings of his theology of representation. Balthasar's theology of representation is economically "performed" in *TD*4, but it is ultimately grounded in his eclectic and original construction of how the two natures of Christ relate via mission. And though it may seem that a lengthy chapter on Christology is outside the scope of this project on representation, it is in fact Balthasar's Christology that is essential to understanding how representation functions, as Balthasar himself says on multiple occasions. For example, if Balthasar offers a Christology like Barth's, which, according to Balthasar, may collapse all human activity into Christ's, then "substitution" may be the most appropriate translation. However, given that Balthasar is keen to correct this tendency in Barth's Christology, "substitution" cannot be the all-encompassing translation of Balthasar's theology of *Stellvertretung*.

Consequently, in this chapter I analyze Balthasar's mission Christology in dialogue with his primary interlocutors (Maximus the Confessor, John of Damascus, Aquinas, Przywara, Buber, and Barth) and explicate the interaction between two central concepts of Balthasar's dramatic theology: the *dramatis personae* and the concrete *analogia entis*. By discerning the eclectic synthesis of the voices, ideas, and logics involved in Balthasar's mission Christology, I offer an overarching Christo-logic of how representation functions. In short, I argue that Christ's representation of humanity is theo-dramatic, that is, universal and personalizing. To do so, I show in the first section of this chapter how Balthasar's mission Christology is reliant upon dialectical and analogical resources. In the second section, I integrate Balthasar's christological metaphysic with the representative–represented relation. In the end, I demonstrate how "representation" fits Balthasar's overarching Christology better than "substitution."

Balthasar's Mission Christology

In *Ecce Homo*, Aaron Riches diagnoses the complexity of discerning the questions of difference and relation in christological debates. If such questions are not considered appropriately, Christ can become a *tertium quid*, a third thing that is neither distinctively divine nor human. As is expressed most palpably in various forms of monophysitism, Christ's divine nature becomes passible and blends into the human nature, or the human nature is destroyed by being absorbed by Christ's divine nature. The same kind of logic pervades Nestorianism. Attempting to preserve the impassibility of the divine and the distinction of the human, Nestorius taught that the two *prosopa*, the Logos and the human Jesus, were unified in the one historical *prosopon* of Christ.[5] Christ, the "prosopon of union," becomes a "quasi-third prosopic reality in addition to the *prosopa* of the *homo assumptus* and of the Logos."[6] Thus, monophysitism and Nestorianism both recapitulate inadequate metaphysical conceptions of the relationship between infinite and finite being.[7] A metaphysical outlook that defines difference as absolute distinction, contrastive, and competitive makes the unification of two distinct natures inconceivable without one absorbing the other or the two synthesizing, producing a *tertium quid*.[8]

A *tertium quid* Christology is precisely what Balthasar seeks to overcome in his mission Christology, as he seeks to walk on another knife edge, here "between Nestorianism and monophysitism."[9] Critical of the polysemy of historical notions of personhood, Balthasar believes that the Chalcedonian definition of Christ will struggle to maintain the distinction-in-union of Christ's two natures without a more precise definition of what it means to be a person. His mission Christology seeks to fill this void by creatively synthesizing the logic of Chalcedon with a variety of ancient and modern voices. In the following construction, we explore how Balthasar develops Chalcedonian Christology by offering a new way of relating concepts through the concept of mission: the divine and the human, individual and person, and representative and represented.

To appreciate Balthasar's argument, we will need to draw upon dialectical logic, and given the controversial reception of dialectic via Hegel, some clarification is in order. Theologians often reject Hegel because of his revision of Christian doctrine, even if they engage him seriously in the process of dismissal.[10] Nicholas Adams reevaluates Hegel by arguing that theologians need to focus on Hegel's "logic" and put aside issues of "ontology."[11] Adams contends that Hegel's dialectical logic is built upon the underlying logic of a Chalcedonian Christ. Chalcedonian logic is a participatory logic of relation ("distinct but in inseparable relation") between the divinity and humanity of Christ compared to the oppositional logic of monophysitism and Nestorianism.[12] According to Adams, Hegel's dialectic mediates the relationship between two terms, denying the absolute opposition of terms in Kantian and Cartesian logic. The terms exist in "motion" with one another. The relation is expressed in a "third," which is not "a third term in a series" or a third thing but the "expression of the 'unity' of the first two terms." Thus, Hegelian dialectic is what denotes differences between a "pair" of terms, while predicating a third that defines the relation of the two. Pairs are, therefore, "triadic."[13]

Although Balthasar's Christology is not Hegelian and he ultimately believes that Hegel's system fails to uphold the necessary difference between God and creation required for genuine participation,[14] there are particular moments throughout the *Theo-Drama* and Balthasar's Christology that depend upon a dialectical logic of participation.[15] Matthew Levering argues that "we can expect von Balthasar to exploit the same 'dialectical rhythms,' [as Hegel] even while he rejects Hegel's reductive rendering of Christ's personal work and of the triune God."[16] In his *Cosmic Liturgy*, Balthasar positively regards Maximus the Confessor's concept of the motion between two terms and acknowledges its similarity to Hegel.[17] Despite the myriad of definitions of dialectic,[18] I will use Adams's definition just provided.

Even though Balthasar is dependent on his interaction with Hegelian dialectic, the logic of his Christology is intimately involved with ontology. This tension between the meta-noetic and the meta-ontic, as Przywara calls it,[19] elicits the presence of the *analogia entis* in Balthasar's Christology. Logical distinctions require some kind of ontological distinctions,[20] and it is ultimately the ontological distinctions grounded in the *analogia entis* that separate Balthasar from Hegel and maintain the essential difference between the universal and the concrete.[21] Recently, Balthasar scholars have argued that one of the unique features of Balthasar's theology is his unique marriage of dialectic and analogy in various aspects of his theology. Gallaher demonstrates their unity in Balthasar's triune portrayal of the God–creation relationship, and Andrew L. Prevot does so in Balthasar's christological aesthetics.[22] I am focusing specifically on the potential unity of analogy and dialectic in Balthasar's mission Christology. When using the term "dialectic," I am referring to the *horizontal logic* of distinction-in-relation. When using the term "analogy," I am referring to the *vertical ontology* of similarity-in-dissimilarity.[23]

In the following, I examine the four main components of Balthasar's mission Christology, showing how the marriage of dialectic and analogy clarifies the eclectic relationship between the ancient (John of Damascus, Maximus the Confessor, and Aquinas) and modern voices (Barth, Buber, and Przywara) that are present, and I offer a reconsideration of some of the christological dilemmas that are associated with Balthasar's Christology. Ultimately, by discerning the various voices and logics that are present in Balthasar's mission Christology, we will be able to more clearly portray the theo-dramatic (universal and personalizing) relationship between Christ-the-representative and the church-the-represented.

Dramatis personae: *Conscious Subjects, Theological Persons, and Mission*

In the opening of his Christology in *TD3*, Balthasar argues that the fathers' lack of a distinctive Christian ontology of personhood resulted in a mélange of incongruous christological terminology and ideas.[24] Balthasar seeks to repair this problem by developing a theo-dramatic understanding of person (persons he labels as the *dramatis personae*) based on mission, which he uses to integrate dramatic theory with the Chalcedon definition of Christ.[25] Thus, in this first component of our christological construction, I introduce Balthasar's theology of person alongside concepts of the theological dramatic theory. In the end, I show how his conception of person and mission needs to be framed dialectically. The *dramatis personae* are those who are unified by mission in the dialectical tension between historical contingencies and the divine will.

Balthasar's Christology begins with a distinction between a "conscious subject" (a natural individual) and a theological person.[26] As I framed it in chapter 1, the drama of creaturely existence is found in the tension between its self-possession (pillar one) and its fundamental need to give to and receive from others (pillar two). Personhood is *dramatic* because drama indicates the social character of human existence. Drama is about the "dialogue" between "events," "characters," "roles," which together constitute the performance of finite existence.[27]

Balthasar distinguishes *theological* personhood from the concept of a "natural individual" simply as a conscious subject. The unique *who* of a person can only be designated by the absolute Subject, God. Personhood is given when God addresses a conscious subject and "impart[s] a distinctive and divinely authorized mission."[28] Whereas a conscious subject's identity is grounded in the tension between the two pillars of finite freedom, a theological person is defined by a unique mission given by God. The archetype of theological personhood is Christ, whose universal mission is to establish personhood for all other conscious subjects by granting them "personal missions" within his universal mission.[29]

Balthasar scholars have noted that his focus on the uniqueness of each person's mission comes from his devotion to Ignatian spirituality. Christian holiness is not primarily expressed in general terms, but in concrete obedience to a personal mission.[30] Balthasar appropriates this Ignatian understanding of individual mission into his theo-dramatic conception of personhood by synthesizing it with the dialogical philosophy of his contemporaries, primarily relying on Martin Buber and Franz Rosenzweig.[31]

This synthesis can be summarized as follows. At some point in life, an individual conscious subject will encounter the eternal "Thou" in a dramatic event of dialogue. In this event, the individual becomes an "I," a theological person, by being "named" by God, a naming that includes a specific and unique mission. In this event, God gains a genuine partner, a "serious co-actor" on the stage, who can contribute to the drama of creation.[32] Balthasar suggests that theo-dramatic theory needs to transition from theatric "roles" or "functions" to "missions." Modernity might focus on the individual, but it does so in a way that characters are "fungible,"[33] and herein lies the problem for Balthasar. Because subjectively chosen roles are interchangeable and arbitrary, the individual can be replaced. In contrast, missions are assigned by God. For the Ignatian Balthasar, personhood is ultimately expressed through one's *vertical* reception of a divine mission, making the "I" unique and irreplaceable.[34]

In this understanding of personhood defined by divine mission, we encounter a potential issue if personhood is genuinely dramatic. Key to drama and dialogical philosophy is the characters' individuality, interpersonal communion, and freedom. If missions are given entirely "from above," then the divine freedom may replace the human subject's freedom and its relation to the historical stage.[35] In other words, one's vertical movement toward God (the universal) should not absorb one's horizontal relation to the stage (the concrete and particular), which requires that there is some form of inherent difference between God and the world so that the "space of dialogue" is not abolished, as it is in Hegel's monism and German idealism, where the divine or the human community absorbs the "I."[36] One of the precise reasons Balthasar recommends transitioning from the term "role" to "mission" is so that the individual does not get lost in his or her role. Roles are often seen as external to the self, as is the case when one represents an institution, such as a sergeant or president.³⁷ The term "mission," then, needs to be employed in a manner that theological personhood does not replace the freedom and historical particularities of a conscious subject.

Therefore, the first part of our christological construction—the theo-dramatic conception of personhood—invites an explicit dialectical formulation. The pair of terms, conscious subject and theological person, are unified by a third, mission. The distinction between terms is maintained, but the terms are nonoppositional because they participate in the formation of the other through mission. The essential question, "Who am I?," is emphatically answered as one acts in unity with God on the stage of one's existence. Balthasar uses an example: "*La Senne* once compared the character with the piano on which the 'I' plays; the music thus played would be the person. In other words, the acting 'I' cannot be, cannot become itself, except through the medium in which it plays, its instrument, which, again, cannot be isolated from the environment in which it lives."³⁸ Mission is what unites a conscious subject's freedom in a community with a divinely given task. The *dramatis personae*, then, are those who freely act in the creative and unified tension between the world stage and divine activity. We further explore this idea under the theme of emplaced *theosis* in chapter 4.

The One Sent: An Analogical Relation between Divine Procession and Human Mission

Conscious subjects are in movement toward personhood, as the many Old Testament (Sarah, Abraham, Moses, David) and New Testament (Peter and Paul) examples indicate.³⁹ However, if the Son were on the move toward theological personhood like all other humans, then it would signify a kind of Hegelian monophysite formula, where "the 'from above' aspect meshes seamlessly with 'from below' aspect."⁴⁰ Thus, for Balthasar, a divine subject needs to be "supra-personal," being entirely identified with mission: Christ is none other than the One sent (*der Gesendete*).⁴¹ Mission is ultimately the "key to [Christ's] whole existence" because it is an analogue to divine receptivity. The Son is none other than the One who eternally receives from the Father in his procession, which is displayed economically as the exact same openness to being sent.⁴²

In this transition from a theo-dramatic conception of personhood to Christology, we see here how Balthasar is using Aquinas's categories of mission, procession, and being sent. Yet, whereas Aquinas clearly distinguishes between eternal procession and temporal mission, Bruce Marshall argues that Balthasar makes temporal mission constitutive of God's eternal procession.[43] Balthasar's theo-dramatic conception of personhood may be dubious in the case of Christ. Christ—the archetype of the *dramatis personae*—would then be defined by his relation to the drama of creation. Whereas the normal *dramatis personae* are subject to the drama and the social character of their existence, Christ's personhood cannot be primarily conceived this way without resulting in an Arian Christ (Christ's procession is for the sake of his mission) or a Nestorian Christ (his human individuality is isolated or in opposition to his divine personhood). Thus, in this subsection, I review Aquinas's procession/mission distinction, which will enable me to show how an analogical rendering of Balthasar's mission Christology can allow Christ to become identified with his temporal mission without being constituted by it. I also show the subtle way that Aquinas's procession/mission distinction influences Balthasar's understanding of *Stellvertretung*.

In the *Summa*, Aquinas addresses "the mission of the divine persons."[44] "Mission" means to "be sent." "Being sent" has a twofold relation to the one sent: the relation to the sender and the relation to the place. First, the one sent and the sender are in relation through a third term: "going forth." Unlike human missions where a sender typically has authority over the sent—the sent "goes forth" at the sender's command—within the Trinity the sender and the one sent must be equals in divine missions. Second, a new form of presence is introduced between the one sent and the place where they are sent. "New" can mean a presence that was not previously in the place sent or a presence that shows up in a new way. Aquinas is clear that the Son is present to creation prior to the Incarnation, but in the Incarnation he becomes present in a new way. Objecting to the point that "being sent" means "change of place," Aquinas notes that this type of mission does not apply to the missions of the divine persons, who are omnipresent.[45] This objection to "change of place" seems to influence Balthasar's theology of representation in *TD4*, which I will examine momentarily.

Aquinas then further clarifies what it means for a divine person to be sent, noting that there are "shades of meaning." First, there is a distinction between eternal procession and earthly mission. Terms such as "generation" and "spiration" refer to a divine person's eternal procession; "sending" and "giving" refer to a divine person's relationship to time through mission. The Son is not eternally begotten to be sent to the world. On the other hand, Aquinas notes how there are similarities between the terms "mission" and "procession." For divine persons, procession and mission are alike when understood as "coming forth from a principle."[46] Thus, Aquinas can speak of mission as a "procession in time."[47] In fact, Aquinas notes that one of the two ways one might explain the phrase "the Son is sent by being begotten" is to say that the Son's eternal coming forth makes it possible for him to go forth, to be sent in time.[48] This linkage leads Aquinas to speak of a "two-fold procession." The first is understood as a divine person's *eternal* coming forth from a principle (generation), whereas the second is understood as a divine person's *temporal* going forth in time (being sent). Aquinas summarizes, "Accordingly, 'being sent' and 'being given' are terms applying to God only in time; 'generation' and 'spiration,' only in eternity; but 'proceeding' and 'going forth,' both in eternity and in time."[49]

What we see in Aquinas is both epistemological and ontological uses of analogy in his understanding of trinitarian procession and mission. He distinguishes between the meaning of terms, drawing out similarities and dissimilarities between human and divine mission and divine mission and procession. He also makes ontological claims. The coming forth of procession is the eternal, noncontingent generation of the Son, which is the possibility of a contingent, temporal mission.[50]

Can it be said that Balthasar follows Aquinas, or does he detour from him? Kilby, Mackinnon, and Pitstick believe he has moved too far beyond Aquinas.[51] On the other hand, O'Regan and Nichols believe Balthasar faithfully upholds the distinction between economic and immanent activities of God, unlike Hegel,[52] but, according to Nichols, Balthasar's "way of reaching Thomas's conclusion is utterly his own."[53] Balthasar is clear throughout his corpus that he desires to maintain fidelity to Aquinas's general rule of processions holding priority over missions.[54] And so by explicitly interpreting Balthasar's mission Christology analogically, I will demonstrate how Balthasar creatively upholds Aquinas's twofold understanding of mission, but he ultimately does so in a way that invites us to consider the dramatic nature of Jesus's humanity. This is one of the ways Balthasar's theology of mission blends dramatic theory and modern voices with the tradition. I will then show the relevance of the mission/procession distinction to the translation of *Stellvertretung*.

The first aspect discussed above in Aquinas's understanding of mission is the analogy between eternal procession and temporal mission. Just as Aquinas names the likeness between the two as coming forth from a source, so Balthasar similarly names *receptivity* as the commonality between two terms. The Son is none other than the One who eternally receives from the Father in his procession, which is displayed economically as the exact same openness to being sent.[55] If the focus on mission in *TD3* is understood within the similarity-in-dissimilarity of the *analogia entis*, then the Son's temporal mission to creation is one of the free possibilities of his eternal procession from the Father. As the Son is his receptivity of divinity from the Father, so he is his temporal mission to creation—he receives humanity in the Incarnation. The Son's procession is in-and-beyond his mission. The Son does not need to become his mission, as humans do, through dramatic events of dialogue. He eternally is always this Person who receives from the Father, and, thus, acts in unity even as he economically receives humanity through his temporal mission. "Consequently," Balthasar can say, "Jesus's existence-in-mission manifests a paradoxical unity of *being* (and a *being* that *has always been*) and *becoming*" because he primordially exists as a "single being" who is as he receives.[56] It is in this *becoming* aspect of Jesus's humanity that Balthasar unifies Aquinas with the dramatic nature of personhood outlined above, which I examine in the next subsection.

If one were simply reading Balthasar's Christology in *TD3*, it is possible to believe the Son's procession is the result of his mission because he consistently identifies Christ's person and mission. Whereas with Aquinas, a divine person's mission is temporal, it seems in *TD3* that Christ's mission is eternal since mission defines his personhood. To the contrary, *TD3* is a reflection on the *content* of Christ's mission, a construction of a theo-dramatic and Christocentric anthropology, and an establishment of a dialectical relation between Christ's universal and personalizing mission. Therefore, *TD3*'s explicit content is on the economic aspect of Christ's mission. By grasping Balthasar's *theology* of mission and its place in the triune life—mission is an analogy of eternal procession because both signify receptivity, one temporal and one eternal—we can read *TD3* as the Son's temporal performance of eternal receptivity. Therefore, it is precisely Balthasar's theology of mission that safeguards him from overidentifying the immanent and economic.

The second part of Aquinas's definition of "being sent," a new form of presence, is also creatively upheld and relates directly to the translation of *Stellvertretung* as "representation" rather than "substitution." Divine missions do not signify a change of place, since God is omnipresent, but rather signify a new form of presence to a place. In the section in *TD4* regarding the trinitarian foundations for representation, Balthasar seems to covertly reflect Aquinas: "The Son, the 'light' and 'life' of the world, who enters into this 'darkness' of negation by becoming man, does not need to change his own 'place' [*Stelle*] when, shining in the darkness, he undertakes to 'represent' [*vertreten*] the world."[57] Because of the way *Stellvertretung* (representation) includes reference to place (*Stelle*), its theological meaning is more specific than the English equivalent. In German, the question naturally arises: When the Son seeks to act in the place of the world (*Stellvertretung*), why does he not need to change his place (*Stelle*)? The Son does not need to change his place, because the world's location, its "place," is already in him (Col. 1:16).[58] Therefore, just as, Aquinas notes, divine missions cannot signify a change in place without diminishing the omnipresence of God, so the Son does not change his place in the economy because the precise place of creation is in him as the other in God. Substitution seems to signify a change of place, moving beyond Aquinas, whereas representation does not. Noticing this implicit influence of Aquinas is important to grasping Balthasar's *theology* of representation.

This analogical understanding of procession and mission needs to be related back to the dialectical understanding of a conscious subject and theological person. Since we defined the Son's *theological* personhood by his procession, we thus risk absorbing the *dramatic* nature of Christ's human individuality, encountering the logic of monophysitism and monothelitism. And although analogy helps us to avoid collapsing

Christ and creation, we still need the dialectical understanding of theo-dramatic personhood. In the next two subsections, we shall see how it is possible to unite analogy and dialectic in a Christology of mission by expressing the dialectical understanding of personhood within the analogical account of temporal mission and eternal procession.

Christ's Consciousness of Mission: Dyothelitism, Theandric Action, and Theo-Dramatic Action

After showing how mission relates to divine and human personhood, Balthasar proceeds with a Christology of consciousness and incorporates Maximus the Confessor's two-will formula into his mission Christology. Rejecting monothelitism, he reportedly lost his hand and tongue for his refusal to deny the two wills and activities of Christ, receiving the title "the Confessor."[59] Twenty-five years after his death, dyothelitism was declared the orthodox position at the Sixth Ecumenical Council in Constantinople (680–81), which asserted that both the human and divine wills of Christ played a role in the drama of humanity's salvation.[60] Maximus's dyothelitism leaves a pivotal impression on Balthasar's *Theo-Drama*. Balthasar reflects that "the entire theo-drama has its center in the two wills of Christ, the infinite, divine will and the finite, human will."[61] In this subsection, I recount Maximus the Confessor's relation between theandric action and the two wills of Christ, then consider how this informs Balthasar's Christology of consciousness and mission. In the end, I will suggest that the wills of Christ can only be properly understood by uniting the analogical and dialectical formulations of mission above, a unity that culminates in theo-dramatic action.

Foundational to Maximus's dyothelitist Christology is Denys the Areopagite's conception of Christ's "theandric energy" or "theandric action." In the fifth *Ambiguum*, Maximus aims to validate "a certain new 'theandric' energy among us," one that incorporates both divine and human activities in Christ.[62] Maximus consistently repeats the phrase "beyond being," highlighting Christ's transcendence from his humanity, while showing how Christ is fully human in the "whole of his being."[63] Christ possesses every capacity or energy of humanity, like willing, breathing, or walking, but in a particular "mode of existence." Maximus's mode (*tropos*) of existence is the equivalent to the Cappadocian hypostasis. Nature (*physis*) is defined by principles and definitions (*logoi*), which together subsist in concrete and particular modes of being. Christ, then, has human nature's "natural *logos*" and its energies, but in the particular mode of the divine Son.[64] As a result, "he does human things in a way transcending the human, showing, in accordance with the closest union, the human energy united without change to the divine power, since the [human] nature, united without confusion to [the divine] nature, is completely interpenetrated."[65] Or, as Balthasar states, God does human things in Christ "just as far as" possible without confusing the two energies.[66] A "new theandric energy among us" refers to how that which is beyond being acts synergistically in the human *logos*, "exercising the divine and human energy in the same person."[67] The "double energy" of Christ is essential to maintaining the difference between the two natures.

Maximus uses Christ's agony in the garden of Gethsemane as one of the most poignant instances of theandric activity. Maximus suggests that the negation in Christ's phrase, "Let not what I will, but what you will prevail," displays the "perfect harmony and concurrence" of his human will and the triune will of God. Christ has two wills as a result of having two natures,[68] but there is no "opposition" or "double-mindedness" between the two wills, because his human will has been deified in the hypostatic union. In the prayer, we see an event by which the divine will "shapes" the human will further.[69] The theandric activity in the event at Gethsemane displays the perfect harmony of the divine and human wills of Christ for the salvation and deification of humanity.

Balthasar follows the fundamental logic of Maximus, but goes one step further by elucidating how they are one in Christ's consciousness of mission. For Balthasar, Christ possesses divine freedom and the natural human capacity of will, which are fused into a "single activity" through his personal mission.[70] Ratzinger states that "the metaphysical two-ness of a human and divine will is not abrogated, but in the realm of the *person*, in the realm of freedom, the fusion of both takes place, with the result that they become *one* will, not naturally, but personally."[71] I next consider the primary features of Balthasar's Christology of consciousness, and then suggest that it creatively blends the dialectical and analogical formulations of mission above.

Balthasar believes that the fathers and the scholastics overemphasized Christ's omniscience and insists that Christ was not endowed with the beatific vision. Making mission the "measure of Jesus's freedom and knowledge," Balthasar believes that Christ's knowledge varies throughout his life.[72] By "depositing" or "laying up" his divine attributes with the Father, Christ empties himself of direct knowledge of the divine life.[73] Christ's direct knowledge is limited to a general knowledge of identity of Sonship, his mission to reconcile the world with God, and the hour of darkness on the cross.[74] More essential to Balthasar than the "perfect knowledge" of Christ is his existence of "poverty, chastity, and obedience." Christ's mission is fulfilled through intuition, obedience, patience, faith, and hope, which is displayed by the way he daily receives his mission from the Spirit, who presents and guides Christ to the eternal will of the triune God.[75]

Jesus's human freedom is more profound than the freedom of autonomous choice. Balthasar's resistance to the "autonomy motif" distinguishes his understanding of finite freedom from Hegel's. For Balthasar, Christ's human freedom is the capacity to receive his personal identity and mission from the Spirit and act within its scope.[76] Balthasar illustrates this point with an example. When an artist is authentically "possessed" by an idea, then the work will display the personal stamp of the artist. In Mozart's *Magic Flute*, one sees how an "inspired work" can display personal freedom through its distinct style. It is precisely when one is possessed by inspiration that he or she is most free to imprint his or her "personal uniqueness."[77] In other words, Jesus's human freedom is not marked by complete autonomy, but by an active and personalizing reception of his mission.[78]

Within this freedom, the particulars of various historical media can contribute to Jesus's personhood as a dramatic character. Like natural human subjects, Jesus's consciousness is partially constituted by the dialogue, events, and characters around him. The I-consciousness of Jesus must be awakened by others. Mary, partially aware of the Father's mission for the Son, imparts an initial understanding of Christ's identity to him while he is a child.[79] Furthermore, since Christ's mission is one of receptivity, he truly goes through a "historical learning process" through various encounters with humanity, which cause him to become more aware of his mission.[80] Balthasar is keen then to speak of the "becoming" aspect of Jesus's consciousness, when he genuinely undergoes development through dramatic events.

With these components of Balthasar's conception of Christ's consciousness in place, we see how Balthasar places the emphasis on how Jesus experiences consciousness in a similar manner to an ordinary human as he is awakened to his mission throughout his life, which highlights the dramatic nature of his human subjectivity. Yet, however unsystematic it might be, he does not seek to bifurcate this "from below" perspective from Christ's "from above" identity, that is, his theological personhood and the procession/mission distinction. O'Regan notes that one of the places we see the "from above" and "from below" elements of Balthasar's Christology balance out is in his incorporation of Maximus's two-wills approach.[81] And thus by suggesting that Balthasar's theology of the wills of Christ unites the dialectical and analogical conceptions of mission above, I can now synthesize the theological and dramatic commitments of Balthasar's Christology, which culminates in theo-dramatic action.

The first and governing foundation of Christ's consciousness is the analogical relation between Christ's procession and mission. The Son is actively obedient in time, which is an analogy of his receptivity in his procession from the Father.[82] The Son, who is beyond time and space (*maior dissimilitudo*), identifies himself with the finite freedom of a human subject, including the limitations of its time-bound, space-bound, and knowledge-bound context. The Son can indwell the time, tensions, and spaces that pervade creation's positive distance from the infinite because he kenotically determines himself to be reliant upon the Spirit in a similar way that he is reliant upon the Spirit to traverse his triune distance from the Father. Christ's human will exists "in" the free vertical movement of the divine will from "beyond." Therefore, we can say that his nonautonomous human will is ordered to the divine, exercising its freedom within the divine mission of the Son. This formulation is similar to Maximus's understanding of the human freedom of Christ in Gethsemane. By conceiving the relation of the two wills on a vertical plane, Balthasar gives priority to the "from above" *theological* nature of Christ's personhood and upholds the distinction between his procession and mission.

Within the procession-to-mission, eternity-to-time movement (analogical-vertical relation) is a dialectical-horizontal relation between

Christ's divine and human consciousness. The vertical-theological plane gives priority to the divine will, but the horizontal plane shows how the two wills are logically distinct in Christ, existing alongside one another in perfect relation through mission. Therefore, humanly, Jesus undergoes change, as dramatic persons are affected by the characters, scenes, and conflicts of the stage on which they find themselves. His human change remains congruent with his divine consciousness, as he chooses to be obedient to his primordial divine will by faithfully receiving his human experience and sanctifying it. Thus, on the horizontal plane, the *drama* of Christ's human consciousness is dialectically united to his *theological* personhood by obedience to mission, which shows how they are distinct but related through a third term, mission. There is no need then to speak of a balance between the two wills or one or the other being more dominant, because the wills are noncompetitive and noncontrastive, operating in the perfect unity of the mission/person of the one Lord Jesus Christ. And although a dialectical relation is necessary to account for the simultaneity of Christ's being and becoming, a tantalizing conflation or antithesis is bound to occur if they are related solely on a horizontal plane. Therefore, I am suggesting that the horizontal-logical-dialectical relation of Christ's divine and human wills exists within the vertical-ontological-analogical movement of the divine to the human.

We see in Balthasar's Christology that Christ's union of two wills is the performance of theo-dramatic activity, which is a development of Maximus's understanding of theandric activity. Christ unites the theological (absolute, simple, and eternal) and the dramatic (historical, contingent, bound) in his divine-human mission. This relation of the divine-universal and human-particular energies of Christ is the archetype of all theo-dramatic activity and is foundational to how the representative–represented relation functions.

The Concrete analogia entis: *Christ Is the Unity of the Theological and the Dramatic*

Following his discussion on the consciousness of Christ in *TD*3, Balthasar addresses the being of Christ.[83] By identifying Christ as the "concrete analogy of being," Balthasar forges the knife edge between Nestorianism and monophysitism and seeks to overcome the "thorniest problem of Christology," which is maintaining the unity of the two natures of Christ without abolishing the *maior dissimilitudo* between them.[84] In the following, I introduce Balthasar's Christocentrism and how it relates to the *analogia entis*. I then utilize three interrelated components of his notion of Christ as the concrete *analogia entis*—a necessary similarity, a prolonged *maior dissimilitudo*, and the finalized proportion of his two natures—to display how the various voices and logics in his mission Christology integrate and exhibit the final form of theo-dramatic activity.

Balthasar's mature Christology in *TD3* (1978) and *TL2* (1985) is a synthetic integration of his historical interlocutors.[85] Before taking its "theoretical formulation" in *The Theology of Karl Barth* (1951), Balthasar notes that his Christocentric vision was formed "aphoristically" in his earlier works *The Grain of Wheat* (1944) and *The Heart of the World* (1945), which were indubitably influenced by his early patristic monographs (on Origen, 1938; on Gregory of Nyssa, 1939; on Maximus the Confessor, 1941).[86] Balthasar's use of the *analogia entis* in Christology began very early in his theological writings as a response to Barth's emphatic rejection of the *analogia entis*, which Barth calls "the invention of Antichrist."[87] Balthasar believes that Barth misunderstood the *analogia entis*, but he ultimately synthesizes Barth's Christocentric vision with it. Balthasar admits that "Barth is absolutely right that the problem of analogy in theology must finally be a problem of Christology," because Christ ontologically and epistemologically governs the relation between the infinite and finite.[88] Therefore, it is not the *analogia entis* as a neutral theory that governs the relationship between God and creation. It is the *analogia entis* in Christ. Christ, "the living center of history," is the norm of history, anthropology, and ontology.[89]

We can now examine the three main components of Balthasar's notion of the concrete *analogia entis* and how they relate to the various issues that we have been discussing in this chapter. The first component is the implicit similarity between the divine and human. Balthasar asks of the Chalcedonian Christ, "How can such a union be possible given the 'abyss' between two different realities that have nothing in common?"[90] Balthasar responds, "But in light of the foregoing discussion, we realize that the incarnate Word comes into 'his own property' (John 1:11).

Hence, he does not travel merely into a foreign land (as Karl Barth says) but into a country whose language he knows."[91] If there were no analogy, no similarity between the infinite and finite, the Son could not assume human nature. Either Christ's humanity or divinity would be absorbed, changed, or destroyed, resulting in a *tertium quid*. Therefore, Christology requires an implicit *analogia entis*.[92]

Balthasar's ultimate concern, despite his appropriation of Barth's Christocentrism, is to protect the freedom and integrity of creation. He believes Barth's Christocentrism is "constricting" or "narrowing."[93] In contrast, Balthasar desires a Christocentrism like Maximus's that is centered on Christ without reducing the autonomy of creation.[94] Balthasar protects the freedom of creation by defending the concreteness and particularity of Jesus's human nature, and he believes some formulations—namely, Logos-sarx Christology, Cyril of Alexandria, and Barth—can potentially misconstrue the relationship between the divine and human in Christ. In response, Balthasar adopts elements of John of Damascus's Christology and expands them through the concept of mission. The first element he adopts is Damascus's formulation of *enhypostasis*, which Balthasar believes is a more precise construction of Cyril's *mia physis* formula and Chalcedonian Christology.[95]

In his *Elementary Introduction* and *Dialectica*, John of Damascus defines theological terms to set the stage for his trinitarian and christological dogma. He inherited years of controversies over the definitions of the various words (e.g., Cyril's equation of *physis* and *hypostasis*) and sought to consolidate and simplify them. *Ousia* is used to refer to the species, essence, and nature (*physis*), whereas *hypostasis* refers to the particular, the person (*prosopon*), or the individual. *Ousia*, though, is abstract on its own; it only exists in concrete *hypostases*.[96] Thus, Andrew Louth states, "it is hypostasis that is the fundamental ontological reality."[97]

The concept of *enhypostasis* is found in John of Damascus's *Exposition of the Orthodox Faith*.[98] The longest portion of this work explores Christology and seeks to defend the hypostatic union in the wake of ongoing problems with monophysitism, monothelitism, and Nestorianism. Reflecting on the idea of *enhypostasis*, John of Damascus states, "For the flesh of God the Word did not subsist as an independent subsistence, nor did there arise another subsistence besides that of God the Word, but as it existed in that it became rather a subsistence which subsisted in another, than one which was an independent subsistence. Wherefore, neither does it lack subsistence altogether, nor yet is there thus introduced into the Trinity another subsistence."[99] Christ's human nature does not have an independent existence, but only exists as it subsists in another.

A commonly used definition of *enhypostasis* is "in-existent."[100] "At the heart of John Damascene's Christology there lies the *theologoumenon* that the humanity of Christ has no hypostasis of its own, since it is taken up by the hypostasis of the Logos, the second person of the Trinity, and exists *in it*," says U. M. Lang.[101] Tantamount to this conception is the "distinction between that which is in something and that in which it is. This 'restarting' of the definition allows Damascene to make a crucial speculation: that which is *enhypostaton* is not identical with its hypostasis; rather it is that which is seen and is real *in* the hypostasis."[102] As a result, a two-sons Christology is refuted by John of Damascus since there is no human Jesus except as he exists in the divine Logos, while monophysitism is avoided because Jesus's humanity is genuine within the divine Son.[103]

By synthesizing the developed enhypostatic Christology of John of Damascus and Przywara's *analogia entis* with his mission Christology, Balthasar seeks to offer a Christocentrism that avoids monophysitism and upholds the integrity of creation. To do so, he insists on the analogical similarity of Christ's two natures and establishes this similarity via his mission-ontology of divine and human personhood. The hypostatic-in of the Logos's relation to human nature occurs as it comes from the Christocentric-beyond, from the vertical procession-to-mission movement. Christ's two natures are in unity because Christ's humanity exists in the divine Son's mission (i.e., it is "enhypostatic"). There is no human Jesus outside of the divine Son's mission, and the human Jesus's mission is entirely oriented toward the divine Son's. In this movement, Christ's humanity is genuine—it is not absorbed—because it does not compete with the mission of the divine Son. Balthasar further clarifies how Christ's humanity is genuine in the next element of the concrete *analogia entis*.

A second aspect of the concrete *analogia entis* concerns how the distance between the divine and human in Christ remains even after the Incarnation. Even as Christ "strides through" the ontological distance between God and creation, incorporating humanity into himself, humanity as such is safeguarded and ensheltered, being both Christ's body and bride—being, respectively, metaphysically one with Christ (Augustine's *Christus totus*) and ontologically differentiated other. No matter the level of unity between the natures of Christ, they must remain "unconfused," even after humanity's divinization.[104] Thus, to speak of humanity's inclusion in Christ, a grammar and ontology of noncompetitive difference is essential to avoid the "mystical absorption" of humanity into God in the Chalcedonian Christ. Christ, the concrete *analogia entis*, redeems and perfects humanity by establishing and maintaining a positive distance from it. As a result, when Christ ascends to "prepare a place" with "many dwellings" for his people (John 14:2), Balthasar speaks of it as humanity's *Einbergung* in Christ.[105] Nichols translates *Einbergung*—a "translation-resistant German word"—as "sheltering engathering," and Gallaher as "ensheltering."[106] Corporeal humanity's bound and limited place is not constricted by Christ, but exists in and is protected by the incorporeal, boundless place of Christ.

Balthasar establishes this sustained distance by incorporating a second aspect of Damascus's Christology, one that emphasizes the importance of Jesus's concrete humanity. Highlighting the problem of what he sees as a Logos-sarx Christology, Balthasar states, "It was possible to emphasize this seizure of power over all flesh (John 17:2) through the Incarnation of the Logos to such an extent that he seemed to adopt human nature in its entirety."[107] Formulations like these emphasize the universal work of Christ for humanity to the extent that the particularities are minimized. Thus, Balthasar believes that *enhypostatic* Christology needs to be coupled with a view that upholds the concrete nature of the Incarnation to avoid monophysitism and monothelitism,[108] a coupling found in John of Damascus and Maximus the Confessor and clarified by the dialectical understanding of personhood.

The Son could not have assumed human nature in the abstract, because abstract human nature does not exist. According to John of Damascus and Aquinas, natures only exist as particular *hypostases* that subsist out of the nature.[109] Aquinas notes that it seems the Son should have "assumed a nature abstracted from all individuals" for his work to be universal. "On the contrary," he responds,

Damascene says (*De Fide Orth*. iii, 11): "God the Word Incarnate did not assume a nature which exists in pure thought; for this would have been no Incarnation, but a false and fictitious Incarnation." But human nature as it is separated or abstracted from individuals is "taken to be a pure conception, since it does not exist in itself," as Damascene says (*De Fide Orth*. iii, 11). Therefore the Son of God did not assume human nature, as it is separated from individuals.[110]

For John of Damascus, Christ's human nature exists concretely, personally, and individually in its mode of union with the divine Son.[111] The way that John of Damascus maintains the unity between Christ's divine and human natures is through the concept of Sonship. Christ's divine Sonship, his distinction in the Trinity, is the reason he could become the "Son of Man" (a concrete individual) without changing his identity, distinction, and individuality of divine Sonship.[112]

As to Logos-sarx Christology, Balthasar believes post-Hegelian emphases on Christ as the "central individual" or "universal human being" tend to abstract Jesus from the rest of humanity.[113] Instead, he follows John of Damascus, stating that "the definiteness of the divine Sonship of Jesus is directly able to make him into a very definite, individual human being."[114] Whereas Gregory of Nyssa defines the "concrete universal" as the human species—thereby denying Jesus the "attributes of individuality"[115]—Balthasar prefers Maximus the Confessor's Christology, which locates the concrete universal in the individual. If Jesus is fully human, then he must have a concrete human will and activity.[116] "This idea of the balance and reciprocity of universal and particular is perhaps the most important in the whole of Maximus's thought," states Balthasar.[117]

To this formulation, Balthasar affixes his concept of mission, which, if combined with our dialectical reading of personhood, can unify what has been discussed thus far. Jesus's human nature only exists as it subsists in relation to the mission of the divine Son, but it is protected by the distance maintained in the concrete *analogia entis*. A *maior dissimilitudo* between infinite and finite being is necessary to the "safeguarding" and perfection of humanity in the "synthetic principle" of Maximus the Confessor's Christology.[118] This sustained distance entails, for Balthasar, that a particular human individual subsists in the divine

Son, not simply human nature in the abstract. Nestorianism seems to arise here in Balthasar's Christology,[119] but this is where an explicit dialectical reading of Balthasar's theo-dramatic conception of personhood can clarify his Christology. Since an individual is only a true person by being assigned a mission and the human Jesus only exists within the vertical movement of the divine Son's mission, then his humanity can be genuine, concrete, and dramatic without remaining separate from divine nature. The horizontal distinction-in-relation between the divine and human agencies of Christ is possible because his human individuality and divine personhood are unified in the one mission of the Lord Jesus Christ. In monophysitism and monothelitism, the divinity of Christ is in competition with his humanity. Instead, Balthasar suggests that the eternal Word makes space for and personalizes the humanity of Jesus by uniting its concrete particularity to the eternal mission of the divine Son. Thus, on a vertical-ontological level, Balthasar upholds both the traditional distinction between Christ's procession and mission (Aquinas) and gives priority to *theological-universal* movement of God to the world (Barth and Cyril). Yet, he seeks to marry the theological tradition to the dialogical personalism of modernity by making space for the *dramatic nature* of Christ's human personhood, which I am suggesting should be read on a horizontal-dialectical plane of distinction-in-relation.

Our construction thus far leads to the third and concluding aspect of the concrete *analogia entis*. Christ is the perfect synthesis, proper proportion, and unified distance between the divine and human. "In this sense Christ can be called the 'concrete analogy of being,' *analogia entis*, since he constitutes in himself, in the unity of his divine and human natures, the proportion of every interval between God and man," says Balthasar.[120] In every place where Balthasar speaks of Christ as the concrete analogy of being, he uses the term "proportion" to describe the final unity-in-distinction of the two natures of Christ's person.[121] In Maximus the Confessor's words, Christ can "synthesize" the natures while maintaining the "unconfused" formula of Chalcedon.[122] For a Thomistic-Przywarian Christ, the term "perfecting border" signifies how Christ is the "middle of creation" in himself, sanctifying and perfecting the God-creation proportion.[123]

In this final aspect of the concrete *analogia entis*, the culminating grammar of our Christology adjoins the horizontal plane of distinction-in-relation within the "in" of vertical analogy, as the two planes meet once and for all in the unity of Christ's person in mission. Because Christ's human nature subsists concretely and personally in the mission of the divine Son—the vertical-universal movement—it meets perfectly with the horizontal distinction-in-relation of Christ's two natures, synthesizing them into theo-dramatic action, a participatory, noncompetitive action that unifies the universal and the particular, the divine and the human. The logical distinction-in-relation of dialectic takes place in the ontological similarity-in-ever-greater-dissimilarity of the concrete analogy of being. This formulation allows us to distinguish logically between Christ's human and divine activities in the economy of redemption, while the two actions remain in ontological unity because they occur within the personal and capacious movement of the divine Son's mission. By incorporating both planes of thought in the person of Christ—he is the finalized proportion between the divine and human—we can see how Balthasar's Christology is dependent on both analogical and dialectical resources.

In conclusion, although Rowan Williams believes Barth corrects this issue in later volumes of the *Church Dogmatics* in his *analogia relationis*, he notices that the divine and human activities are often displayed "in competition for one logical space."[124] Przywara, Williams suggests, offers what Barth does not, by affirming "a non-rivalrous difference."[125] Furthermore, Williams notes (O'Regan offers a similar conclusion) how Balthasar's incarnational metaphysics, owing to the influence of Barth, Hegel, and Przywara, proffers "a model of divine being-in-the-other that allows full scope for the tension between the conditioned and the unconditioned and thus allows us to see grace—and incarnation—as the proper crowning of creation and created action, without compromising divine liberty."[126] With a parallel vision in mind, I have shown in the first half of this chapter how Balthasar creatively extends Chalcedon by blending the Chalcedonian vision of thinkers such as Maximus, John of Damascus, and Aquinas with more modern voices such as Przywara, Buber, and Barth to display the theo-dramatic dimensions of Christ's activity. By discerning the various voices, concerns, and logics in Balthasar's Christology, I can now propose a theo-dramatic interpretation of Balthasar's theology of representation.

Inclusion in Christ: The Theo-Dramatic Representative

The trinitarian and soteriological development of representation in *TD*4 is preceded by a christological foundation in *TD*3. Balthasar's theology of representation is not simply a soteriological concern, but is involved with traditional christological developments. The work of Christ (motifs 2, 3, and 4) is united with the person of Christ (motif 1). In the section in *TD*4 where Balthasar promises an exact elaboration of the concept of representation, he refers back to his mission Christology in *TD*3, where he incorporates the traditional head/body and "in-Christ" formulas from Pauline theology.[127] A particular section entitled "Inclusion in Christ" provides the structure for Balthasar's conception of *Stellvertretung* in *TD*4, but there is little explicit integration between the two volumes, which may be part of the reason that Balthasarian scholarship on representation has not thoroughly analyzed its relationship to his Christology. Furthermore, Karl-Heinz Menke remarks that Balthasar Christology and understanding of *Stellvertretung* is not easy to grasp because Balthasar makes Christ the universal concrete with an aesthetical "display of the form" (*Schau der Gestalt*), not with a rational, logical system.[128]

Consequently, by giving attention to the theo-dramatic nature of Balthasar's mission Christology, I can now situate the Christ–creation relation primarily in representative–represented terms and show how the critiques developed from *stauro*-monistic readings of Balthasar's theology of representation do not adequately discern the theological foundations of his theology of the cross. For example, Schumacher, in the only published article exclusively devoted to examining representation in Balthasar, believes that Balthasar's theology of representation "is obscured . . . by a subtle reversal of the Creator–creature relationship so that the creature rather than the Creator becomes the primary referent."[129] She focuses primarily on the action of Christ on the cross and his descent, not considering the broader development of representation in Balthasar's trilogy. Similarly, those who reductively translate Balthasar's conception of *Stellvertretung* into the language of penal substitution (Brown, Coffey, Pitstick) also miss the inherent unity of the Incarnation and the cross in Balthasar's dramatic soteriology.

In the following, I argue that "representation," in comparison to the common use of "substitution," is the best translation of Balthasar's conception of *christological Stellvertretung*. Representation more accurately depicts the broad relationship between Christ and those he represents because it encompasses the metaphysical and participatory nature of this relationship. Substitution can be used appropriately as a subtheme of representation in *soteriological Stellvertretung* (chapter 3), but I show here below that it cannot account for Balthasar's broader biblical, traditional, and unique christological commitments without being attached to the concept of representation. By using the various components of Balthasar's mission Christology and applying emerging conversations about the universal and concrete in Balthasar's theology, I define Christ as the theo-dramatic representative. *Theo*-dramatic signifies his universal-vertical representation of humanity, because Christ's relation to creation is primary, intrinsic, and differentiated, acting in-and-beyond those he represents. At the same time, without a horizontal consideration of Christ's universal action and particular human action, I show how the problems associated with monophysitism and monothelitism arise, replacing or absorbing human action. Therefore, I consider how the dialectical relationship between Christ's two natures makes it possible to conceive universal representation as theo-*dramatic*. That is, Christ's representation is personalizing because he acts with humanity by imparting his mission to human persons in the Spirit.

The Universal Representative: Christ Acts in-and-beyond Humanity

The universal nature of Balthasar's theology of representation is expounded in *TD3* and *TL2*, where he explains Christ's relation to human nature. By highlighting the two concepts he uses to elucidate the universal nature of Christ's representative activity and using linguistic arguments from Sölle's theology of representation, I argue that the christological translation of *Stellvertretung* as "representation" is more appropriate than "substitution." I suggest that Christ acts "in-and-beyond" humanity, which accentuates the vertical dimensions of Balthasar's Christology, as humanity's universal—intrinsic, primary, and differentiated—representative.

The flesh of Christ—the christological "in" of the hypostatic union (the vertical movement of Christ to creation)—mediates the relationship between the representative and the represented.[130] Incorporating Irenaeus, Balthasar argues that the "flesh" of humanity is naturally weak and transitory, revealing the "chalice character of humanity"—its natural openness and need to be recapitulated by Christ.[131] Furthermore, in connections Balthasar makes between Christology and representation after the *Theo-Drama*, he notes that an "essential presupposition" of the "mystery of *Stellvertretung*" is that the Logos assumes flesh *because* the flesh is what connects individuals with the entire human species.[132] Throughout his early and late works, Balthasar accepts the "the real and organic unity of nature" or the "natural communion of material beings," which he believes is established by the biblical understanding of humanity's inclusion in Adam, Augustine's *Totus Christus*, and an Aristotelian-Thomist understanding of nature.[133] Therefore, the *Stelle* of Christ's action is first and foremost the flesh, including the entirety of humanity's "personal and social situation."[134]

The second aspect of Christ's relation to human nature that Balthasar discusses is Christ's supremacy over humanity—the christological "beyond" of the hypostatic union. Christ "towers above" the natural relation between the individual and the species: "Christ does not enter human nature as a mere subject but as someone who is superior to the whole nature (where 'nature' means the species and the sum of individuals)."[135] To establish Christ's relation to human nature "from above," Balthasar relies heavily on the Greek fathers and adds his mission Christology to this approach. Not only is Christ able to affect the human nature through the natural connection between the individual and the species, but he does so by a "real, supernatural inclusion by virtue of his mission."[136] As the place of the world is ultimately in Christ, humanity is naturally oriented toward and recapitulated by Christ, its representative. Thus, when Christ is crucified and resurrected, humanity is crucified and resurrected.

These two elements accentuate the theological and Christocentric foundation of Balthasar's conception of the representative–represented relation. Thus, when Balthasar speaks of the *admirabile commercium* and *pro nobis*, he qualifies it as "*echte Stellvertretung*," a "genuine representation" or, as translated in the English edition of *TD3*, "genuine action on our behalf."[137] Representation and the dramatic exchange between Christ and humanity presuppose an inner, "organic" relation between Christ and human flesh.[138] In *TD3*, Balthasar makes it abundantly clear that his conception of representation that focuses on the organic and ontological unity of Christ and humanity distinguishes his theology of representation from penal substitution, which he labels as a "Protestant version of the doctrine."[139] Karl Rahner believes that one of the primary problems with the term *Stellvertretung* is that it implies "an artificial association of two self-constituted realities [Christ and humanity],"[140] but Balthasar seeks to thwart this problematic relation in his conception of the term.

The ontological relation of Christ and the human flesh is the basis for connecting Balthasar's understanding of christological *Stellvertretung* with representation instead of substitution.[141] Substitution is problematic when the referent is strictly the Christ–creation relation, because a substitute's action is often considered a replacement for the original subject (teacher, athlete, etc.) and, thus, is often a secondary role. A secondary and replacement understanding of *Stellvertretung* is evident in translations such as Bailey's "place-taking." Even if a substitute teacher's action is inclusive of the original teacher's curriculum, his or her role is still secondary because it is temporary and unnecessary. In addition, the original and substitute teachers' agencies are largely exclusive. When the substitute is acting, the original teacher no longer is.

Christ is a representative because he is ontologically intrinsic, primary, and essential to the represented. If Christ is ontologically extrinsic to creation, as implied in the term "substitute," then creation and God operate in two independent ontological spaces. Such an Arian, secondary, attenuated conception of Christ does not represent the thrust of scripture (Acts 17:28; Col. 1:17), the tradition's witness to Christ, or Balthasar's Christocentric vision. Christ is ontologically intrinsic to creation and the contingencies of finitude. He does not travel to a new place when he represents humanity in his incarnation, life, death, and resurrection, but "acts in, with, and for" a reality that he already governs and sustains as the eternal Logos (John 1:1). His role is primary, as creation's representative, because creation already lives, moves, and exists in him

(Rom. 11:36). The term "representation" captures this essential relationship between the infinite and the finite.

Additionally, if a substitute is understood as a replacement (i.e., a Republican is elected in the place of a Democrat), then the substitute is on the same ontological or functional plane as the original subject. Roles are interchangeable in substitution logic, and the original role-filler is ultimately replaceable. The logic of substitution as replacement does not draw the distinctions necessary to safeguard the two subjects, as Sölle argues.[142] Balthasar does not make this connection to *Stellvertretung*, but he is clear in his theo-dramatic conception of personhood that the modern replacement logic of roles is removed in his conception of mission. Representation, because it allows for an inclusive and incorporative relationship, does not have these problematic implications. A representative's role is to advocate, act, sustain, and increase the space of those whom he or she represents. By differentiating the two subjects, their actions on the stage are noncontrastive and noncompetitive.

By framing Balthasar's theology of representation within the Christology we have just outlined, we can speak of Christ's activity that is "in" humanity's place, effecting salvation from within, while the transcendent-beyond of his eternal being allows him to do something that humanity could not do for itself. Christ may be ontologically intrinsic to creation, but he is also ontologically differentiated. Since Christ represents humanity within the similarity-to-dissimilarity of his two natures, he can represent humanity without threatening the existence of either nature. There is an "infinite distance that lies between the grace of Christ and our imperfect and shoddy activity."[143]

It is within Christ's ontological difference that we can speak of Christ's unique work *pro nobis* (*solus Christus*). As I shall argue in chapter 3, Christ can substitute for humanity's sin and defeat sin once and for all (soteriological *Stellvertretung*) because he is humanity's representative (christological *Stellvertretung*). Christ's work is exclusive (he dies instead of humanity) because it is inclusive (humanity has died in him). Kathryn Tanner calls this the "for us" and "without us" of Christ's activity.[144] "Without us" could imply a replacement, competitive logic, as Sölle believes is the case with Barth.[145] My alternative language of "beyond us" and "in us," adapted from Przywara's *analogia entis*, is offered to more explicitly avoid such connotations. As representative, Christ acts *beyond* the sphere of the represented, yet his action is always to benefit those *in* him by preserving and increasing their sphere.

In conclusion, the relationship between Christ and creation in our governing metaphysic explains the universal nature of Christ's *theo-dramatic* representation. I set the stage for a universal understanding of Christ's representation of humanity by locating it first and foremost in (1) Balthasar's Christocentric vision and (2) a communicatory understanding of the flesh. "For the Fathers, however, [these] two aspects are inseparable, the first being the efficacious principle; the second being the condition of the possibility of this efficacy," summarizes Balthasar.[146] The translation of christological *Stellvertretung* as "representation" encapsulates the intrinsic, primary, and differentiated relation of Christ to creation. By constructing a theology of representation on the foundation of Balthasar's Christology, we can see that he does not reverse the Creator–creature relationship. Any judgment of Balthasar's theology of representation that does not incorporate this foundation fails to see how it is developed by Balthasar outside of *TD4*.

The Personalizing Representative: Christ Acts with Humanity

If Christ simply assumed humanity "from above" or became the "universal personality" or "ideal" (which Balthasar associates with Platonic rationalism, Meister Eckhart, and modern idealism), then individuals may be absorbed by Christ, recapitulating the problems of monophysitism and monothelitism.[147] Consequently, the universal relation between the representative and represented expressed through Balthasar's Christocentrism needs to be qualified by the other voices and ideas at play in his mission Christology. In other words, Christology must not simply be done "from above"—the universal-vertical nature of Christ's work—but "from within," which speaks to the dramatic, horizontal, and personalizing dimensions of his work.[148] By conceiving the place in which Christ acts as a personalizing place and interpreting the representative–represented relation dialectically, I argue that Christ's representation of humanity is theo-*dramatic* as he incorporates the personal, historical, and particular of the *dramatis personae*.

First, Balthasar's way of conceiving the place or "sphere" of humanity's existence in Christ elicits in interpreters a way to articulate the dramatic relationship between the representative and represented. For Balthasar, Paul's "all-encompassing and many-faceted [in-Christ] formula" is "held together by a single center." What is this center? For Balthasar, it is "nothing other than the sphere of life and action created by the extension of the universal mission of Jesus."[149] Refuting a Hellenistic "ego-centric mysticism" that absorbs all human personality into the divine, Balthasar interprets the sphere of Christ's action as a "personal sphere of influence" (*personale Wirksphäre Jesu*), the "acting area" (*Spielraum*), and the "personal and personalizing area" (*personaler und personalisierender Raum*).[150] As a result, Balthasar describes Christ's universal inclusion of humanity in the following terms: dramatic, personalizing, communicative, realistic, an inner effect, and synergy.[151] The extension of Christ's work by his Spirit to his body and bride is not simply forensic, cognitive, or eschatological.[152] It is a sanctification that is "authentic, inner, and ontic," as Balthasar puts it, distinguishing himself from Barth's soteriology and ecclesiology.[153]

By connecting Balthasar's account of how humanity is included in Christ to the dialogue philosophy we have traced, we see that the space where an "it" becomes an "I" through an encounter with a "Thou" is not just any space but is a place or sphere opened up by Christ. Christ, the universal acting place of humanity, becomes the "personalizing medium," the theo-dramatic stage that constitutes the I–Thou relationship in which individuals become persons.[154] O'Regan says it this way: "Christ does not so much designate a sphere of beings to be saved as touches each of them individually."[155] When persons encounter Christ, they become personalized and endowed with missions. Thus, in the event, they are not assumed and become "one thing" but enter the body of Christ becoming persons in the Person.[156] As Gallaher states, "Creation is ensheltered in the Trinity, where it has a certain 'acting area' in the realm of infinite freedom of the Son. In this filial 'space which is not a space,' creation can exercise its finite freedom."[157] As part of the universal mission of Christ, the person is not only an individual conscious subject but a theological person with a unique mission, a theo-dramatic person.

Sölle's polarization of representation and substitution does not apply to my formation of the two concepts, but we do need to inquire if her critique of substitution (understood as replacement) applies to Balthasar's theology of *Stellvertretung*. Critiquing Barth, Sölle states,

> Our place is "occupied" by Christ. I have been "relegated" by Christ and "placed" in another sphere. Barth speaks of our "deposition" and of our being "forced." These are substitutionary terms. Barth equates representation and substitution, and impelled by his objectifying tendency, turns Christ into a replacement. The relationship—established by the act of representation between Christ the Representative and us who are represented—is not conceived in personal terms.[158]

For Sölle, the issue with Barth is that he used spatial concepts, such as place, which are difficult to detach from substitution's replaceable and interchangeable logic. According to Sölle's alternative conception of representation, we need to be careful to not absolutize Christ's representation of humanity, which would remove human responsibility.[159] Similarly, Rahner's precise concern with the term *Stellvertretung* is that popular usage of the term (e.g., "Christ takes our place") implies a logic of replacement, which compromises human freedom.[160]

Given Balthasar's personalizing conception of place, Sölle's and Rahner's concerns do not seem to apply to Balthasar's use of spatial metaphors, which further signifies why it is important to discern the broader Christo-logic of Balthasar's theology of representation. The universal nature of Christ's action accounts for the way the work of Christ for humanity is unique and complete; Balthasar's mission Christology cultivates an appreciation for human action and responsibility. As I have argued, in agreement with Sölle, the term "substitution" can invoke inadequate imagery: a new actor arrives on the stage to replace or "take the place" of a current actor, making the subject and object compete for the same acting space. In contrast, the term "representative" connotes subject–object participation. A representative performs for the represented by protecting and creating places for the other person, such as with a parent, doctor, or educator. The representative's action for the represented need not inhibit the activity of the represented. Therefore, by developing Balthasar's theology of *Stellvertretung* in relationship to his Christology, we can see that Sölle's critique of Barth's Christology and Rahner's concern with the potential replacement logic of *Stellvertretung* do not apply to how Christ's "action in our place" functions in Balthasar's theology.

This personalizing relationship between the represented and representative can be further clarified by our dialectical reading of Balthasar's mission Christology, along with a concrete view of human nature. I have shown in this chapter the relationship between a Chalcedonian Christ and a dialectical logic of participation.[161] Although the two terms are distinct (like Christ's human and divine natures or the subject and object of thought), they always exist in motion with one another through the relation of a third term.[162] Our development of a dialectical relationship between Christ's divine and human natures in Balthasar's Christology makes it possible to show how Christ's universal work on humanity's behalf does not need to contradict the personal, historical, and concrete contingencies and responsibilities of human persons. In the following, I relate the two terms—universal and personal—by a third term, the Spirit, and the two terms—represented and representative—by mission.

Since human nature only exists as it subsists in a particular *hypostasis* (John of Damascus, Aquinas), which includes a concrete will and activity (Maximus the Confessor), Christ's universal work of redemption ultimately extends to human persons by the Spirit.[163] The dramatic import insists that the action of the subject and object are always in relation, and this relation is maintained by the Spirit, who imparts to each person a unique mission. Balthasar states, "Christ's Holy Spirit, working in a mysterious way, universalizes Christ's historical, risen reality as the *universale concretum*, thereby enabling its radiance to penetrate 'to the ends of the earth.'"[164] The unity of humanity is not an external reality in Christ, a biological datum, or an abstract reality, but the ethical, social, and theotic performance of the reality created and enacted in Christ and extended through his body.[165] The Spirit, whom I entitle the "Continual Representative," is the unity of the universal Head and the personalized body, the church (chapter 4).

Since the universal mission of the Son is to restore and recapitulate humanity—a humanity that exists as individuals who become persons as they receive a mission—then the representative and represented are distinct but related by the Son's universal mission. In the same way that Jesus's human nature is personalized in the divine Son's mission, so the mission continues as it is personalized in the *dramatis personae* via personal missions. Christ's universal mission and its personalization through particular missions are distinct-but-in-relation in the One Lord Jesus Christ, which is similar to how his own human individuality and divine personhood relate. The represented and representative are in dialectical relation on the theo-dramatic stage. Humanity's place is not taken over, but now exists in relation to Christ's performance on the stage.

Finally, just as Christ represents humanity in-and-beyond its place, so it is invited to participate with-Christ. Christological "for us" extends to christological "with us." Christ draws humanity into his personal acting area, inviting people to share in his dying and rising so that the "We in Christ" is reciprocated with "Christ in us." Inadequate Christologies and metaphysical constructs cause the human "I" to be alienated, whereas Balthasar's understanding of Christ "leads [individuals] from alienation to authentic personal being."[166] Christ's death on humanity's behalf is objective, unique, and corporate. It is "in-and-beyond" humanity. He does something humanity could not do for itself (Rom. 3) and humanity has died in him once and for all (2 Cor. 5:14–15).[167] At the same time, his death is dramatic and personal. Christ's work *pro nobis* draws humanity into a "mystical fellowship of death," which "embraces" and "demands" the death of those in him (Rom. 12:1).[168] If one were to look at Paul as an example and apply Balthasar's mission Christology, one would see that though Christ "has left him [Paul] intact as a conscious subject, he has also *expropriated* him in order to *personalize* him . . . the *en* becomes a *syn*, a participating in Christ's dying and rising and in his work (*synergoi*)."[169] Thus, Balthasar conceives a noncompetitive, roomy understanding of "expropriation" (*Enteignung*). By drawing persons into himself, Christ liberates them from self-alienation that they might be personalized and sent forth in service to their neighbors.[170] The theo-dramatic representative extends the pattern of his life to the represented, as the body participates with-Christ to restore creation to its place in God.

I have applied emerging conversations about the universal and the concrete in Balthasar's theology to our conception of representation, which advances Balthasar's theological vision of representation. The vertical-ontological dimension of our christological formulation accounts for the universal nature of Christ's representative action, and the horizontal-dialectical dimension accounts for the participatory and personalizing nature of the representative–represented relation. In both the universal and personalizing aspects, it is apparent why "substitution" is an inadequate translation of Balthasar's theology of christological *Stellvertretung*. Overall, there are aspects of Balthasar's theology of the cross that align with substitutionary, penal, or forensic logic (chapter 3), but these must be heavily qualified within a more comprehensive understanding of Balthasar's Christ–creation metaphysic.

Conclusion

In the first part of this book, I have constructed a theology of representation and a dramatic exchange formula from a sympathetic and constructive, and in some places critical, interpretation of Balthasar's trinitarian and christological metaphysic. By doing so, I have desired to show how representation, understood as the relationship between place, action, and actors, is a *Grundkategorie* of Balthasar's theology and the integrative element of Balthasar's dramatic soteriology. I have also provided a theological foundation for a definition of representation as action in, with, and for the other and have developed a more comprehensive grammar for how the representative–represented relation functions. By constructing these foundations from Balthasar's doctrine, I can now turn to the dramatic action of Christ, developing both parts of our dramatic exchange formula by employing the metaphysic and grammar laid out. The integration of these two parts—theology and soteriology—will provide a more systematic treatment of Balthasar's theology of representation, expose places of concern, and develop the nascent areas of Balthasar's theology of representation.

PART 2
DRAMATIC ACTION
He Acts in Our Place That We Might Act in His Place

CHAPTER THREE

DRAMATIC REPRESENTATION
Recapitulation, Suffering, Tragedy, and Liberation

If any one confesses not that the Word of God suffered in flesh, and was crucified in flesh, and tasted death in flesh, and was made firstborn of the dead, in so far as he is life and giver of life, as God; let him be anathema.

—Cyril of Alexandria, *The Anathemas of Cyril in Opposition to Nestorius* 12

Balthasar opens *Mysterium Paschale* with Gregory Nazianzen: "Our task now is to consider that problem, and that teaching, which so often are passed over in silence, but which—for that very reason—I want to study with all more eagerness. That precious and glorious divine Blood poured out for us: for what reason and to what end has such a price been paid?"[1] Standing "at the heart of [his] dogmatics"[2] is Balthasar's reply: a shambolic synthesis of the darkly robed penal language of the Reformers, the judicial proceedings of Anselm's courtroom, and the mystical spirituality of the Greek fathers, making it problematic to overly define "representation" or confine Balthasar into a single model, as some do.[3] For example, Alyssa Lyra Pitstick believes Balthasar works with a penal substitution model, specifically, a "quantitative penal substitution,"[4] even though Balthasar explicitly recommends removing "penal" from the concept of representation.[5] *Stauro*-monistic interpretations of representation offer a much different account of Balthasar's soteriology, one where penal substitution may be the dominant category. Balthasar does indeed focus on sacrificial, expiatory elements, but he also makes use of themes of restoration, recapitulation, liberation, and *theosis*, complicating reductionist or categorical readings. I will include these themes by accounting for a broader trinitarian and christological theology of representation. "God's entire world drama is concentrated on and hinges on this scene [of the cross]. . . . Here, more than ever, it is clear that the boundaries between the theological 'loci' and 'treatises' must come down," Balthasar states. "All these elements are involved simultaneously: each has its role, each belongs on stage."[6] Any interpretation of Balthasar's dramatic theory of redemption—the first half of our exchange formula—must consider the various movements, dynamics, and relationships that are included in Christ's action for, in, and with humanity.

To reiterate, the objective of *TD4* is to give an exact elaboration of the concept of representation. But, besides a few places where Balthasar expounds this concept, there is no place he provides a detailed elaboration.[7] Therefore, the objective of this chapter is to provide a broad soteriological elaboration of the concept of representation. By labeling Balthasar's theology of representation in the context of his soteriology as a "dramatic representation,"[8] I proffer a synthetic account of atonement. Since Balthasar's synthesis is not simply a comforting (or apathetic) acceptance of a "pluralism" of atonement theories but is instead a "magnificent polyphony,"[9] I interpret dramatic representation under three subheadings, which I explore in the final three sections of this chapter: recapitulation (context of the cross), suffering (event of the cross), and liberation (outcome of the cross).

Immediately upon any attempt to interpret Balthasar's theology of the cross, one encounters apparent contradictions and a blending of categories. To clarify these, one must discern the movements and subsequent countermovements in the *Theo-Drama*, as Rowan Williams suggests of a "dramatic exegesis" of scripture.[10] Thus, to provide a soteriological elaboration of representation, an interpretive key is needed to help resolve the dramatic tensions in Balthasar's construction. After I introduce the interpretative key in the first section, the rest of the chapter unfolds the drama of redemption, and I point out where the interpretive key and the resources from the previous chapters help clarify various movements. I also note suggestive solutions and problematic concerns. Balthasar's work should not be idolized, and there are some parts that need to be corrected.[11] Most notably, one of Balthasar's hermeneutical moves causes representation to venture into absolute tragedy. And although a tragic interpretation of the cross is significant to Christian discourse, Balthasar does not provide the necessary limits to contain Christ's dramatic representation, and it will be necessary to provide a countermovement in the final subsection of this chapter.

Theo-Dramatic Hermeneutics: Toward the Ever-Greater Totality

In the first two chapters, I proposed analogical and dialectical readings of Balthasar, which drew on the influences of Przywara, Ulrich, and others. I now add Balthasar's "friend and master," Henri de Lubac, to our interpretation of Balthasar.[12] In *Our Task*, Balthasar acknowledges the importance of de Lubac's "rediscovery of the doctrine of the fourfold sense of Scripture" and how he would be unable to understand and communicate divine revelation without it.[13] De Lubac's monumental four-volume work *Exégèse médiévale* is the foundation of the "theo-dramatic hermeneutic" Balthasar develops in the *Theo-Drama*.[14]

According to Balthasar, there is a hermeneutic toward the "ever-greater totality" of revelation illustrated in Ignatius of Loyola, Anselm, and the "Johannine comparatives," implicit in the early church apologists, and explicitly embodied in Irenaeus's writings.[15] The theologian's free movement toward the *semper maior* is the summative principle of Balthasar's theo-dramatic hermeneutic and the signal that Balthasar's soteriology should be interpreted dramatically. Balthasar outlines this operative principle in *TD2*, but it remains covert for the remainder of the voluminous *Theo-Drama*. I will now provide a summary and suggest that it provides an alternative way of reading Balthasar's dramatic soteriology, which I then analyze in subsequent sections.[16]

Balthasar does not provide a "thoroughly substantiated" hermeneutic, but "a kind of formal framework."[17] In order to penetrate Balthasar's dramatic soteriology, two elements of this framework need attention.

First, scripture is a "dramatic instrument" and "interprets its meaning and so performs its own hermeneutics. And in doing so it also outlines the form of theological proof."[18] As a theologian interprets scripture—the process that Balthasar calls "theological proof"—he or she becomes involved in the theological drama, which points to the ever-greater totality of revelation. This process of theological proof is formed through the four senses of scripture: *historical, allegorical/spiritual, tropological/moral,* and *anagogical/eschatological*. Introducing his usage of these senses, Balthasar states,

> But on the basis of all we have said, it is clear that the "spiritual" sense is not some second meaning above or behind it [the historical sense]: the "spiritual" sense is the central, christological sense that is always contained in the "historical." This "spiritual," christological, and pneumatic meaning can inwardly unfold itself as the Good News of God-given grace, which as such wants to incarnate itself in the faith and life of the man who hears it (the "moral" or "tropological" sense) and directs his gaze ahead to a fulfilment (the "anagogical" or eschatological sense), which is made plain in the Risen Christ and is as yet hidden in the believer, as a present reality embraced in hope. All these aspects are interrelated and merge into one another; the four classical senses to which we have referred are not fixed stopping places: there are many intermediate points. Nor is the sequence itself irreversible: thus the moral appeal issued by God's gracious action can presuppose the eschatological aspect of perfection, containing it as one of its elements.[19]

What will become essential to Balthasar's understanding of representation is the phrase "the central, christological sense that is always *contained in* the historical." Theological proof must not only start with the historical sense, but also keep it as a "permanent point of reference."[20] The circular movement between historical fact (exegesis) and theological proof (dogmatics) is the attempt to discern the historical facts, and this hermeneutic also demonstrates that "this fact contains a meaning that embraces, consummates, and transcends every other projected meaning."[21] That is, the goal of theological proof is to uncover the "total meaning," which is "always more"—in-and-beyond—than the historical sense. Summarizing, Balthasar states, "For although, in one respect, the written word as such can never contain the 'breadth and length and height and depth' of the incarnate Word—as scripture itself clearly testifies (John 20:30, 21:25)—this testimony, since it is inspired by the Spirit, is always more than itself: what seems on the surface to be a book is inwardly 'spirit and life.'"[22] Hermeneutics, then, is not some rational, removed incident between an "uninvolved spectator and reporter,"[23] but it is the dramatic discovery of the ever-greater meaning contained within the historical sense. Balthasar explicitly uses this method in his construction of the cross in *GL7*,[24] but it silently lurks behind the theo-dramatic scene of the cross in *TD4*. This hermeneutic resolves apparent contradictions and shows a coherence within Balthasar's account.

Second, the theo-dramatic hermeneutic contains an ever-greater movement not only from the historical to the theological meaning, but also from theological meaning to the triune God. The *Deus semper maior* eternally transcends the senses of scripture, clothing the total meaning in the garbs of analogy and mystery.[25] The hermeneutical centrality of the *analogia entis* highlights Balthasar's intention in the *Theo-Drama* to write with the cautious stroke of Anselm's pen in *Cur Deus Homo*. Anselm feared misrepresenting something so "beautiful in its logic, beyond the reasoning of men."[26] Theological proof can only "circle around" the mystery, which is a phrase often repeated in the *Theo-Drama* to caution against systematization.[27] Christian revelation is full of paradoxes, and theologians should fear "compress[ing] the mysteries of Christianity into a small textbook that can be taken in at a glance. Such fantasies burst like children's balloons before the infinity of God and his self-revelation."[28] Those who participate in a theo-dramatic hermeneutic will find that the contradictions in the theological meaning are so severe that "there are many who [will] refuse even to look in the direction of totality."[29] Balthasar's study of Gregory of Nyssa seems to have influenced his own style, so that his description of Gregory could apply to his own writing: "Here again Gregory is not the eclectic compiler, which some would like to make him out to be. He is the conscientious philosopher who is wary of one-sided systems where an excess of clarity holds sway, who prefers the apparent contradiction to the simplistic solution."[30]

Despite Balthasar's insistence on a dramatic and unfinalized theology, some Balthasar scholars believe that he writes with an excessive precision, displaying the epic feature of a factual systematician that his dramatic project detests.[31] Perhaps Balthasar expects his readers to remember instinctively the underlying appeal to mystery. Karen Kilby states, "On the one hand we find the profound insistence on theological humility, and on the impossibly rich, transcendent, mysterious nature of the subject matter; but on the other hand there is Balthasar's theological procedure, which silently presumes his own comprehensive grasp and control of the material."[32] Ben Quash also recognizes that Balthasar "is simply not consistent in his attempts to safeguard the vital unfinalizability of the supra-form."[33] In particular, Balthasar's dramatic soteriology *prima facie* confirms these concerns. Despite saying that his intention is not to erect a system, Balthasar confidently describes the history of atonement models, then fastidiously dismisses aspects of each of them for not fulfilling every feature of the five soteriology motifs of scripture.[34]

At the same time, a deliberate reading of the *Theo-Drama* as a dramatic exegesis of scripture offers an alternative hearing of Balthasar's project. The discipline of reading scripture in light of its "dramatic process" takes time. "I may begin by simply following the movement of the text as it stands; but that will alert me to deeper movements or rhythms within it, relations between whole blocks of material, all the way in which a text can display subversions and tensions within its own progression—the ways in which it can put itself in question," says Williams.[35] Balthasar's theological use of the genre of drama rather than the epic style of systematicians signals the need to read his theology in this manner. Adams's heuristic for reading Hegel could be adopted for reading Balthasar's *Theo-Drama*:

> Themes are not presented melodically, but as germs whose purpose is to be generative rather than tuneful. These themes do not only contrast with each other: they contain within themselves—and display from the outset—myriad possibilities for development. . . . The development is long, dramatic, and often urgent. The germs can be utterly transformed, and can blossom into forceful moments of astonishing reimagining and drama. The restatement at the end is not only a resolution of the argument (although that too), but is also a new moment of hearing. What is formally "the same" is heard as different, because of what happened during the development.[36]

If Balthasar readers do not read the *Theo-Drama* dramatically, they will fail to notice the various movements and countermovements, the movements from oppositional logic to dialectical and analogical reasoning. For example, directly following his outline of the history of atonement models and the problems associated with them, Balthasar moves into his dramatic soteriology, where he employs many of the concepts he previously dismissed. So, Balthasar will offer a critique of "external, juridical" notions of punishment in the history section,[37] then later in his dramatic construction the Father's punishment of the Son is active and forceful.[38] What must be taken into account is that his one-sided critique is being used, but now in dialectical unity with another concept (punishment/consequence, wrath/love, and forsaken/relation). This chapter is not an attempt to demonstrate painstakingly that Balthasar does this well, but to offer an alternative interpretation of Balthasar's soteriology, a dramatic one. I expand on the relationship between a dramatic understanding of language and representation in chapter 4.

Recapitulating Representation as the Context of the Cross

The "central action" of Balthasar's dramatic soteriology is the cross,[39] and the "central fact" of the cross is representation.[40] The cross and representation rest on two foundations: the Trinity and the covenant: "The Cross was not an event that came straight down from heaven but rather the culmination of God's covenant history with mankind (epitomized by Israel)."[41] Starting with the covenant, Balthasar's search for the meaning of the cross moves in two directions. First, as Balthasar considers the covenant, dramatic dimensions are contained in the historical vision. Hidden underneath the biblical, covenantal history between God and Israel is a metaphysical foundation, a trinitarian doctrine of creation, portrayed as the interplay between infinite and finite freedom.[42] Second, the breach of the covenant results in the true drama between God and humanity, which Balthasar describes using terms such as "justice," "wrath," and "expiation." In both directions, Balthasar appears to be using the language of scripture and tradition to point to a greater meaning grounded in a trinitarian doctrine of creation and God's eschatological goal for creation, but these moves, especially the latter, can elude the reader. Therefore, I offer an account of these two movements, which establishes that the historical covenant points toward Christ's recapitulating work of restoring creation. As a result, I argue in what follows that recapitulating representation can include judicial and penal grammar as a secondary theme.

The Tension between Infinite and Finite Freedom: The Unholy Distance

The notion of infinite and finite freedom is explored in depth in *TD2*,[43] but it is in *TD4* that its dramatic tension is heightened in the tragedy of evil. According to Balthasar, the "ultimate tensions of the drama of human existence" can only be understood in the context of "freedom, power, and evil."[44] Keeping an eye on the covenant, we will see that freedom, power, and evil reveal the unholy distance between God and humanity, all of which is enclosed in a trinitarian doctrine of creation.

The image of the Trinity can be analogously located in the two pillars of finite freedom. "Man cannot exist and act on the world stage except in this polarity," according to Balthasar.[45] These two pillars form two contradictory shapes of being: every being is free "to-be-for-itself" (first pillar) but at the same time finds completion and wholeness in God and others (second pillar).[46] For Balthasar, the historical covenant points to this relationship between infinite and finite freedom. Finite creatures have genuine freedom, yet a freedom that is ultimately only fulfilled by infinite freedom.

The first pillar highlights humanity's power. Balthasar calls this "freedom as autonomous motion."[47] Humanity's freedom "is the most fundamental expression of power, and, in this sense, power is eminently part of the goodness of creation."[48] Power, according to Balthasar, is the ability to make decisions. It is therefore "a central topic of theo-drama. And theo-drama is concerned with the interplay of finite and infinite freedom. As I shall go on to show, this interplay is impossible without the making of decisions at the fundamental level."[49] Although autonomy and power are ultimately good, they must be governed by goodness, a goodness defined by self-giving. Therefore, Balthasar would go so far as to say that "absolute power is identical with absolute self-giving."[50]

The second pillar highlights the giftedness of finite freedom and, thus, its necessary dependence on God.[51] As Balthasar summarizes, "It does possess itself, yet it is not its own gift to itself: it owes itself to some other origin. Thus it can never catch up with its own ground, nor with its essence; it can only attain fulfilment beyond itself."[52] Therefore, the fullness of finite freedom is realized it its indebtedness to infinite freedom. Balthasar calls this "freedom as consent."[53] No matter how free humanity is, the second pillar of humanity's existence cannot be circumvented. Essential childlikeness, an inherent dependence upon infinitude, is a fundamental aspect of humanity's existence. Once again, this highlights the receptive notion of humanity's existence, which is analogous to the Son's "mode of receptivity."[54] Ultimately, what is needed is a "philosophy of prayer": "*Prayer*, essentially is the attitude of a beggar, as the parables about prayer dramatically describe this: one must keep on dinning into God's ears, indeed one must become a nuisance to him, begging for the 'minimum of existence.'"[55] These two pillars define Balthasar's understanding of finite freedom in relation to infinite freedom.

"Having dealt with freedom and power, we inevitably come to the topic of evil. For only in the context of evil does the dramatic tension of personal and social existence finally explode," declares Balthasar.[56] Evil is a possibility on the basis of the two pillars of human existence. In essence, when finite freedom chooses to make the autonomy pillar absolute, therein lies evil. Humanity's freedom is characterized by gift, indebtedness, and thanksgiving (Ulrich). Not only is it to realize this stance toward God, but the second pillar is also orientated in self-giving toward others. When this second pillar is ignored, then humanity contradicts its fundamental nature of existence and closes in upon itself.[57] "If it is to avoid self-contradiction, it cannot affirm itself as a loving source unless it acknowledges that it owes its being to a profound abyss of freedom (God's love), which has given it this being-in-responsibility, *and* simultaneously affirms and makes room for the freedom of others (love of neighbor)," summarizes Balthasar.[58]

Though Balthasar characterizes evil in a variety of terms, one concept emerges from his elliptical style: distance. In chapter 1, I introduced an ascending distance taxonomy according to which the four forms of distance are like planes in an ascending hierarchy, with the higher-level planes containing the lower: immanent divine distance, economic divine distance, natural human distance, and sinful human distance. Immanent divine distance is that interpersonal distance between the Father, Son, and Spirit, which includes and transcends all the other distances. The natural human distance is the natural distance between God and creation, which Christ strides through in the Incarnation. This natural form of distance is the basis for a more tragic distance, the sinful human distance, which is the result of sin. The sinful human distance is the object of the Son's triune work on the cross, which presents an economic divine distance. The sinful human distance and the economic divine distance and how they relate to the immanent divine distance are the primary subject of the rest of this chapter. To set the context for the suffering of Christ, it is helpful to have a brief overview of the sinful distance between God and humanity.

What happens when humanity contradicts its fundamental character? The dramatic distance between God and humanity becomes tragic.[59] The natural distance between God and creation becomes a "deeper *diastasis* of sin,"[60] an "unholy distance" (*unheilige Distanz*).[61] The portrayal of this dramatic, unholy distance could not be starker. Throughout his works, this distance takes many forms: godlessness, enslavement, annihilation, and suppression. In his early work on Gregory of Nyssa, he notes that if humanity "turns away from [its] source with a desire to belong to itself, it no longer merits the name of being. This profoundly ontological privation of being is sin, which is veritably an annihilation."[62] Essentially, by refusing to reciprocate the Son's "mode of receptivity," humanity "reveals that abyss in the creature whereby it contradicts its character as analogy and image, a character that arises necessarily from its position within the trinitarian relations. As a result, the creation of the most positive God-lessness on God's part has produced a real, negative godlessness."[63] It must be clear, however, that the negative godlessness of creation is distinct from the positive divine godlessness of love, which "undergirds it, renders it possible and goes beyond it."[64] The distance between God and creature is naturally characterized by movement and openness,[65] but finitude's desire to become complete in itself "freezes the movement of finite freedom, which can only remain vital in the current flowing from the infinite source to the infinite goal (the two are identical)."[66]

To summarize, a theo-dramatic interpretation of the *Theo-Drama* uses the historical lens of the covenant to point to a metaphysical lens, a trinitarian doctrine of creation. The covenant's primary theme, which is much more important than its commandments, is humanity's inherent dependence upon the Infinite. It cannot exist in any other way. When humanity contradicts the character of its freedom, the natural distance between God and creation opens up to an unholy and tragic distance.

Recapitulating Representation in Dramatic Terms:
Justice, Wrath, and Expiation

The second aspect of the covenant involves God's response to the abyss created by humanity. As one unfolds the language of justice, wrath, and expiation, therein lies the true dramatic nature of Christ's representation. In his usage of these terms, Balthasar certainly employs the rhetoric of the penal substitution model, yet the hidden interpretative key is vital to demonstrating how it might be qualified within a theology of representation. Therefore, the objective of this subsection is to set up the context of Christ's dramatic representation on the cross by providing an overview of Balthasar's usage of the terms "justice," "wrath," and "expiation," while showing that they belong within an ever-greater movement toward the restoration of the created order and its initiation into the triune life by means of Christ's recapitulating representation of humanity. Though this ever-greater movement is nebulous in Balthasar, its incorporation into our theology of representation challenges *stauro*-monistic interpretations of Balthasar's theology of redemption and offers an alternative way of reading his dramatic soteriology.

Balthasar specifically distinguishes himself from Karl Rahner, who is critical of the notion of "expiatory sacrifice" and Anselm's satisfaction model.[67] Rahner attributes these ideas to later New Testament theology and not to the "original, ineducible, and first revelation of Christology" given to the first disciples of Jesus.[68] His primary reason for rejecting these theories is God's immutability: How can God change from a wrathful God to a reconciled God? This God is mythical.[69] According to Rahner, God must be the original cause of his own reconciliation.[70] "The pure initiative of God's salvific will" is the foundation of Jesus's life, death, and resurrection, rather than the death of Jesus being the cause of God's salvific will. Ultimately, the death of Jesus becomes the sign that "causes what is signified."[71] Balthasar agrees with Rahner that it is not an angry God needing to be reconciled but a loving God who freely initiates reconciliation. At the same time, he states, "It would be wrong to take the almost countless scriptural references to God's anger with the sinner, and those that speak of judgment (particularly in the New Testament), and submerge or dissolve them in 'God's free, salvific will.'"[72] Thus, Balthasar believes that Rahner, like so many who ignore the patristic exchange formula, "lacks the decisive dramatic element."[73] Similarly, Kevin Vanhoozer believes modern atonement theories that focus on the cross as a manifestation of God's love and forgiveness "dedramatize" the cross.[74] According to Rowan Williams, the importance of dramatic representation in Greek theater is that it takes familiar narratives, in this case God's love, and does not simply tell but "enacts" these narratives through dramatic events to convince its listeners that perhaps they do not know the narrative as well as they had thought.[75]

Balthasar believes Anselm does employ some of the necessary dramatic components, and justice is a major part of his system.[76] "The juridical component has an abiding and legitimate place within theodrama and its theological presentation. No theology is to be rejected as unbiblical or unspiritual because it employs juridical categories," says Balthasar.[77] Balthasar departs from the fashionable dismissals of Anselm, supporting Anselm throughout his works, while simultaneously synthesizing Anselm into his own dramatic system.[78] According to Anselm, because God's freedom is regulated by his righteous justice (*rectitudo*) and his righteous justice shows its form in the "universal order," then God cannot uphold his honor while allowing disorder (sin) to reign without some form of repayment or punishment. To simply forgive humanity would be dishonorable to God's righteous order and the freedom bestowed upon humanity.[79] Following Anselm, Balthasar summarizes, "It is impossible for God to announce to the world a law of reward for the good and punishment for evil, and then let this law operate so to speak without his own active participation. Having established the world order, he cannot renounce his freedom nor retire from his obligation to punish and forgive."[80] Balthasar links Anselm's theology with the Old Testament theology of *sedek, mishpat,* and *shalom* much earlier in *GL6*. God's *sedek* (righteousness/justice) and *mishpat* (justice) are linked to Anselm's *rectitudo*, signifying "the right that must at all costs be put into force on the earth" to maintain and bring forth *shalom*, an age of salvation and peace for all of creation.[81] Isaiah links the three together well: "Then justice [*mishpat*] will dwell in the wilderness, and righteousness [*sedek*] abide in the fruitful field. And the effect of righteousness will be peace [*shalom*], and the result of righteousness, quietness and trust forever" (Isa. 32:16–17).[82] This earlier linkage between Anselm and the Old Testament in *GL6* helps to demonstrate how Balthasar's theology of justice points toward restoration; unfortunately, the linkage is absent in *TD4*.

Darrin W. Snyder Belousek's *Atonement, Justice, and Peace* has shown that those, such as Anthony Bartlett, who lump Anselm's model into penal substitution categories have misunderstood the internal logic of Anselm.[83] "Whereas God's justice does aim at Jesus's death in Calvin's model, for it is precisely Jesus's death in humanity's place that satisfies God's justice, that is not so in Anselm's model: God's justice aims at the restoration of God's honor (and, ultimately, creation's order)," states Belousek.[84] One must not associate the means through which God deals with the consequences of sin first and foremost with a "penal righteousness," but with a "saving righteousness" that motivates the God of love to represent humanity in the flesh and bring forth restoration.[85] In other words, Anselmian, juridical categories are located within the covenant of love, peace, and salvation, and, thus, juridical and relational categories do not need to be dichotomized.[86] The logic of juridical and relational is not oppositional, because the two terms are dialectically unified by God's restorative goal for creation.

The second dramatic term to understand is "wrath." God's wrath against humanity's sin is one of the "constant themes of Scripture" and, therefore, occupies a central role in Balthasar's dramatic soteriology.[87] Unlike many modern theologians, Balthasar has no problem advocating for the wrath of God: "Within the horizon of the Old Testament, it is unthinkable that the 'Day of the Lord,' which brings everything to light, could be a revelation solely of mercy and not also of wrath. Contrary to the unconsidered utterances of modern theologians, we must maintain that 'anger is an essential and ineradicable feature . . . even in the New

Testament picture of God.'"⁸⁸ At times Balthasar uses language of curse and punishment to describe God's wrath,⁸⁹ but he overall describes it as the "necessary corollary" of love, "suspended love," a "function of mercy," and God's jealous protection of the covenant.⁹⁰ He quotes Lactantius, who in Balthasar's estimation is unduly overlooked by modern theologians: "If God is not angry with the godless and unrighteous, he cannot love the God-fearing and righteous."⁹¹ Following Abraham Heschel's lead, Balthasar believes that "this 'pathos' is not an 'attribute of being,' some 'immutable quality' of God, but an aspect of his personal engagement for creation and covenant. It is his 'constant care and concern,' distinguishing him from other national and covenant gods."⁹² God's wrath is his forceful action to bring about his eschatological desire for creation's order, peace, and salvation.

God's justice and wrath lead to the ultimate heightening of the covenant and unveil the dramatic nature of Christ's representation: expiation. The juridical, lawsuit theme of the covenant "opens out into a universal theo-dramatic dimension."⁹³ In regard to the unholy distance between God and humanity, can God continuously pour the gift of being into the finite if it rejects God? Although God temporarily sustains creation in such an unholy state through his covenant faithfulness, Balthasar's answer is an emphatic no.⁹⁴ God takes the first pillar (the relative autonomy of freedom) of humanity seriously.⁹⁵ The *guilt* and *consequences* of sin cannot simply be ignored; expiation is required.⁹⁶ Returning to the exegetical, literal sense of scripture, Balthasar states, "In continuity with the Old Testament, again, expiation is seen in terms of 'blood,' without which 'there is no forgiveness' (Heb. 9:22); but what is meant here is death (Heb. 9:15), possibly violent death, or, more accurately, the surrendering of life (John 10), which leads back to the former meaning."⁹⁷ The cross is not simply the revelation of an already reconciled God, but the cross is the dramatic action of God's love that brings reconciliation and expiation.⁹⁸ "A harmless, 'epic' doctrine of redemption is insufficient" to defeat the tension, the sinful abyss, caused by humanity's sin—a dramatic "reconciliation-event" is required.⁹⁹ The need for expiation and not simply a "sovereign act of divine forgiveness" is essential to this restoration (Rom. 3:25; Heb. 9:12, 15, 22; 1 John 4:10).¹⁰⁰

In this sense, one could think Balthasar makes penal substitution the primary model of redemption. However, according to Belousek, penal substitution primarily focuses on propitiation—appeasing God's wrath—and secondarily on reconciliation.[101] Balthasar translates the Greek word *hilastērion* in Romans 3:25 as "expiation," and not "propitiation," in all cases except one.[102] George Hunsinger observes that expiation and propitiation do not need to contradict one another, as long as propitiation does not mean that God is appeased by inflicting punishment: "It would be an error to suppose that 'propitiation' and 'expiation' must be pitted against each other as though they were mutually exclusive. The wrath of God is removed (propitiation) when the sin that provokes it is abolished (expiation)."[103] In other words, although the "shedding of blood" (Rom. 3:25)—the suffering and death of Christ—is essential to redemption, it is aimed at liberating humanity from sin and death (expiation), which removes the wrath of God (propitiation).[104] Essentially, the central feature of the exegetical, literal sense of scripture is the hour of judgment on the cross, and this converges into the primary, dogmatic theme, which is the *pro nobis* formula. Rather than bifurcating God's love and God's wrath, Balthasar believes the former is the hidden motivation of the latter, and both are aimed at defeating the unholy abyss.[105]

Reading these three dramatic components—justice, wrath, and expiation—as themes of the love of God clarifies Balthasar's dramatic presentation of Christ's representation on the cross, making recapitulating *representation* the primary theme and *substitution* secondary. The focal points of wrath, death, and forsakenness in Balthasar's dramatic depiction of the cross in *TD*4 are problematic unless interpreted through the underlying presupposition: *Irenaean* recapitulation.[106] Though the theme of recapitulation is indisputably present in the *Theo-Drama*,[107] it is puzzling that it takes so little space in *TD*4, especially given that Balthasar published a thematic selection of Irenaeus's writings a year after *TD*4 was released, and a good portion of the selected writings is on recapitulation.[108] Even so, I argue in the final two sections of this chapter that it is vital to interpret Christ's representation on the cross through the context of my chapter 2: Christ, the concrete *analogia entis*, universally recapitulates creation through his perfect obedience to his mission, which is to represent the final, eschatological relationship between infinite and finite freedom. The economic covenant is fulfilled—recapitulated—through Christ's economic mission, which is an ever-greater revelation of his eternal *eucharistia*, his "eternal Yes to the gift of consubstantial divinity."[109] To say it in Ulrich's words, "being's movement of finitization [its essential act of gratitude] is recapitulated in the incarnate Word of God."[110] In this way, Christ's active obedience through his life, death, resurrection, and ascension recapitulates humanity, fulfilling the second pillar of humanity's existence. Although this ever-greater theological movement is possible to make using Balthasar's theology, there are moments where the grammar he uses to describe the drama needs to be carefully reconsidered. Ultimately, what must be clear is that the place of Christ's action on the cross (substitution) is contained in the ever-greater Christ–creation metaphysic (representation).

In contrast to this alternative reading, Pitstick will say of Balthasar's theology of redemption that "the place exchanged, the fate assumed is Sheol." She continues, "For Balthasar, then, Christ's redemption is *quantitative substitution in Sheol*. . . . This position is certainly different from the traditional Catholic understanding of the redemption through Christ's death on the cross as being satisfactory in virtue of the preeminent qualities of his person."[111] Because of Balthasar's use of the word "expiation," Pitstick believes Christ's sufferings are passive, rather than active, which is why she labels his soteriology a version of penal substitution. Ultimately, for Pitstick, suffering can only be passive, as in penal substitution, or active, as in the traditional Catholic account.[112]

Pitstick is correct that there is a passive nature to Jesus's suffering in Balthasar that can be problematic, but she does not seem to notice the historical development of Balthasar's thought and the various movements and countermovements of Balthasar's dramatic depiction. In *GL7* (1969) and *Mysterium Paschale* (1970), Balthasar speaks more freely of the Father's active punishment of the Son. The Son is passively obedient as the Father unloads his wrath against the world's sin on the Son.[113] In *GL7*, Balthasar goes as far as saying that the Father crushes the Son on the cross (Isa. 53:10).[114] Thus, Pitstick, who focused heavily on these two sources, believes that suffering is the "formal principle" of humanity's redemption in Balthasar because of these elements of punishment and active unloading.[115] However, there is an indication in *GL7* that Balthasar is wrestling with this tension of punishment and the love of God. He states that it is important "to guard against both extremes, that of interpreting the suffering of Christ as a punitive raging of divine anger against the innocent victim (as the Reformers tended to do), and that of seeing this suffering as merely the manifestation of the superabundance of divine love."[116]

In the eleven years between *GL7* and *TD4*, this tension becomes further heightened when Balthasar becomes more concerned about defining representation. At least one part of this concern may be attributed to his reading of René Girard, whose arguments related to atonement were not published until the 1970s, after *GL7*. In *TD4*, Balthasar engages with Girard's *Violence and the Sacred* (1972) and *Things Hidden since the Foundation of the World* (1978).[117] Additionally, in 1980 he writes an article on Girard and scapegoating.[118] Although Balthasar goes on to reject Girard's scapegoat mechanism, he does appear to appropriate Girard's critique of punishment in his own construction, which calls into question any reductionist reading of Balthasar's soteriology as penal substitution; Pitstick does not mention Girard in her account of Balthasar.

The basic structure of Girard's scapegoat mechanism is easily grasped. Girard rejects any understanding of the cross as sacrifice, vicarious punishment, satisfaction, or penal substitution. He lumps these categories into one,[119] and he believes a sacrificial reading of the Gospels has discredited Christianity in the modern world.[120] Ultimately, God is not a god of violence or punishment. Any violence in the Gospels originates from humanity.[121] Contained in the history of religions and cultures and unveiled fully at the cross is the scapegoat mechanism. The violence of a community is released upon a scapegoat, which restores peace. By revealing society's scapegoat mechanism, Jesus demythologizes it.[122] Balthasar engages Girard directly on the question of whether God wills the Crucifixion or allows it.[123] Balthasar believes it was Christ's free initiative to give himself up (Gal. 1:4, 2:20; Eph. 5:2, 5:25) for the sake of the world (motif 1), and this is located in the one divine will of love (motif 5).[124] Christ's economic obedience should be "understood as a spontaneous 'offer,' so that there can be no question of the Son being 'forced' to do something by a will that is exclusively the Father's."[125] From his reading of Girard onward, it is very clear that one should not overemphasize punishment categories. However, if Christ is in ontological solidarity with humanity, then Balthasar believes some form of penal element must be employed.[126] Thus, even though in the drama itself it may appear that the Father and Son are pitted against one another as in the penal substitution model,[127] in this precise place they could not be more intimate and unified. They are acting *with* not *against* one another for the sake of the world's reconciliation.[128] In short, penal language is in full force in places of Balthasar's dramatic soteriology, but it is used in a qualified and equivocal manner.[129]

What must be clear, then, is that a theology of representation is the category that can contain the dramatic language Balthasar uses in his theology of the cross. In contrast to a *stauro*-monistic interpretation, *TD*3 (Christology) and *TD*4 (atonement) must be clearly tied together. Our christological interpretation of Balthasar's theology of representation is essential here. The divine and human in Christ are not on the same ontological plane, leading to an either/or understanding of passive and active suffering. Rather, Christ's human nature is contained in the *maior dissimilitudo* of his divine nature. The only way the human flesh is healed is through the distinction-in-union of the Chalcedonian Christ—the cross might be central in the economy, but its foundation lies in the Incarnation.[130] Thus, although in the horizontal dimension of his mission Christ may appear passive, it is one polarity within the vertical movement from Christ to creation. Passive suffering and passive obedience are dialectically related within the divine Son's active movement to humanity. Since Christ's representation is not primarily a cross-based event but depicts the eschatological place of humanity in Christ, then the passive and dramatic language is simply one part of a greater exchange between Christ and humanity. As Riches states, "To say that Jesus endured 'every human suffering' does not mean that he specifically suffered everything that every person ever did or could suffer, but that he 'sums up' in his Passion the sufferings of the world, mystically including them in his own suffering and recapitulating them in the form of perfect love."[131] A quantitative transferal of sin and suffering is simply one aspect of the hypostatic-in, which is unified, healed, and restored in the hypostatic-beyond.

In summary, the link between an Anselmian restoration to the covenant, an Irenaean recapitulation, and Balthasar's theo-dramatic theology of representation is vital to grasping the various dogmatic and dramatic components present in the context of the cross and to indicating how recapitulating representation can include penal and judicial language as secondary themes.[132] Although some argue that themes of violence and wrath in Irenaeus are only a "polemical instrument" and Balthasar may thus move beyond Irenaeus,[133] it is also clear that by reading Balthasar's language within a trinitarian doctrine of creation and its necessary ontology of recapitulation, however covert it might be, the dramatic components are better interpreted through God's eschatological goal for humanity. The only way to detect this stealthy operation in *TD*4 is Balthasar's theo-dramatic hermeneutic: As one moves through the historical sense (covenant and wrath) into the theological sense (infinite freedom, finite freedom, and unholy distance), hidden therein is a deeper, eschatological meaning involving the restoration of creation (motif 3) and its initiation into the triune life (motif 4) through and in the recapitulating representative (motif 2), which originates in the love of God (motif 5).[134] Ultimately, it is true that Balthasar does not offer a scrupulous construction of this performance, and a countermovement will need to be made. Before offering the countermovement, I will examine Balthasar's depiction of Christ's suffering on the cross.

The Dramatic Action of the Suffering Representative

In the same year *TD*4 was published, Balthasar delivered an acceptance speech for an honorary doctorate at the Catholic University of America. In this speech, he provides what may be the most compressed statement of his theology of the cross:

> Please believe me that in stating this I do not defend some kind of fundamentalism or biblical literalism, but the inspired spiritual phenomenon, the active, unified comprehension that is gained from the New Testament. The issue is not the letter but the content. To give an example: Already in pre-Pauline tradition and then, even more, by him and by John, but also in some of the words of the synoptics, the meaning of the Passion is understood as Christ's *representative suffering for us* (*qui propter nos homines et*

propter nostram salutem . . .). If you relativize and flatten these statements, the entire Catholic faith collapses.[135]

The dramatic character of Balthasar's soteriology rings loudest in the vicarious sufferings of Christ, which lie at the center of the New Testament faith and are the means of humanity's restoration.[136] Furthermore, this climactic scene on the stage of the world becomes a "super-action," taking place in the life of God.[137] "This indispensable concept (representation) introduces into theology something that Anselm had pondered deeply but had formulated in a rather narrow way: the process of reconciliation, at the center of which stands Christ (and hence Christology), is dramatic, both within the Godhead and in the relationship between God and man," says Balthasar.[138]

Suffering is certainly at the heart of Christ's mission, but Balthasar desires to veil from the audience's view a comprehensive grasp of the "the hour" of his death.[139] He notes that it must be clear that "the 'hour,' from which Jesus so consciously lived, is certainly the hour and 'the power of darkness,' but the important hour, which the Father has set for him and which he reserves to his knowledge and management."[140] As an example, Balthasar will ask: Was the hour caused or allowed by God? Does the Father or the world unload "the unimaginable load of the all the world's No to divine love" on the Son?[141] Balthasar is content in many places in the *Theo-Drama* to emphasize both sides of these questions, because one should leave the tensions of the hour in the ever-greater movement toward the triune mystery.[142]

However, in other places, Balthasar seems to offer a complete view of what is happening behind the curtain. By contemplating Balthasar's climactic depiction of the cross and the suffering it entails, we will observe two ever-greater movements from the historical meaning to the theological meaning where Balthasar offers a complete viewing of the mysterious hour of Christ's death. The first is seen in Christ's relationship to the unholy distance created by humanity's sin, and the second, the most dramatic of all, is seen in the relationship between the Father and the Son. Similarly to what we saw in the second section of this chapter, these hermeneutical movements will help clarify Balthasar's understanding of the cross and representation. In the first case, it provides valuable nuances; the second takes dramatic representation too far into the life of the Trinity.

Sin and the Crucified: Representation of the Unholy Distance

Balthasar highlights the centrality of the fathers' exchange formula, and yet he believes they ultimately do not "follow it through as radically as the New Testament requires," missing out on the "whole dramatic potential of this central element of the theo-drama."[143] Crucial to both Eastern and Western fathers' soteriology is Jesus's assumption of human nature and its necessity for redemption. Related to the Incarnation is the type of flesh Christ assumed: Did he assume an unfallen or fallen/sinful nature?[144] In the nineteenth century, Edward Irving claimed that Jesus's human nature was "fallen."[145] Following Irving, Barth brought the fallen argument to a larger audience;[146] the issue is still debated.[147] In relation to the fathers' exchange formula, Balthasar believes Paul's soteriological texts (e.g., 2 Cor. 5:21; Gal. 3:13; Rom. 8:3) cause the fathers to emphasize Christ's fallen or sinful human nature: "Many fathers see Paul's assertion that Jesus was 'made to be sin' and 'a curse' for us (2 Cor. 5:21; Gal. 3:13) as referring to this assumption of sinful human nature: thus Gregory of Nyssa (*Vita Moysis* 2, 33) and Gregory Nazianzen, who says that in this way Jesus became *autoamartia* and *autokatara* (the epitome of sin and a curse—*Or* 37; PG 36, 284)."[148] E. Jerome Van Kuiken's research demonstrates that the Greek fathers use both fallen and unfallen language, yet the terms "fallen" and "sinful" have different meanings.[149] Whereas some defenders of an unfallen flesh equate fallenness with sinfulness, Thomas A. Noble shows that in Irenaeus, Athanasius, Gregory of Nazianzus, Gregory of Nyssa, and Cyril of Alexandria a fallen nature (the "ontological" effects of the fall) is not synonymous with a sinful nature (the "moral" effects): the latter through Christ's assumption of the former is sanctified in his incarnation, life, death, and resurrection.[150] As Cyril of Alexandria states, "He became human and clothed himself with our nature.... In order that he may kill our 'earthly members,' that is, the passions of the flesh, and destroy the law of sin that rules in our members, and that he may sanctify our nature as well."[151] Yet, in what way does Balthasar follow the Greek fathers and in what sense does he attempt to move beyond them?

Though Balthasar discusses a variety of fathers on this issue, Gregory Nazianzen is his primary interlocutor. Gregory believes Christ became a "slave to flesh" so that he might save it.[152] Christ represents humanity by submitting to its condition. He appropriates humanity's disobedience by becoming a curse (Gal. 3:13) and sin (2 Cor. 5:21). Using Christ's forsakenness as an example, Gregory says that Christ is not uttering his own forsakenness by the Father, but humanity's forsakenness because of its condition.[153] In this way, Christ represents humanity by assuming and playing the role of humanity's condition, but he was not "changed into these things."[154] Gregory summarizes, "But as the 'form of a slave' he comes down to the same level as his fellow-slaves; receiving an alien 'form' he bears the whole of me, along with all that is mine, in himself, so that he may consume within himself the meaner element, as fire consumes wax or the Sun ground mist, so that I may share in what is his through the intermingling."[155] It is important to notice the sanctifying elements in this quote: Christ assumes the "alien form" (flesh) and "consumes" the "meaner element" (sinful flesh) so that humanity might share in his nature.

Balthasar notes that those who took up Gregory's phrase "he bears the whole of me, along with all that is mine,"[156] such as Augustine, Maximus the Confessor, and John Damascene, "restricted it to the consequences of sin and the punishment due to sin, whereas sin itself is *not* taken on by him."[157] For example, when qualifying Christ's appropriation of flesh, John Damascene states, "And it was in this way that our Lord appropriated both our curse and our desertion, and such other things as are not natural: not that he himself was or became such, but that he took upon himself our personality and ranked himself as one of us."[158] For this reason, Balthasar believes the church fathers' understanding of exchange is not "internal," "dramatic," or "ultimate" enough.[159] However, this reading is complicated by Gregory Nazianzen's first letter to Cledonius the Presbyter, where Gregory equates the "Word was made flesh" with Paul's texts on Christ's sinful flesh (2 Cor. 5:21; Gal. 3:13), and by Gregory of Nyssa, according to whom Christ is depicted as being made sin, which is the serpent.[160]

Balthasar believes a more dramatic proposal arrives from the Protestant theologian of the cross, Martin Luther: "It is as if Luther's thought, from its very beginnings, was bent upon filling precisely the gap that patristic theology had left open in the *admirabile commercium*."[161] Although Balthasar is critical of Luther because he missed the divinization aspect of the fathers' exchange model, he believes Luther's theology takes seriously the literal sense of the biblical text (2 Cor. 5:21; Gal. 3:13; Rom. 8:3).[162] Luther's sermon on Galatians 3:13 shoots straight at a sophist target: theologians of glory. What did Paul mean by "Christ became a curse *pro nobis*"? Luther proclaims, "But just as Christ is wrapped up in our flesh and blood, so we must wrap him and know him to be wrapped up in our sins, our curse, our death, and everything evil." Though Christ is certainly innocent, Luther does not distinguish humanity's sin from the innocence of Christ: "Whatever sins, I, you, and all of us have committed or may commit in the future, they are as much Christ's own as if he himself had committed them. In short, our sin must be Christ's own sin, or we shall perish eternally." Christ did not simply bear the *consequences* of sin. Christ becomes "the highest, the greatest, and the only sinner." As the basis for humanity's justification, Luther proclaims, "This is the most joyous of all doctrines and the one that contains the most comfort."[163] Barth also notes Luther's dramatic portrayal, formulating his own understanding of Christ as the "bearer and representative of sin" emphasizing a "genuine and actual" solidarity with sin.[164]

The crucial question for Balthasar is this: How far does Jesus's solidarity with humanity go? For Balthasar, liberal christologies can limit solidarity to social or psychological aspects—the emphasis is on Jesus's solidarity with the poor and outcast. For Balthasar, this type of solidarity is important, but it is too "external" on its own.[165] As we will see momentarily, the boundary between solidarity, exchange, and substitution theologies is "very narrow" if construed properly.[166] Balthasar addresses Jesus's relationship to sin in a variety of places,[167] but perhaps none is more significant than what is provided in *TD*4 when he speaks of the "nature of 'representation'" in the context of "sin and the crucified."

How does Jesus relate to humanity's sin? Here is where Balthasar's hermeneutical key is of importance. Balthasar uses the literal sense of scripture, as Luther does, and integrates it with the theological sense. According to Balthasar, Jesus becomes identified with "darkness" (*Finsternis*) and the "sinful God-distance" (*sündige Gottferne*) or the "God-distance of darkness" (*gottferne Finsternis*).¹⁶⁸ The English translation of *TD4* conceals the notion of distance here because it translates *Gottferne* as "alienation" (*Entfremdung*).¹⁶⁹ Although Balthasar does also describe the distance between the Father and Son created by sin as a "mystery of darkness and alienation" (*Mysterium der Verfinsterung und Entfremdung*),¹⁷⁰ the English translation misses the heightening of the literal sense (sin and curse) to the theological sense (distance). Even so, what *precisely* does Jesus assume, become, or represent? What place does Jesus act in? Balthasar's answer is the dramatic, unholy, and sinful distance created by humanity's No.

The economic place of Christ's action is included in Balthasar's triune framework of distance. To reiterate, creation is "within the distinction/difference between the Hypostases" (*innerhalb der Differenz der Hypostasen*), and, consequently, creation's unholy distance is also located in "the 'place' of intra-divine difference" (*der "Stelle" der innergöttlichen Differenz*).¹⁷¹ Therefore, when Christ acts in the place (*stellvertreten*) of creation's unholy distance, he does not need to alter his place. "He can do this on the basis of his place within absolute, divine difference from the bestowing Father," states Balthasar.¹⁷²

It is difficult to perceive how Balthasar actually moves beyond the Greek fathers. First, how the unholy distance is sin and not the consequence of sin is unresolved in Balthasar, unless he is attempting to give sin an independent, ontological existence, which would certainly be crossing into heterodox territory since he locates this unholy distance within the triune life. Additionally, although Balthasar wants to get as close as possible to identifying Jesus and sin, and at one point he calls for a "true identification,"¹⁷³ he does clarify that there is some form of distinction between Jesus and the actual No of sin (John 8:46; 2 Cor. 5:21; Heb. 4:15; 1 Pet. 2:22). Overall, he is content to leave the precise relationship between distinction and identity undefined. Christ's representation of sin is still vicarious and alien in some sense.¹⁷⁴

On the other hand, Balthasar distances himself from the Greek fathers in two ways. First, when Balthasar addresses Christ's ontological solidarity with the unholy distance, he exclusively does so in his theology of the cross. When the Greek fathers speak of Christ's fallen flesh, however, they speak of its sanctification through his incarnation and active life.[175] For Athanasius, as John Behr notes, Jesus's suffering is "not sequentially, but simultaneously" transformed into freedom. Thus, "his voluntary, active, 'impassible' acceptance of 'suffering' reverses the effects of [creaturely] suffering."[176] The recapitulation process starts with the Incarnation and extends through Christ's entire life, but Balthasar does not deal with the soteriological implications of Christ's assumption of the fallen flesh until the cross.[177] The second distinction is related to the *pro nobis* formula. What Balthasar is attempting to make precise is that Jesus's "for" is defined as ontological solidarity with humanity—there is no distance between Jesus and the abyss created by human sin.[178] Ultimately, where it seems Balthasar wants to move beyond the Greek fathers is to emphasize Jesus's true, inner experience of the sinful state, rather than simply the external carrying of it. Unlike a sacrifice whose relationship to sin, guilt, and its consequences is external, Christ is in no way distant from sin. Balthasar moves from the literal sense, which he sees as a simple "psychological unloading" of guilt upon Christ like a sacrifice, to the theological sense, an ontological unloading.[179] He summarizes, "Jesus does experience the darkness of the sinful state, not in the same way as the (God-hating) sinner experiences it (unless the sinner is spared such experience) but nonetheless in a deeper and darker experience. This is because it takes place in the profound depths of the relations between the divine Hypostases—which are inaccessible to any creature."[180] In this sense, Jesus does not simply represent humanity on the cross, but he genuinely represents and experiences the distance between God and creation created by human sin.

Dramatic Representation: Forsakenness, Death, and Hell

The "central fact" of Balthasar's Christology and soteriology is Jesus's representative death in humanity's place, and the source of this death is rooted in Jesus's unfathomable cry of dereliction.[181] The most genuine place of Christ's representation *pro nobis* is found in the "mystery of darkness and alienation between God and the sin-bearing Son."[182] Christ's representative suffering in this concentrated scene is located in the fluid self-giving and self-receiving love of the triune life, not in the judiciary courtroom or the violence between a mob and a scapegoat. By describing the apogee of Christ's action on the cross—how the sin of humanity affects the Father and Son's relationship—we will see why "substitutionary representative" is the most appropriate phrase to describe this particular event and why Balthasar's dramatic depiction of the cross raises some concerns.

Balthasar describes the trinitarian event on the cross in this way: "It takes place at a point where the estranged world, having been drawn into all seriousness into the relationships within the Godhead, seems to create a contradiction in God."[183] Because Jesus drinks the full chalice of darkness, alienation, and sinful distance, the "divine light of love" no longer can reach him. Rather than use verbs such as "balancing," "canceling out," or "weighing" to describe the exchange, Balthasar uses terms that portray the cessation of movement in the triune life: light to darkness, hope to hopelessness, grace to gracelessness, reliance to forsakenness, intimate distance to sinful distance.[184] Many of these movements appear as a series of puns in *TD4* (*sich verlassen/verlassen; vergeben/vergebens; Vergeblichkeit/Vergebung*).[185] The trinitarian language of mutual love, givenness, and receptivity we put forth in chapter 1 is circumvented on the cross. Balthasar states, "On the Cross, the constant relationship between them has assumed the modality of 'forsakenness' by the Father and hence of irremediable 'lostness' on the part of the Son; as a result, the Son experiences the loss of a horizon of meaning and being such as no ordinary creature can either possess or lose."[186] Consequently, there is an impenetrable difference between Christ's suffering on the cross and humanity's suffering caused by sin because the sinful distance between humanity and God creates a new distance between the Father and Son.[187]

Paradoxically, the economic intimacy of the Father and Son could not be more perfect than in this triune action. The impenetrable unity of the Father and Son is maintained in the unifying Spirit, even in the Father's abandonment of the Son.[188] Additionally, God does not need to change because the Son's abandonment is grounded in God's kenotic abandonment of self in his eternal procession.[189] Balthasar summarizes, "In the end, therefore, it is the human expression of a shared love-death in a supereminently trinitarian sense: the One who forsakes is just as much affected (in his eternal life) as the One who is forsaken, and just as much as the forsaking and forsaken love that is One in the Holy Spirit."[190]

Forsakenness, the loss of relationship with God and others, inexorably results in death. When humanity contradicts its fundamental pro-existent character, which is "laid up" in Christ, it experiences spiritual and physical death.[191] In relation to Christ, Balthasar notes, "Of course we can say that the Son dies 'because of sin,' but at a deeper level he dies 'because of God,' because God has definitively rejected what cannot be reconciled with the divine nature."[192] Therefore, in his full representation of the essence of humanity's sin, Jesus dies: "In that same way that, upon earth, he was in solidarity with the living, so, in the tomb, he is in solidarity with the dead."[193] But, how should we interpret this death? And, in what way did Christ represent humanity in death? Balthasar's theology of Holy Saturday is of key importance.[194]

Whereas Holy Saturday has traditionally been understood as a triumphant event, Balthasar believes the sufferings of the crucified Lord are prolonged to the furthermost abyss, the realm of the dead.[195] He describes the traditional understanding as the "motif of the light shining in the darkness." "In this schema," he states, "Christ in his descent is depicted as someone who is active in the extreme: 'I have entered by foot into Hades and bound up the strong and led men into the heights of heaven.'"[196] However,

> We must go farther than this: according to the sense of the classical Old Testament texts, the dead person is lifeless, powerless, without effect, and above all without contact with God or thus either with his fellow human beings. In Sheol, in the Pit, all that reigns is the darkness of perfect loneliness. But to be without contact with God *means* to be without the inner light of faith, hope and love—which, as long as the bonds of death have not been broken through, are limited in the Old Covenant to earthy and mortal life (Is 38:11; Ps 6:6, 88:11–13): "For Sheol does not praise you; death cannot extol you" (Is 38:18).[197]

Why is it that Balthasar seeks to move the traditional understanding of Holy Saturday further? In the pits of Sheol, the dead are in a partial state of the *poena damni* (the "punishment of damnation," i.e., loss of the vision of God). Balthasar describes this place as a "realm of (eternal) darkness, as 'dust,' 'silence,' an existence without strength, without activity, without enjoyment, without knowledge of what takes place on earth, without the praise of God, without return, an existence in nothingness and oblivion."[198] The vision has not been fully lost because the dead still wait in the hope of Christ. For Christ's movement of redemption to be complete, Christ must travel here, to the place of the dead, not as the triumphant victor, but as a dead man. Furthermore, only the One whose life is perfect pro-existence, the One who beholds the *visio beatifica*, can experience the full effects of the *poena damni*. In this way, he represents death in the place of the dead.[199] "If Jesus has suffered on the Cross the sin of the world to the very last truth of this sin—godforsakenness—then he must experience, in solidarity with the sinners who have gone to the underworld, their—ultimately hopeless—separation from God, otherwise he would not have known all the phases and conditions of what it means for man to be unredeemed yet awaiting redemption," says Balthasar.[200] In *Mysterium Paschale*, Balthasar describes Christ's act among the dead as an act of solidarity.[201] However, he says that *Mysterium Paschale* was "hastily written," and "the term 'solidarity with the dead' was a compromise," and is replaced with *Stellvertretung* in *TL2*, but he does not explain why.[202]

These nuances to Balthasar's developing usage of representation in the context of the cross and Holy Saturday are crucial to the objective of giving an exact elaboration of representation, one that includes subthemes of solidarity and substitution. The term *substitutionary representative* is probably the best English term to encapsulate Balthasar's theology of the cross and Holy Saturday, and for three reasons.[203] It seems that one reason why "mere solidarity" or "mere substitution" is insufficient without "representation" is that they imply that Jesus experiences the same partial *poena damni* as the dead.[204] He would simply be a dead person among dead people. Balthasar asks of mere solidarity: "But if I suffer from cancer, what good does it do for me if someone else lets himself be stricken by the same illness in order to keep me company?"[205] Only a differentiated, divine Subject can play the role of the representative of suffering and death and experience the full *poena damni*. This act is exclusive to his triune personhood. Christ is "entirely alone" in his trinitarian suffering and death.[206] At the same time, as it pertains to the suffering aspect of Christ's dramatic representation, "mere representation" does not seem to be enough either. The logic of penal substitution does come back to surface. Balthasar states that "God's anger strikes him instead of the countless sinners."[207] That is, the dramatic and suffering action of Christ is substitutionary because Christ bears the ultimate consequence of humanity's sin as its representative and suffers death in solidarity with humanity. Rahner's and Balthasar's participatory notions of representation have much in common, but they diverge here, where Balthasar emphasizes the dramatic, substitutionary, and exclusive components of Christ's action *pro nobis*. It is not enough for Christ to merely "act on our behalf" (*Repräsentation*), as a universal mediator.[208] In order for redemption to be complete, Christ must also "act in our place" (*Stellvertretung*) and that place is the full ontological weight of humanity's death.[209]

The second reason Christ's atoning work needs the concept of representation is that it does not exclude the actions of the persons for whom he is substituting. Typically, the substitute and the one substituted for act in exclusion of one another (the substitute takes the place of someone and does their work for them), whereas Christ's action cultivates humanity's participation (chapters 2 and 4) and can be resisted. In fact, Christ's experience of the full *poena damni* makes it possible for humanity also to experience the full *poena damni*.[210] Balthasar states, "Only after God has uttered his absolute Yes to man can man utter his absolute No to God: genuine atheism is a post-Christian phenomenon."[211] Therefore, the dramatic interplay between God and creation is not diminished but "heightened" after the cross.[212]

The third reason why representation is needed is that mere substitution directly benefits the one substituting (the substitute receives the reward for his or her substitution), whereas Christ's work directly benefits humanity. Hence, the term "substitutionary representative": Christ's work is on humanity's behalf and for its benefit but also in its place. That is, he dies in the place of humanity (substitute), but it benefits humans and includes their participation (much like an attorney's representation of his or her client is inclusive).

Finally, although it is beyond the scope of this work to present a full-scale interpretation of impassibility in Balthasar's theology, and I am generally sympathetic with an interpretation such as O'Regan's,[213] the way Balthasar speaks of the forsakenness of Christ seems to move beyond the limits of the various linguistic resources that he employs.[214] Balthasar takes the literal, historical words of Christ's cry of forsakenness and discovers a "deeper and darker" meaning of Christ's suffering, which "takes place in the profound depths of the relations between the divine Hypostases."[215] By making this final ever-greater movement and placing the "conditions" for forsakenness in the context of the immanent Trinity, making Jesus's abandonment timeless, and subsequently employing language such as the Father "strikes,"[216] Balthasar sweeps aside his earlier conclusions about the equivocal nature of the language of punishment and the hidden mystery of the hour of judgment. He stretches an analogical reading of triune distance to the breaking point when he makes God the Father's forsaking of God the Son direct, active, and absolute. Separation becomes concrete in God, taking epic undertones,[217] making the free self-offering of the Son impossible. Although it may be said this dramatic action takes place in the unified will of the Father and Son in the triune place of distinction, which is held together by the Spirit, it would seem more sensible to be rhetorically cautious and say that God the Father allowed the Son to be forsaken and experience suffering and death as the consequence of his assumption of the unholy distance. The subject of Christ's suffering and forsakenness is his economic oneness with the unholy distance, not his eternal Father's paroxysm. As Thomas Weinandy states, "The wrath of God is simply God's approval of what sin rightfully demands."[218] Rowan Williams sees this kind of reading of Christ's suffering operating in Balthasar: "The Father cannot intervene to save the Son without betraying his purpose, and so betraying himself."[219] However, when the movement from the historical to the theological meaning changes from Christ's free assumption of the unholy distance to forsakenness in the immanent Trinity, then the former is difficult to reconcile with the latter. Furthermore, it would seem the liberating outcomes of the suffering of Christ would be in jeopardy if forsakenness were raised into the immanent Trinity and were timeless. How does God forsaking God liberate and restore humanity? If the Father forsakes humanity's representative in the triune life, then does that not separate humanity from its source? In the next section, we will now look at the outcome of Christ sufferings, liberation from death, asking if Balthasar's tragic depiction of Christ's suffering can be contained in Christ's eucharistic being.

Liberation from Death: Tragedy Contained in Christ's Eucharistic Being

Death, a prominent theme of the *Theo-Drama*, is defeated through the sufferings of the crucified Lord. Christ liberates finitude from its return to nothingness and restores it back to the infinite reciprocating life of God. In his dramatic depiction of the cross, Balthasar incorporates the insights of the genre of tragedy. However, for reasons I shall discuss, his conception of eternal forsakenness moves beyond his own recommended limits of the tragic insight, trapping humanity in death. Therefore, I offer an amendment to Balthasar's theology of the cross using his own theology. As O'Regan acknowledges, "A Balthasarian view of impassibility can sustain correction and welcome supplement."[220] I locate Christ's suffering on the cross in Christ's eucharistic being, which is dramatically performed in his recapitulating activity as the representative of finite freedom. Dramatic representation, it shall be argued, is situated in the action between finite and infinite freedom and, particularly, in death's despotic reign. By placing dramatic representation in this context, I shall show how humanity's liberation from death occurs through Christ's representation of finite freedom's second pillar of existence, and the character of this representation is dramatic, but does not succumb to absolute tragedy. This historical tragedy does not introduce any new form of separation or distance to the Father, Son, and Spirit's perfect distance of peace, unity, and beauty.

Death and Liberation: From a Tragic Reading to Absolute Tragedy

The theatric bond between death, tragedy, and liberation is an underlying concern of Christ's representation of humanity.[221] Death is finitude's most venomous and dreaded enemy and must be central to any dramatic model of redemption: "Death stands, unuttered, behind every play, and often enough it becomes its explicit subject matter, and not only in tragedy either."[222] Thus, the antagonist in the drama of finite freedom is death; the protagonist is God, fighting to liberate finitude from its self-enclosed contradictions. It is in this manner that renderings of the cross must carefully portray the tragedy of Christ's death by employing the metaphysical and grammatical resources we laid out in the first part of this book. In the following, I analyze Balthasar's theology of Christ's forsakenness by introducing the theological use of the genre of tragedy and Balthasar's understanding of the possibilities and limits of how Christian theology can use tragedy. I then argue that Balthasar extends the tragic vision too far into the inner life of God, which causes his tragic reading of the cross to move to absolute tragedy.

The use of the genre of tragedy in Christian theology is contested. Donald MacKinnon remarks that the gift of classic literature is the significance it gives to human evil and perversity, reminding Christians that to speak of the cross is to reflect on the genre of tragedy seriously.[223] David Bentley Hart is critical of MacKinnon's theological appropriation of tragedy, for any depiction of the cross that displays God condoning society's sacrificial mechanisms makes a metaphysics of beauty, peace, and harmony implausible by introducing violence into difference.[224] Although some, such as Hegel and Kierkegaard, believe that individual sacrifice is worthy of a universal good,[225] Hart believes that a theology of the cross must pass Karamazov's test: "If the universal final good of all creatures required, as its price, the torture of one little girl, would that be acceptable?"[226] According to Francesca Aran Murphy, Hart fails to see the theological contributions of the concept of tragedy. Therefore, Hart finds no redemptive elements in Christ's suffering, but only in his obedience, overlooking the fundamental insight of Anselm.[227] Ben Quash also critiques Hart. Quash believes that Hart rejects tragedy based on a narrow conception of its meaning and does not take the historicity of the cross seriously, but Quash wonders if Balthasar perilously ends up on the opposite end of the spectrum.[228] Considering that *The Beauty of the Infinite* is partly attributed to Balthasar's influence on Hart,[229] it is a great irony that one dismisses tragedy while the other believes Christ is "the heir of all the tragedy of the world,"[230] finding redemptive significance in Christ's suffering and obedience.

The debated nature of the genre's importance to Christian theology is at least partly because of different conceptualizations of what tragedy is.[231] For our purposes, I use Ben Quash's broad definition of tragedy, because it encapsulates the narrower meanings Balthasar uses below: "The tragic may be summarized as the woundingly 'embroiled' character of human action."²³² He notes that "embroilment often takes the form of a warping of what we intuitively regard as the natural relation between *capability* and *culpability*."²³³ "Tragic heroes" are often caught in an internal conflict between two values (guilt/innocence, freedom/necessity, etc.). In the case of Saul, Quash remarks that it might be a story of true tragedy showing the marks of "culpability without capability" and ends with no clear resolution.²³⁴ Tragedy, then, is broadly about a tragic hero's internal embroilment with two values that are in opposition to one another, which normally results in the hero's death.

It is essential that we demarcate this broad definition of tragedy in a way parallel to Balthasar's more specific employment of the genre, which he provides in *TD*1. Based on the work of Albin Lesky, Balthasar distinguishes three different modes of tragedy, suggesting that it is only appropriate for Christian theology to use two. The first mode is the "tragic situation." In this mode, a tragic hero is caught between conflicting values, which causes death before leading to some form of reconciliation between the opposing powers. The second mode is the "closed tragic conflict." The hero is also caught between two "equally valid opposites." However, in this mode, the way out of the tragic situation is less foreseeable. Reconciliation does eventually occur, but it needs "a higher level," a transcendent power for resolution, whereas in the first mode the reconciliation occurs within the tragic situation itself.²³⁵ The third mode is the "closed tragic worldview." "Here the structure of the world is seen as ultimately one of antagonistic and mutually annihilating forces and values." For Balthasar, this mode is "absolute tragicism" because it is "inwardly at war with *itself* (and lacking a governing highest value) makes the conflict seem meaningless along with man, caught in its toils."²³⁶ Hart's rejection of the genre of tragedy seems to be a rejection of this third form of tragedy, because the tensions of the tragic situation are projected on to the metaphysical, making the tragic situation fateful and external. Hart states, "These irresoluble contradictions within moral order belong often to a civic order of injustice, which tragedy dissimulates by displacing the responsibility for civic violence to a metaphysical horizon of cosmic violence; the sacrificial structure of the polis is presented as the sacrificial order of the world."²³⁷ Yet, Murphy believes Hart confuses tragedy with melodrama. "Robert Heilman used to distinguish tragedy and melodrama by the fact that the melodramatic protagonist is an undivided, pathetic *victim*, whereas the tragic hero is internally *divided*," says Murphy. "By assuming that tragedy is simply about suffering as victimisation, and therefore wanting to brush it under the carpet of eschatological joy, Hart exhibits a confusion of tragedy with melodrama."[238] Rather than melodrama or tragedy, I call this third mode "absolute tragedy," which affirms a metaphysical reality that demands suffering, death, and tragedy.[239]

Balthasar suggests that Christian theology can employ only the first two modes. He believes that the Christian "interpretation of the tragic comes within a hair's breadth of the third of the categories mentioned, while remaining just clearly distinct from it."[240] God can associate himself with the tragic situation in his free self-giving in Christ without confirming a tragic metaphysic. Thus, for Balthasar, "genuinely tragic situations are possible for Christians," as long as a "nontragic Absolute is the indispensable precondition of the tragic."[241] This nontragic Absolute is trinitarian distance—the dramatic distance of the Son's eternal generation can contain the drama of creation.[242] As a result, the hope of using the first two modes of the genre of tragedy is in their power to represent the tragic and to come as close as possible to absolute tragedy, while still challenging social and religious mechanisms that condone violence.[243]

With this background in mind, the question can now be asked of Balthasar: Is his dramatic project, with its linguistic resources (analogical, dialectical, hermeneutical), able to endure eternal forsakenness? Three correlated ways can be identified to show how Balthasar fails to contain the tragic reading of the cross in his depiction of Christ's forsakenness, causing his account to valorize absolute tragedy. After outlining these, I show in the next subsection how a firm countermovement—using and amending the dramatic resources in *TD*5—offers the tragic reading that Balthasar suggests Christian theology can employ.

First, Balthasar lacks the rhetoric necessary in his dramatic portrayal of the cross in *TD*4 to protect himself from making a tragic reading of the cross a necessity. Quash is adamant that the historical tragedy of the cross can be considered Christian as long as the dungeon Christ enters is "a dungeon not of his own making, but nevertheless one of his choosing."[244] What is needed to protect Christ from absolute tragedy is a rhetoric of freedom: Christ is "both the offerer and the offering" (Augustine)[245] and the "judge, the judged, and the judgement" (Barth).[246] If Christ's culpability, his oneness with the unholy distance of sin, is a triune gift given out of free love and not an external obligation the Son must fulfill to the Father, then the tragic insight may prove fruitful. As John Behr notes of Athanasius, impassibility does not mean that the Word is uninvolved, but that any suffering that is related to his assumption of human flesh is the "Word's active, willing acceptance of our human condition" not a passive, forced event.[247] The dramatic action between Father and Son is best interpreted in a trinitarian economy of free love, not an "Arian vision of the Divinity."[248] Situated in this place, Christ's gift is not a victimized, fated necessity, but the *drama's* free action.[249]

At first, Balthasar follows this rhetoric: Christ is not the victim of the Father's punishment, but is both the giver of the gift and the gift itself—the protagonist who hands himself over (John 10:18).[250] Nevertheless, he bypasses this understanding of the Son's free self-giving and the imprecise nature of the rhetoric of punishment by displaying the Son's death in the climax of the drama as passive. Balthasar's Christ appears to be a victim of not only the world, but also of the Father. If hell, for Balthasar, is a dungeon that free creatures choose and not a place God actively sends anyone, then should not the cross and descent be consistently depicted similarly?[251]

Another way Balthasar lacks the necessary rhetoric is that Christian tragedy should be read paradoxically. David F. Ford also believes the category of tragedy is important to Christian theology, showing that tragedy is a critical side of the polarity between sorrow and joy in Paul's Second Letter to the Corinthians, and, therefore, the category should not simply be thrown out in the joy of the Resurrection.[252] However, Ford's question for MacKinnon can also be asked of Balthasar: "Yet one question that the letter prompts one to ask MacKinnon is whether he has done justice to the joyful note of abundance. Paul describes himself and others as 'sorrowful, yet always rejoicing' (6:10); can MacKinnon's emphasis on tragedy fully affirm the second half of the paradox?"[253] Kevin Taylor believes that Balthasar is able to affirm both sides of the paradox, arguing that for Balthasar "the Truth of Greek tragic insight remains, yet it is now relativized within the larger fullness of Christ's truth."[254] Although it may be permissible to speak of tragedy and suffering on the cross paradoxically, both "heightening" and "minimizing" tragedy, is Balthasar as effective at this as Taylor suggests?[255] A large portion of *TD*5 attempts to maintain this paradox,[256] but Balthasar's ever-greater movements undermine this effort. Most conspicuously, Balthasar will say that any economic death in *TD*4 is contained within a "positive death" in *TD*5, locating the tragedy of the cross in the eternal self-emptying of God.[257] The Son's self-giving (the positive death) is undergirded by the Father's own self-giving, which eternally generates the Son. Yet, if the Father's generating ceases by eternally forsaking the Son, then the Son's positive death is no longer continuously generated by the Father's self-emptying. This is absolute tragedy, because it collapses historical forsakenness into eternal forsakenness, preventing one from reading the cross paradoxically.

The second way Balthasar struggles to escape absolute tragedy is that he moves beyond the limits of the *analogia entis* by introducing a new form of distance into the triune life. In *TD*1, Balthasar notes that a hero's death is only truly tragic if the hero transforms completely from one pole to the opposing pole. The tragedy is further heightened if in the hero's alteration, he or she does not "heal the wound": "Christian theology alone can prevent the tragic dimension from this self-destruction."[258] Rowan Williams believes that Balthasar's Christ can be the "supreme tragic hero" without creating a contradiction in God. In his complete abandonment to the unholy distance of sin, Christ finds himself abandoned by God on the cross, but never "strictly abandoned" because it occurs within Christ's abandonment to the triune will. Consequently, Williams concludes, "This 'tragic' rupture [can] occur without entailing a kind of tragic division within God."[259] Carpenter offers a similar understanding of how tragedy is "relativized" by Christ's ever-greater surrender.[260] Finally, though, Carpenter's and Williams's interpretations fail to convince because the analogous and dialectical dimensions of Christ's dramatic representation are missing in *TD*4. Instead of keeping forsakenness as a horizontal dimension of the Son's mission, Balthasar lifts forsakenness to the transcendent-beyond. Created distances, though, cannot apply to the primordial divine distance because the analogous difference between the two is what makes the former a possibility. It is not the Son's representative suffering that is ultimately tragic, but the disruption of the infinite beauty and unity of the Father, Son, and Spirit by finite perversion and contradiction. When infinity collapses into finite sin and violence, eliminating the *analogia entis*, then the tragedy of Christ's representative suffering is uncontainable.

Third, the ultimate test to determine if Balthasar's theory of representation moves to absolute tragedy is related to "healing the wound," which is liberation from death. There is a strong linkage between dramatic theory, a hero's death, and liberation from death:

> The dying man can make his death the highest expression of his existential will, as in the case of a martyr or the person who sacrifices himself to some lofty ideal. By means of this final act, whether he suffers it or seeks it out, he can imprint a meaning, retrospectively, on his whole existence. Thus in the drama it is generally only the last act that rids the preceding one of its fluid and provisional character and confirms the entire action.[261]

In fact, tragic situations, as distinct from absolute tragedy, insist that a tragic hero's death and suffering leads to the "creation of a new order."[262] Although Balthasar acknowledges forms of historical, political, structural, and social suffering, the aim of his focus of liberation is primarily eschatological, centering on liberation from death;[263] Quash and Walatka rightly criticize this limitation.[264] By concentrating on death, Balthasar believes liberation theology "reveals the dramatic situation of the Christian in this world as perhaps nothing else does."[265] Assuming this to be the case, the self-attested assessment Balthasar must pass in the final act is this: Does the action of the universal protagonist overcome the unyielding antagonist, death (1 Cor. 15:26; Rom. 8:10)?[266] As the drama of human existence borders on tragedy, finds itself overcome by the power of evil, death, and suffering, can it find "genuine liberation from the tragedy of death?"[267] Given Balthasar's conception of receptivity in the Trinity and its analogy in creation, eternal forsakenness makes humanity's liberation from death inconceivable. If finite freedom introduces a new form of distance in God, impeding the exchange in the eternally begotten Son, who himself is the "exchange" between heaven and earth, then creation and Christ become trapped in death.[268] Although Balthasar will say, "For in itself, however baffling it may be to the finite mind, the all-embracing reality within which 'tragedy' is played out is—eternal blessedness,"[269] it is not evident how eternal blessedness meshes with other statements, such as "infinite pain" in God or "this atoning torment must have consisted in unfathomable depths of forsakenness by the Father."[270] Even more alarming, Balthasar insists, "this abandonment is more profound than anything we can imagine and, according to the Christian understanding, underpins everything in the world that can be termed 'tragic.'"[271] It is these kinds of statements that make the third form of tragedy that Balthasar sought to avoid most visible, projecting tragedy into the divine life. In Balthasar's construction of the final act, the tragic hero is powerless to heal the wound.

A Necessary Countermovement: Death Is Liberated through Christ's Eucharistic Being

In a sense, Balthasar employs a model like Rowan Williams's: What kind of divine life would make the dramatic action in *TD4* possible?[272] Williams is correct that the "dramatic representation" involved in tragedy must not be reduced to "paradoxical safety" and the Resurrection does not simply explain or fix human suffering, but he still recommends that the "tragic imagination" needs certain limits to "contain the representation of suffering."[273] As we just observed, though it is conceivable to read *TD4* in light of the eternal blessedness of *TD5*,[274] Balthasar is still keen to speak of a new divine distance and an eternal cry of forsakenness, even in this context,[275] which was shown to move beyond the containment of the tragic insight. For our purposes, the historical tragedy of the cross does not need to introduce a new distance into God to liberate humanity from death.[276] With a countermovement to the tragic action of *TD4*, there is a way to conceive the historical sense of the cross, including its tragic dimensions, in the theological sense without collapsing divine and creaturely distance. The tragedy of the cross, I argue, is contained in Christ's eucharistic being, which is dramatically performed in his recapitulating activity as the representative of finite freedom. Consequently, Christ liberates humanity from death.

Christ's representative suffering of the unholy, tragic distance is located in the place of the eternal "blood circulation"—self-giving and self-receiving—of the triune life, particularly, in Christ's eucharistic being.[277]

Although Christ is crushed under the full weight of sin in his concrete representation of finitude and the ever-flowing life between the Infinite and finite ceases, the distance of the triune life remains uninterrupted and is preserved in pure harmony, peace, and unity. Any separation is located only in the context of finite freedom and infinite freedom. More specifically, Christ's suffering on the cross is contained in the *semper maior* of his eternal eucharistic being—his "eternal Yes to the gift of consubstantial divinity"[278]—maintaining the distinction between Christ's eternal procession and temporal mission. It is possible to maintain an emphasis on Christ's forsakenness without disrupting the simplicity of immanent divine distance by expressing the economic divine distance of forsakenness within the horizontal dimension of the Son's mission. Forsakenness is dialectically related to Christ's economic obedience as humanity's recapitulating representative. Both forsakenness and obedience are horizontal expressions that together exist in Christ's mission, his vertical-beyond movement into the economic-in. His historical cry of forsakenness *pro nobis*, then, is a revelation of the depths of his eternal pro-existence, not a revelation of an eternal cry of forsakenness or ever-greater suffering.[279] Yes, Christ freely "made a dungeon of himself" and his life is lived in tragic tension by representing the unholy distance, but he does not immanently become a tragic contradiction because economic tragedy (economic divine distance) is surpassed by the ever-greater, excessive fullness of divine self-giving (immanent divine distance). In a much earlier publication entitled "Tragedy and the Christian Faith" (1965), Balthasar more effectively shows the harmony between the historical and theological senses of scripture: "His gift of his flesh and blood in the Last Supper, coincides with the deed of the uttermost hatred, the slaughtering of this flesh and the pouring out of this blood."[280] And, this eucharistic inaugural address is grounded in his eucharistic gift of divinity back to God.

It is in such a context that finitude is liberated from the tragedy of death. As the Son historically surrenders to death, signifying his eternal surrender of divinity, he is concurrently and endlessly generated with life through the Resurrection (in the Spirit) as he is in his trinitarian procession.[281] Instead of splitting Christ's death and resurrection into two distinct moments in his narrative of salvation, as Moltmann does,[282] Balthasar should have imagined one simultaneous action, as in Athanasius.²⁸³ As the representative of finitude, Christ descends to its place of death, and in this dry and desolate place, he restores the flow of being through his endless generation from the Father. The Son is liberated from death in the Resurrection, which is an image of the triune God's eternal self-reception—underneath the splattered blood, the historical sense, is the sharing of eternal life, the theological sense.²⁸⁴ Balthasar states, "The blood of the cross flows 'back and forth,' forever reconciling earth and heaven to one another."²⁸⁵ It is the perfect eucharistic action of the self-giving (sacrificial) Son, the recapitulating representative, that is pleasing to the Lord, and this liberates humanity by filling the second pillar of finite existence. It is not the blood of the sacrifice alone that liberates humanity, but the aroma of Christ's eucharistic being (Eph. 5:2). This account takes the second pillar of humanity's existence seriously by redeeming humanity in the place of its freedom rather than from the outside. Christ fulfils the gift-character of humanity by recapitulating and incorporating it into his triune thanksgiving.²⁸⁶ Thus, the interpretative key finds Christ's perfect self-giving on the cross pleasing to God, showing the historical tragedy to be a theological aroma.

In summary, when Christ freely takes humanity's place of death, he dramatically performs his eternal eucharistic being—his eternal gift-giving to the Father in the Spirit. His complete givenness to the second pillar of finite freedom becomes an action, an absolute Yes, in the place of humanity's disobedience and self-contradiction.²⁸⁷ The economic covenant is fulfilled—recapitulated—through Christ's economic mission, which is an ever-greater revelation of his eternal *eucharistia*. By acting in humanity's place, he recapitulates finite freedom, and thus Christ and humanity are simultaneously resurrected, restoring finite freedom to the life flow of God. Death is liberated not negatively through the Father's eternal abandonment of the Son, but positively because the Son in his surrender to death "eucharistically fills up the cosmos with triune life."²⁸⁸ So, Balthasar can say, "[The reversal from alienation to proximity] is made possible by the fact that the Son's God-forsakenness is drawn into the love relationship within the Trinity. The Son 'takes the estrangement into himself and creates proximity': nearness between God and man on the basis of the union between Father and Son that is held fast through every darkness and forsakenness,"[289] without needing to speak of an unequivocal, unfathomable, eternal forsakenness.[290]

We can now see what is meant by dramatic representation and how, in the tragic drama of redemption, it includes elements of representation and substitution. Christ's representation of humanity is dramatic because (1) it includes various movements and countermovements to grasp its meaning, resisting trite systemization, and (2) it incorporates inclusive and participatory elements—drama is social in nature—as we will see in chapter 4. Representation with substitution language allows for taking, filling, and acting in the place of humanity. By taking the sinful distance of darkness and its ultimate consequences and representing death and suffering, Christ, the recapitulating representative, is then able to act in this place *pro nobis* by filling it with his divine life, transforming it from a place of deadly distance to a place of intimate distance, liberating humanity from death.[291] Christ's action on the cross (substitution) is contained in the ever-greater Christ–creation metaphysic (representation). By integrating the trinitarian and christological metaphysic with Balthasar's dramatic soteriology, we can see how representative and substitutionary logics are needed.

Conclusion

I have sought to construct the first half of the dramatic exchange formula by clarifying and amending Balthasar's account of the drama of redemption. Balthasar's dramatic search for the meaning of the cross reveals a complex, idiosyncratic, and even contradictory framework that attempts to weave together various strands of Christian thought. His theo-dramatic hermeneutic contains various ever-greater movements from the historical to the theological meaning, and many of these ascents allure Balthasar's audience into a renewed vision of the blood circulating between the triune life, the cross, and humanity. The theo-dramatic hermeneutic attempts to represent the mystery of the triune God *pro nobis*, yet continuously draws attention to *Deus semper maior* who eternally transcends any theological vision. Although Balthasar offers the triune vision to contain the tragic history represented in Christ's suffering, death, and forsakenness, he sets his sights too far, and tragedy ascends into the life of God, creating a new distance between the Father and Son and destroying the analogy between God and creation. Only an uninterrupted, eternal, simple God could descend to such a depth to contain, represent, fill, and restore all the abysses of finitude's nothingness, while in himself remaining sheer, immutable, and infinite beauty, truth, and goodness. The theo-dramatic project must be transcended by and in the ineffable simplicity of triune love. We can now turn to the second half of the exchange formula, elucidating the participatory notion of Christ's dramatic representation.

CHAPTER FOUR

EMPLACED *THEOSIS*

The Spirit as the Continual Representative

In this we know that we abide in him and he in us, because he has given us of his Spirit (1 Jn 4:13). He then is the one meant when we read, Love is God (1 Jn 4:8, 16). So it is God the Holy Spirit proceeding from God who fires man to the love of God and neighbor when he has been given to him, and he himself is love.
—Augustine, *The Trinity* 15.5.31

So far we have discussed a theology of representation primarily in relation to Christ's universal work for humanity. To fulfill the aim of making it a *Grundkategorie*—that is, both universal and concrete—we now shift to the dramatic nature of Christ's work and the relevance of representation to the church, incorporating our governing trinitarian metaphysic and Christology. Balthasar, Sölle, and Bonhoeffer link christological representation to human responsibility for others, an interconnection Sölle insists is imperative if a "doctrine of representation" is to progress.[1] What our theology of representation aims to advance, then, is a metaphysic that ineluctably cultivates human action for others. Christ's representative agency opens out for human representative agency. Yet, Sarah Coakley warns of the danger of idolizing *imitatio* theology, where humans "attempt directly to *imitate* the life of the Trinity." "Because we are embodied, created beings, we may indeed (through the graced aid of the

Spirit) 'imitate' Christ, the God/*man*; but we cannot without Christ's mediation directly imitate the Trinity itself."[2] Therefore, as I expand Christ's representation to the *communio sanctorum*, I also seek to avoid producing a moral exemplar model of atonement.

In this chapter, I develop representation in relationship to humanity's initiation into the triune life, motif 4 of Balthasar's dramatic soteriology.[3] Anytime Balthasar speaks of *theosis*, it is immediately followed by the actions of the *communio sanctorum*. For example, in *TD*4 Balthasar addresses *theosis* under the heading of "Freedom Liberated" and directly following is "Christian Discipleship." The conclusion of this section is that Christ's work *pro nobis* is handed over to his followers, who now must act in the place of others.[4] This link between holiness and service for others is certainly part of Balthasar's incorporation of Ignatius of Loyola in the *Theo-Drama*, however implicit it may be.[5] Divinization, humanity's participation in the triune life, is often displayed as creaturely and ecclesial action and fruitfulness,[6] whereas its eschatological incorporation into the triune life is left a mystery of faith. This is seen most unequivocally in *TD*5. In a section titled "Embedded in God," Balthasar shows how humanity's initiation into Christ's eternal place flows directly into the church becoming a place for others, which includes action on their behalf.[7] Balthasar also believes that "the presence of Christ is continually brought about" through the Spirit's work in the institutional church,[8] but I focus here on the subjective and missional nature of the church's representation through individuals because Balthasar, as O'Regan argues, is particularly concerned about personal holiness and discipleship, which the institutional office supports.[9]

In the first section of this chapter, I construct the dramatic exchange formula pneumatologically—Christ acted in our place that humanity might act in his place *in the Spirit*—and "emplace" humanity's divinization by explaining how the Spirit is the "Continual Representative" of Christ.[10] And although Bonhoeffer offers a better account of how representation functions socially than does Balthasar (see final subsection of this chapter), Rowan Williams notes that Bonhoeffer's theory of *Stellvertretung* lacks the necessary trinitarian and pneumatological elements.[11] Building on Balthasar's trinitarian theology of representation we developed in chapter 1, I seek to draw out the pneumatological elements of representation: Christ's action *pro nobis* cultivates a dramatic community that acts for others through the indwelling work of the Holy Spirit. In the second section of this chapter, I make the category of representation more concrete by delineating types of representative action, linguistic and social. I aim to show that (1) representation not only shapes doctrine, but the nature of theological knowledge and the theological task, and that (2) Balthasar's dramatic vision is latent: he primarily speaks to the vicarious spiritual actions of the saints, leaving room for us to develop the more social nature of dramatic action.[12]

The Continual Representative, *theosis*, and the *communio sanctorum*

In chapter 2, I explained how the objective and universal work of Christ for humanity is linked to a dramatic dimension, which includes the participation of his body, the church. More specifically, Balthasar extends Christ's representation of humanity to the theotic activity of his people, who now are expected to represent others.[13] However, he does not overtly mediate Christ's representation and ecclesial representation through pneumatic representation. Therefore, to further develop the thesis that Christ acts in humanity's place so that humanity might act in his place, a qualification is necessary: both parts of the equation are completed *in the Spirit*.[14] According to Weinandy, the patristic phrase to describe deification is "by the Son in the Spirit."[15] As Athanasius states, "So then, in the Spirit the Word glorifies creatures, and after he has divinized them and made them sons of God, he leads them to the Father."[16] There is a sense in which the Spirit "acts in the place of" Christ through the continuation of the triune mission. As the Spirit descends, the ascension of human nature into the triune life is sustained and made perfect. In dialogue with various fathers (Gregory of Nyssa, Basil the Great, Cyril of Alexandria) and modern thinkers (Balthasar, Williams, Eugene Rogers), I elucidate this pneumatic framework by explaining how the Spirit represents humanity, which cultivates a community that acts for others and emplaces *theosis* in the missional activity of the *communio sanctorum*. I close this section by relating human agency to the horizontal and vertical dimensions of Balthasar's mission Christology.

The Spirit as the Continual Representative and the Church as the Sacramental Representative

Balthasar's corpus has an unquestionable Barthian ring. Yet, when it comes to the concept of humanity's divinization, its ontological participation in the triune life, a fundamental departure from Barth ensues.[17] In Balthasar's early book on Barth, he states that Bonhoeffer "tried to unify a theology of actualism with a theology of being-in-Christ, that is, an ontology of the Church."[18] For Barth, however, humanity's status in Christ is not the day-to-day reality of the human person "in the flesh." Though he says that a person can live free from sin intermittently throughout the *Church Dogmatics*, he mostly is asking, "Where is this 'new man' to be found?"[19] Barth states that "[sanctification] does indeed involve the creation of a new form of existence for man in which he can live as the loyal covenant-partner of God who is well-pleasing to and blessed by him. But these are far-reaching and pregnant words if we take them literally. They sound like 'idle tales'. . . . Where is man in this new form of existence, as the loyal covenant-partner of God? Who of us is this man?"[20]

McCormack, describing Barth's view of the Christian life, calls it a life "in transition." Though it may be true that a person, in Christ, is the "new creation," when one looks at one's own "physic-psychical existence," there is no evidence of new life.[21] Barth uses the word "impartation" sparingly when describing the relation of Christ's holiness to believers' holiness, primarily following the Reformers, especially Luther and Calvin,[22] in emphasizing the alien, imputed righteousness of Christ. To Barth, the only impartation of holiness in the flesh is in the fact that humanity can "look to Jesus" for its sanctification. The fact that a person can look to Christ for his or her sanctification is the imparted holiness of Christ. Justification and sanctification are already perfected in Christ.[23]

Balthasar asks of Barth, "Why should the real and ontic sanctification of the creature through grace be postponed for the future aeon alone and only be treated as merely a forensic sanctity here and now in the face of all the statements of revelation? Why this restriction to the cognitive side of things alone?"[24] Balthasar recommends a move from a "forensic" understanding of sanctification to one that is "authentic, inner, and ontic,"[25] and this ontological sanctification finds itself functionally in the actions of the *communio sanctorum*. Barth will later object to the mediatorial and representational role the saints play in Balthasar's works about Thérèse de Lisieux, Elisabeth de Dijon, and Reinhold Schneider.[26] In the 1961 *Afterword* added to *The Theology of Karl Barth*, Balthasar notes that Barth understands the representational character of saints as a replacement for Christ's work.[27] A similar issue surfaces between Barth and Bonhoeffer. Bonhoeffer sought to give the church and individuals a more concrete, active, and mediatorial role in the work of salvation, bridging Christology and ecclesiology by his usage of *Stellvertretung*. The significance Bonhoeffer extended to the church was too "Catholic" for Barth.[28]

Colin Gunton, Robert Jenson, Eugene Rogers, Alan Torrance, and Rowan Williams all recognize the underdevelopment of Barth's pneumatology, which leads to an insufficient soteriology and fails to indicate how salvation is incorporated into and mediated through the life of the church. Human agency for Barth is simply human agency.[29] Dismissing a conception of the Spirit as simply the mediator of revelation, Williams states, "It seems, then, that for Barth Spirit is what closes the hermeneutical circle."[30] The Spirit is limited to relaying information about the Logos. Rather, Williams continues, "the Spirit's witness . . . is precisely the formation of 'Son-like' life in the human world; it is the continuing state of sharing in the mutuality of the Father and Son."[31] For Williams, the Spirit is a dramatic communicator, imparting the reality of humanity's new form of existence created in Christ.

Balthasar conceives the role of the Spirit in similar terms when he develops his pneumatology in *TL3*.[32] The Spirit is the Revealer, "bearing witness" to the truth. This revelatory act is an event that includes both the mediation of knowledge and the Spirit's "*movement into* someone." When the Spirit moves in human persons and dwells with them, the Spirit simultaneously carries them into the triune processions. Therefore, Balthasar believes "'truth' is simultaneously 'grace.'"[33]

The Spirit's work is to draw humanity into the "risen Christ's Sonship," and this Sonship is a place of activity, movement, and mission.[34] In Gregory of Nyssa's *Life of Moses*, he speaks about the paradox of resting and motion when it comes to the spiritual life. As one "stands" on the rock of Christ, he or she is drawn into a life of motion, action, and ascent, because Christ himself is a "place" of movement.[35]

In other words, the Spirit incorporates Christ's form in believers, not from "the remote standpoint of a dispassionate believer, but by being drawn into the form itself. . . . This is because the 'aesthetic' view is now complemented by the 'theodramatic,' which inserts itself into the total Christian experience."[36] Thus, the Spirit's witness to humanity is theodramatic: it communicates the finished work of Christ and the form of triune activity to humanity. This theology of the Spirit is another component of Balthasar's theology that separates him from Barth's "christological narrowing."[37]

Eugene Rogers's *After the Spirit* shows how scripture relates the Spirit's work to human places. He constructs a pneumatology of triune indwelling and, analogically, human indwelling. Ephesians, Romans, and Colossians all use the language of the Spirit dwelling in particular places and people. In fact, incorporation "in Christ" is followed by the church being the dwelling place of the Spirit (Eph. 2:22). This indwelling is physical, historical, and concrete "as the seed in the womb, the priest in the temple, or the householder in her home." Rogers continues, "You do not need a theory of premotion to see that even as late as Thomas Aquinas (who learned it from Aristotle) to 'inhabit' is to habituate, to dwell dispositionally or by training in limbs and muscles physically readied, for love's sake, to act. To inhabit is to habituate, to render love bodily."[38] A gnostic, discarnate Spirit found solely in mystical or spiritual space misses the incarnational shape of the Spirit's mission.[39]

Stellvertretung encapsulates the nature of the phrase "in the Spirit" in an unparalleled manner by connecting the Spirit's work directly to places and activity.[40] Rogers explains that "'in' is a preposition of place. What is this place? The *koinonia* that the Spirit creates in and with the Trinity. 'In the Spirit' means in *community*, and then in the form of life, in history, in circumstances, in witness, in a person like a mother or saint: the preposition indicates a mode or form."[41] Furthermore, in Basil the Great's *On the Holy Spirit*, the Spirit is given a special relationship to place and action verbs: the place where the Spirit dwells is where individuals and the church are sanctified, gifts are distributed, and gifts are used to nurture and unify the body of Christ.[42] Basil summarizes, "So, the Spirit is truly the place of the saints, and the saint is the proper place for the Holy Spirit, as he offers himself for indwelling with God and is called a temple of God."[43] By linking "in the Spirit" to representation and the dramatic exchange formula, we can discern a connection between the divinization of human nature and the historical places and actions of the church. The interval between humanity's eschatological incorporation in Christ and the historical actions of his body is crossed over in the Spirit.

Therefore, to define "Christ acts in our place so that we might act in his place" pneumatologically is to emplace *theosis*. By emplaced *theosis*, I mean that humanity's eschatological place in Christ comes to dwell in or inhabit particular historical places and people. Because the ascension of the Son and the descent of the Spirit at Pentecost are tacitly paired,[44] the distance between the triune life and creation is traversed. One need not limit deification to a forensic or futuristic sphere, but can look for it in the places, times, and people of a pneumatically indwelled human history. The "where" of the Christian's eschatological place in Christ is found in the places Christ's theo-dramatic form is historicized. As the Spirit alights, humanity is gathered into God's self-giving through the Son, and the self-giving and mutual indwelling of God extend to the life of the church. These economic actions that take place in the action of the trinitarian processions re-present triune beauty, goodness, and truth in creation.

Now that I have established what emplaced *theosis* is, I can define overtly the meaning of "Continual Representative." By labeling the Spirit as the Continual Representative, I mean that the Spirit acts in the place of the Son's humanity by expanding the boundaries of his body and incorporating its members into his activity. The Spirit represents *Christ* by "universali[zing] Christ's historical, risen reality as the *universale concretum*, thereby enabling its radiance to penetrate 'to the ends of the earth.'"[45] At the same time, since the Spirit is continuing Christ's work of representing humanity, the Spirit represents *humanity* by acting in-and-beyond it.

If representation is to apply to the triune identity and mission, it must be inclusive of the three persons of God (doctrine of inseparable operations) and, by virtue of the hypostatic union, of the body of Christ (the church), undermining Barth's critique of Balthasar and Bonhoeffer about the church replacing Christ. The Spirit does not substitute for Christ, vitiating the *opera Trinitatis ad extra indivisa sunt*. Rather, the Spirit continually perfects Christ's work in his body (*totus Christus*).[46] Likewise, the church does not substitute for Christ, but Christ's representative agency is emplaced in the activity of the church through the power of the Spirit.

Finally, by completing the dramatic exchange formula with this pneumatology, we can include the church in the Spirit's continuation of Christ's mission of incorporating humanity into the triune life and climatically conclude that the church is the sacramental representative of Christ.[47] A sacrament signifies humanity's sanctification by pointing toward the cause (Christ), embodies the form (grace/virtues/mission), and witnesses to the end of humanity's sanctification (glorification).[48] Vatican II's constitution *Lumen gentium* calls the church the "universal sacrament of salvation" because it is the "sign and instrument" of the world's salvation.[49] By acting on Christ's behalf in the Spirit, the church is a means by which Christ's dramatic form of existence is imparted to humanity and is a living, totemic witness to God's eternal goal of incorporating humanity into the place of Christ.[50] Ecclesial agency is incorporated into divine agency and is the fruit of divine agency. The same Spirit that spans the immeasurable gulf of the distance of sin between the Father and Son can gather the church's sacramental actions into the Son's eternal eucharistic response and make them fruitful.

Emplaced theosis: *The Missional and Incorporating Activity of the* communio sanctorum

When addressing *theosis* in the Greek fathers, Balthasar believes Cyril of Alexandria "must occupy center stage."[51] In Cyril, divinization includes humanity's incorruption, sanctification, and adoption[52]—"adoption" being the primary term he uses to represent the "basis, means, and result" of divinization.[53] Christ is the Son by nature, whereas Cyril uses adoption to signify that humanity's sonship is by grace.[54] Cyril comprehensively states his soteriology in his commentary on John 17:18–23: as humanity is adopted into the Son in the Spirit, becoming children in the Son, it is simultaneously gathered into ecclesial unity and sent on mission.[55] Ben Blackwell summarizes, "For Cyril sanctification and empowerment for mission are thoroughly situated in the context of divine indwelling."[56] In the following, I shall continue our development of Balthasar's dramatic soteriology by showing how the Spirit continues the mission of Christ by uniting the places, actions, and missions of the *dramatis personae*. To speak of a pneumatically indwelled human person/community—an emplaced *theosis*—is to speak concretely of the missionary character of the *communio sanctorum* as action in, with, and for others, resulting in humanity's incorporation into the place of Christ.[57]

Gregory of Nyssa, the "father of fathers" as entitled at the Second Council of Nicaea, influenced Balthasar early on in his life.[58] In his homilies on the Song of Songs, Gregory of Nyssa uses an analogy of the archer and the arrow to describe the trinitarian process of divinization. When the Spirit indwells Christians through the arrow of love, they become the arrow by which God infuses love in others. Martin Laird states of this analogy that "the deeds and discourse of the bride take on the attracting, transforming power of the Word and become a vehicle of the Word's incarnational dynamic."[59] "Becoming like God" does not refer to becoming "God's essence, but to his personal exchange of love."[60] The grammar of triune identity, relations, and missions is assimilated into the shared life and activity of God's people. Accordingly, one becomes like God by being regenerated in the "Son's *processio* from God in his *missio*, which goes to the utter 'end' of love (Jn 13:1). This is why we too, if we are begotten of God, are called to give our lives for the brethren (1 Jn 3:16)."[61]

Mission is what unites a conscious subject's freedom in a community with a divine task. The *dramatis personae* are those who freely act in the creative and unified tension between the world stage and divine activity. Balthasar's focus on drama, roles, and ever-greater fruitfulness inculcates the distinct roles and activities of particular people in particular places. The category of representation is significant here because it unites through mission the relationship between existents, places, and divinely shaped activity. Thus Balthasar states, "The being of the theological person coincides with the person's role and influence in the community."[62] Christians are divinized as they play their divinely given roles through acting on the stage in which they exist.

Christian action in, with, and for others—love for neighbor—is theotic because it takes the form of and is a witness to God's own life of self-giving and self-receiving love. The trinitarian grammar of event, generation, creativity, and receptivity demonstrates that divine action occurs in a community that works toward the forgiveness, restoration, and liberation of others.[63] By action, I do not simply mean social or political action. As we saw in chapter 1, the Son was active even in his receptivity, his procession from the Father. Emplaced *theosis*—the theotic activity of the *communio sanctorum*—includes an Ignatian unity of contemplation and action.[64] "With Ignatius, Balthasar sees the creaturely 'ascent' to God as nothing other than the 'descent' of mission, of being sent by God to accomplish some definite task in the world," says Jonathan Martin Ciraulo.[65] For example, after years of resting in God, Basil the Great leaves the monastery to institute his "social vision" in the world, "bringing with him the fruits of his silence and prayer."[66] For Basil, the fruit of love of God, *theosis*, is concrete action for one's neighbor.[67] In the final section of this chapter, I show in more detail how contemplation/language and social action function as acts of representation.

The pneumatic fruit of ecclesial and personal missions, which are Christ's mission,[68] is incorporation, creating a theotic community that shares in both the exchange and unity of the triune God. "The Spirit gathers human beings in him, and distributes gifts to human beings, as a gift upon the gift that Spirit returns to the Son," says Rogers. "This process incorporates or in-members human beings into a *community* constituted by the exchange of gift and gratitude, in which persons delight to receive what they have."[69] In his *Long Rules*, Basil instructs monastic communities on the social nature of Christian community: "For nothing is so proper to our nature as to share our lives with each other, and to need each other, and to love our own kind."[70] In fact, Basil remarks that dwelling in a place with other Christians "preserves the distinctive mark of the saints as narrated in the Acts, about whom it is written, 'All who believe were in one place, and they had all things in common' (Acts 2:44)."[71] The Spirit distributes gifts to individuals for the sake of the community. "Consequently," Basil states, "in community life the activity of the Holy Spirit in one person must pass to everyone together."[72]

Incorporation into the triune God generates a community of exchange and ever-greater possibility, which shares in triune pro-existence. The infinite self-giving of one Person generates unqualified space for the other, which through the ongoing movement of God's life simultaneously bears fruit in both the acting Subject and the generated other. By acting in humanity's place, the "uncreated 'other in God'" creates a triune place for the "creaturely 'other in God'" to offer its missional activity, conceiving a community of ever-greater exchange.[73] By extension, human acts of representation also create possibilities for others.[74] By using their freedom for the sake of the others, actors affirm and heighten their own freedom and potentiality, generating a greater future. "However we try to portray the unimaginable eternal life in the communion of saints, one element of it is constant: we shall be filled with astonished joy, constantly being given new and unexpected gifts through the creative freedom of others; and we for our part shall delight to invent other, new gifts and bestow them in return," states Balthasar.[75] Therefore, representative actions in the *communio sanctorum* do not depersonalize, substitute for, or replace others, but create identity, meaning, and possibility for others.

Finally, incorporation into the triune life brings unity. Returning to the language of Christ's prayer for his people in John 17:18–23, we see that the missional activity of God through his people incorporates others into variegated unity. Trinitarian grammar is functionally operative in the sanctification of God's people. Cyril of Alexandria reflects, "When Christ cites the essential unity that the Father has with him and he has with the Father as an image and type of the inseparable friendship and concord and unity of kindred souls, he wants us to be blended with one another, so to speak, by the power of the holy and consubstantial Trinity so that the entire body of church may be one, ascending in Christ by the joining and concurrence of two peoples [Eph. 2:14–16] into one perfect whole."[76]

In the baptism of God's people, the fig leaves (the sinful distance) are washed away, eliminating humanity's loneliness and shame, and are exchanged for the vestments of Christ (restored distance), as humanity is sewn into a corporate body and participates in the fullness, beauty, and unity of the shared life of the saints. Through the distribution of its gifts, its acts of dispossession, the *communio sanctorum* incorporates itself and others into the fullness of the mystical body of Christ.

I have been developing the way *theosis* and representation considered together might function in Balthasar's dramatic soteriology. To summarize what has been said so far: *theosis* is the emplaced activity—contemplation and action—of a self-giving and self-receiving people, whose common mission is to incorporate others into the fullness, unity, and beauty of triune community. The *dramatis personae* are those indwelled by the Spirit of God in particular places and actions through divine missions. The category of representation is significant to this formulation because it unites the place and action of Christ's universal mission to humanity's concrete places, actions, and missions through the continual agency of the Spirit.

The Spirit's Theo-Dramatic Prayer: Fruit in-and-beyond Human Agency

In this final subsection on the relation between *theosis*, the Spirit, and representation, I assimilate into our conversation Balthasar's reflection on the possibility of prayer being grounded in trinitarian grammar and Paul's teaching on the Spirit's innermost indwelling. Balthasar states,

> All the profound mysteries of Christian prayer revolve around this indwelling of the Spirit of God in the soul; so that, once again, we see that the very possibility of Christian contemplation is founded entirely on the doctrine of the Trinity. Mysteries such as these are not merely theoretical and theological; they are thoroughly practical. It makes a great difference to the act of contemplation whether I see myself as an isolated subject, who, albeit assisted by God's grace, endeavours to understand something of the mysteries of revelation; or whether, in faith, I have the conviction that my inadequate attempt to understand is supported by the wisdom of the Holy Spirit dwelling within me, that my acts of worship, petition and thanksgiving are borne along and remodeled by the Spirit's infinite and eternal acts, in that ineffable union by which all human doing and being has been lifted up and plunged into the river of eternal life and love . . . it is part of the contemplative's act of faith to cling to this: "for we do not know how to pray as we ought, but the Spirit himself intercedes for us with sighs too deep for words," by calling Abba, Father, not somewhere outside or above us, but actually in us and from within us. This cry is heard by him who "searches the hearts of men," who "knows what is the mind of the Spirit," as if the Spirit's cry were the cry of the "saints" themselves (Rom. 8:26–27, 15; Gal. 4:6).[77]

Human performance—the emplaced enactment of its theotic mission—is not meant to be a meritorious "work" or a version of the moral exemplar model of atonement (i.e., Christ acted for others, so humans should act for others). Rather, human action for others is the fruit of pneumatic representation, the ongoing prayer of the Holy Spirit on humanity's behalf. Christ's representative action is complete, yet the continuous action of the Spirit in-and-beyond the *communio sanctorum* is historically and eschatologically endless, because it is excess, a gift of beauty, generosity, and consummation.[78]

The Spirit protects ecclesial action from being a meritorious work because the Spirit acts on the church's behalf, even in its lassitude (Rom. 8:26–27).[79] As humanity's historical existence (*Dasein*) lags behind its essence (*Sosein*) in Christ, the Spirit continues to recapitulate its existence by acting in-and-beyond its place. The Spirit does not replace or make up for humanity's indifference toward the suffering of others; such determinism would remove the dramatic import.[80] Yet, the Spirit receives humanity's fragmented action and, in the midst of it, acts for and with it to be fruitful. The Spirit's dramatic prayer for humanity is part of his continual activity and Christ's heavenly intercession on humanity's behalf. Humanity's action, recognition of inaction, and confession for help all occur through the Spirit's ongoing prayer. Even as Christian speech, which is the church's linguistic action, runs up against its limits and ventures toward nothingness, which is the silence of its own dispossessed narrative, Christ acts for humanity in the Spirit giving it speech. As Rowan Williams so fittingly states, "And, ultimately, what the various languages of revelation propose or imply is that our most fully aware and deliberate and freely accepted silences, when the speaker's agenda is most manifestly suspended, are moments where truthfulness is most evident, where there is the most potent and appropriate act of 'representation.'"[81] Knowledge of God, as stated in Przywara's reading of the Augustinian tradition, is the "rhythm of what passes away," yet God "works through and sustains this rhythm in its entirety."[82]

Humanity is not enshrined or protected from God's judgment on irresponsibility, fragility, and passive fixity. Yet, to confine the Spirit to conscious human agency is to misunderstand the God who transcends human consciousness. God is *superior summo meo* ("higher than the highest peak of my spirit") and *interior intimo meo* ("more intimately present to me than my innermost being").[83] Przywara amalgamates this

Augustinian phrase with the *analogia entis*: humanity's "essence is in- and-beyond existence."[84] Stated in the grammar I am employing in this research, God transcends the distance between a person and his or her theotic mission. Thus, even as the body lags behind its mission, place, and identity, it is preserved in the Spirit's prayer and actively represented in its Head.[85]

The Spirit's agency, then, is theandric or theo-dramatic, working "in- and-beyond" the confines of human agency. In the same way that the Spirit dwells in the divine Son, uniting his divine and human energies (chapter 2), so the Spirit is sent to rest on the church, guiding it to its divine mission in the world. The Incarnation "opens up the triune God's involvement in the whole world drama, which Irenaeus calls God's 'becoming accustomed' to dwelling with man and which Thomas designates as the indivisible 'missions' of Son and Spirit into the whole of history— before and after Christ."[86] Even so, the horizontal activity of the saints (dramatic, historical, linguistic, contemplative, and social) occurs "in" the vertical descent of the Spirit to draw humanity into the "beyond" activity of the Spirit's work, humanity's eternal place in Christ.[87] Dramatic action is a joyful, glorious, and fruitful response cultivated by the Continual Representative. Yet, the dialectical relationship between the divine and human is still not collapsed into one in-activity.[88] Ulrich states that, because God is unbound or, in our terms, is supra-space, then the Spirit can be co-local with the Christian community without being identified with it. No matter the proximity of relation, the distinction between divine and human action remains, because the church is both Christ's body and bride. The Spirit works to synthesize the divine and human activities into one common mission, performing a participatory, noncompetitive theo-dramatic action.

Finally, the Spirit's representative prayer for humanity is historical, because the Spirit bears the Head's fruit in his body and bride, and also eschatological, because the Spirit's ecclesial fruit anticipates humanity's eschatological existence. In the same way the Spirit represents Christ by opening up places for divine agency on earth, so the Spirit represents humanity by welcoming humanity into the roominess of the triune life, humanity's infinite and ever-greater place that Christ has prepared for it (John 14:2–3).[89] "The final form" of the *communio sanctorum* is participation in triune pro-existence.⁹⁰ Balthasar states in the closing paragraph of the *Theo-Drama*, "What does God gain from the world? An additional gift, given to the Son by the Father, but equally a gift made by the Son to the Father, and by the Spirit to both. It is a gift because, through the distinct operations of each of the three persons, the world acquires an inward share in the divine exchange of life; as a result the world is able to take the divine things it has received from God, together with the gift of being created, and return them to God as a divine gift."⁹¹ The fruition of Christ's dramatic exchange has once and for all been consummated in the Spirit, because humanity is incorporated into its source, fully emplaced in the infinite flow of triune love.

In summary, the construction of a dramatic exchange formula alongside a pneumatology inspired by various patristic and modern thinkers demonstrates how the category of representation should not be limited to the topic of Christology. Christ's representation of humanity is continued and completed by the Spirit through the *communio sanctorum*. As Chau states, "Balthasar's commitment to a Church that understands itself in terms of representation and substitution emerges in his belief that the life of the evangelical counsels must be retrieved with new seriousness in this age and culture."⁹² Although Christ's universal representation is unique and unparalleled, it includes the activity of his body through the Continual Representative. Our christological metaphysic accounts for ecclesial activity by placing Christ's representational activity in both universal and personal missions. Imitation of Christ's moral example may occur in the life of the Christian community as the fruit of the Spirit's representation of humanity. The Father is the source of human activity; the Spirit enables human activity and incorporates it into divine activity; the Son is the perfect synthesis of divine and human activity.

Dramatic Action: Linguistic and Social Representatives

Not to move from the general relationship between *theosis* and representation to specific types of representative action would disregard the personalizing and dramatic nature of Christ's representation of humanity. We've seen that Balthasar's, Bonhoeffer's, and Sölle's rehabilitation of the representation category links the objective understanding of Christ's representation with Christian ethical action for others. Moreover, both Balthasar and Sölle insist that the comprehension of the universal vicarious representation of Christ is reliant upon there being some analogy of representation in human relationships.[93]

In the *Prolegomena* to the *Theo-Drama*, Balthasar highlights the elements of drama that need to be included in a theological dramatic theory. We have already explored some of these: actors (the *dramatis personae*), roles (divine and human missions), and movements/countermovements (hermeneutics). An element not yet explicitly discussed is the function "death on behalf of someone else" plays in drama, and the shape it will take in the *Theo-Drama*. "Death is passive but can be active. The most exalted way to make it active is to die on behalf of someone else," Balthasar states.[94] Thus, it is in drama that Balthasar locates the connection between human action for others and Christ's action *pro nobis*.[95]

Balthasar makes a turn from what is a primary element in drama, "bodily death on behalf of others," to "spiritual death on behalf of others," which he connects to a distinctly Christian incorporation of the dramatic element.[96] According to Balthasar, the best illustration that ties the dramatic to the Christian is Bernanos's *Dialogues des Carmélites*.[97] The fictional screenplay is a development of Gertrud von Le Fort's novel, *Die Letzte am Schafott*, which was inspired by the story of the martyrs of Compiègne. The majority of the martyrs of Compiègne were Carmelite nuns who were guillotined during the Reign of Terror for refusing to surrender their monastic vows, which were abolished in the French Revolution. Bernanos tells the story of the fear and courage involved in the nuns' commitment to martyrdom. Two scenes are of significance. First, the main character, anxious and fearful Blanche, is accepted into the Carmelite monastery by aging Prioress Cressy. Balthasar describes the exchange that happens between Blanche and the prioress near the prioress's death:

> The gravely ill prioress "takes her over" and says that she is ready "to give my own poor life" to protect Blanche from the threat that hangs over her [the fear of death]. She is taken at her word, frighteningly so. Instead of dying the edifying death the community expects, she dies in the most terrible mortal fear. "As if the good God had given her the wrong death, as

one gets one coat from the cloakroom attendant rather than another. . . . We do not die for ourselves; we die for one another."[98]

Later in *TD5*, Balthasar will even correlate the prioress's suffering with Jesus's on the cross, describing her suffering as "the most bitter abandonment of God."[99] Second, in the final stanza, Blanche, who had fled the monastery out of fear of martyrdom, ends up joining the other nuns at the bloody scaffold, singing "Veni Creator Spiritus" ("Come, Creator Spirit"). Balthasar reflects on this scene: The "natural fear" of death in the martyrdom of the Carmelite sisters is taken into a "supernatural fear of the Mount of Olives and embedded in the mystery of the communion of saints, where it belongs."[100]

At the end of Balthasar's dramatic soteriology, when he addresses "The Dramatic Dimension of the Communion of Saints," he closes this section and the dramatic soteriology as a whole by returning to the story of Blanche. Though Balthasar stresses the "visible actions" of the saints, he is clear that it is the "invisible actions," namely, suffering and prayer, which extend the greatest fruitfulness.[101] He continues,

> Such action extends even to the place of purgation: the person undergoing the fire of Purgatory cannot intercede for others (although he will be able to do so in heaven), but there is nothing against our showing uninterrupted solidarity with him through our intercession and sufferings on his behalf. How can such purgation, which is so much the result of personal culpability, be transferred to another? This is one of the mysteries of divine justice and mercy; in all probability—as in other matters—God has many different ways and means of achieving the same goal.[102]

The *communion* of the saints is one of suffering, as we see exemplified in the stigmata of St. Francis of Assisi, the dark night experience of St. John of the Cross, and Adrienne von Speyr's Holy Saturday experiences. The passive suffering of the saints is made active by being fruitful for others.[103] Balthasar extends death on behalf of someone else to the dark night of the soul, where the saint suffers with Christ by vicariously representing someone else. One person's suffering is transferred spiritually in an equal or greater extent to the saint.

The originality of Balthasar's dramatic soteriology, which extends to the church's mediation of the triune mission, is attenuated through the priority given to the spiritual vicarious action of the saints. Many commentators remark that the social and political possibilities of Balthasar's dramatic vision are unrealized.[104] Both Quash and Williams say this is attributed to Balthasar's epic, rather than dramatic, understanding of history.[105] Williams states of Balthasar, "There is the teasing and challenging abstraction from the specific calls to 'stake' an identity in dialogue and action," but he suggests that Balthasar's ontology is too original to be forgotten and "undoubtedly needs to be politicized."[106] Walatka provides the most thorough analysis of this judgment of Balthasar's thought, showing that it is "partially right and partially wrong."[107] Nevertheless, I argue in what follows that whatever spiritual suffering the saints may experience should be displayed as the result of their active engagement with the world or the natural fear of their impending death—death that the triune mission does not instigate, but incapacitates in the Resurrection. In his interpretation of martyrs of Compiègne, Balthasar extends the notion of Christ's eternal abandonment to the body of Christ, venturing back into the mythological notions of an angry God needing to be appeased.[108] If we are to restore the category of representation, Sölle insists it needs to be dissociated from the "magical," specifically, "from the notion of mystical exchange of deeds and their consequences."[109] In other words, the advancement of the category of representation requires a different interpretation of the martyrs of Compiègne, which I return to in the final subsection below.

Thus, the objective of the final two subsections of this chapter is to continue to develop the category of representation by making the actions of the saints more emplaced, that is, concrete and particular, not denying the possibility and profundities of spiritual vicarious action,[110] but developing the more social nature of drama and action that is left inchoate in Balthasar. Two forms of representative action take shape here. The first is linguistic representative action. Although Balthasar may have never formulated it in his written work this way, there is a sense in which he acts out his life as a representative through dramatic theology and linguistic representations. The second is the social and political nature of representation. Following Balthasar's recommendation, I elucidate this kind of representation using the theology and life of Dietrich Bonhoeffer, and I also consider the lives of other Christian witnesses and martyrs.[111]

Balthasar as a Linguistic Representative: Dramatic Theology and Linguistic Representations

Balthasar's theology of representation is mutually involved with Balthasar's own practice of theology. A "linguistic representative," understood as one who acts in, with, and for others through linguistic representations, is a category that discloses the task of dramatic theology. In the following, I develop the various substrates that underlie the meaning of this label: the dramatic nature of theological language, the relationship between action, place, and linguistic representations, and the relationship between the Spirit, language, and *theosis*. Finally, I suggest that Balthasar understood his own mission, his theotic role, to be a linguistic representative and that the *Theo-Drama* be read as a form of linguistic representation.

Language is dramatic. In *TD2*, Balthasar suggests that theological language operates as drama, as distinct from epic and lyric; his typology of genre is borrowed from Hegel.[112] When theology functions by the epic mode of language, it ushers the events of the past (scripture, councils, etc.) into the present through utmost precision, systematically speaking "about God" in written, universal facts. However, when theology speaks in the mode of lyric, it addresses God as a "Thou" through the personal prayer life of an individual (i.e., the Ignatian exercises) by awakening the past in the present subjective conscious of the individual.[113] When taken to an extreme, the mode of lyric can lead to the "involutedly lyrical obsession with an asocial and atemporal subjectivity."[114] In between these "two streams of Christian utterance"[115] lies the dramatic mode of language, which considers the dynamic exchange of time, subjects, events, and language.

Drama is ineluctably social, and thus dramatic theology is a social task.[116] Rowan Williams aggrandizes the dramatic/social nature of language in *The Edge of Words*: "The encountered environment is 'real' for us as and only as it insists on establishing itself in our language and stirring that language to constant readjustment and new kinds of representation."[117] Language is inextricably tied to place—inhabited time, culture, and language—and, thus, to be truly emplaced, language needs to move from the "epic to the dramatic" (in Balthasar's words) or from "description to representation" (in Williams's words).[118]

Linguistic representation is more than description ("cataloguing elements in what is perceived"[119]). This type of language is "designative," as developed in a post-Cartesian mindset by Hobbes, Locke, and Condillac.[120] Designative language is after the fact, simply describing a reality that is already there. Williams and Charles Taylor both believe language is invariably more. Explicitly influenced by Ludwig Wittgenstein's argument on the social nature of language,[121] Taylor believes language is "constitutive" and "performative" (J. L. Austin's term); that is, it is generative through the creation and formation of new possibilities for its participants.[122] Williams is also influenced by Wittgenstein, who understood "philosophy not as theory or doctrine but as an activity."[123] By representation (close to Hegel's *Vorstellung*[124]), Williams means "the widest possible category of 'mental goings-on' that can be seen as appropriating the stimuli of an environment as part of a continuing conscious life—or, in the more metaphysically ambitious language [he has] sketched, as fusing the agency or energy of this particular bit of the environment with my own agency, allowing the external stimulus to shape my action, yet also shaping the stimulus in particular ways as I make it my own."[125] For Williams, linguistic representations are the product of one's interaction with his or her place; the embodiment of which creates the possibility for new meaning, form, and action.

Amalgamating Balthasar, Williams, and Taylor, dramatic theology, understood as linguistic representation, is the continuous moving forward of language through its receptivity from its linguistic partners of the past and the social encounters in the present, resulting in the shared transformation of the future.[126] Language is an existent's (*Wesen*) expression of and exchange with its place (*Stelle*). When a *Wesen* fully inhabits and acts in his or her *Stelle*, one fruit is linguistic representation. Acts of linguistic representation display the unity of *Stelle* and *Wesen*, and such unity is also social.

This dramatic theory of language we are developing is quite similar to Ulrich's conception of "metaphysics as reenactment" (*Metaphysik in der Wiederholung*).[127] Metaphysics as reenactment is the "retrieval" or "repetition" of "the movements of thought that have occurred in history."[128] Reenactment happens this way: "To receive the word of a thinker, and to 'hear it back' into the 'ground' from which it arises and comes to pass, to follow the path by gathering up the ground, *without* fixing the fact or the ground in place and calculating their distance from each other, and without closing the 'difference.' What is being carried out in this movement is nothing other than human existence."[129] Because of this, Ulrich resists the systematization of knowledge for its "anti-time and anti-space" character.[130] Instead, philosophers and theologians are to receive knowledge and the tradition and then reenact it through their own concrete relation to space and time; their knowledge is related to their own movement of finitization. In other words, the reception of the tradition ("thinking") takes the same shape as the reception of being ("thanking").[131] Therefore, according to D. C. Schindler, there is a "mysterious exchange that happens at the heart of knowledge." This exchange includes "'life,' because it involves in every respect the increase of 'organic' tensions that result from things being irreducibly different and yet intrinsically related; 'giving' because it occurs in the multifaceted event of a spontaneous receptivity encountering receptive spontaneity; and 'exchange' because exchange is the only way to avoid both a reductive unity and a dualistic difference."[132]

Consequently, language is action in, with, and for the other. If language were simply epic, descriptive, or designative, it would reduce language to action upon the other. The goal of linguistic exchange would be to accurately depict an environment, which would often entail an information giver and information receiver; a clear boundary between the two persists. In contrast, linguistic exchange, if understood in the way we are developing here, is participatory, fluid, material, and complex. Our knowledge of how representation functions as pro-existence between beings shapes our understanding of how knowledge is exchanged. In *Leben in Der Einheit von Leben und Tod*, Ulrich makes a similar connection by explicitly connecting knowledge and *Stellvertretung*.[133] In fact, Martin Belier believes that "what is at issue in the 'metaphysics as re-enactment' is the foundation of a *philosophy of vicarious representation*."[134] A subject acts in the place of an object and liberates it through the exchange of knowledge, while simultaneously the subject receives itself through this gift-giving.[135] In the exchange of language, the knower and the known act in and for the *Stelle* of the other (*ineinander und füreinander*), not "displacing, trampling, or crushing" the other, but freeing them to stand in their own place.[136]

Though analogous, contemporary neuroscience resembles something of what is trying to be said here: through the exchange of verbal and nonverbal information and energy, communicants create new neuron openings for one another—they act in, with, and for one another in creating meaning.[137] According to Daniel J. Siegel, in this process of exchange, "two differentiated individuals can become linked as a part of a resonating whole. This is called interpersonal integration."[138] The performance of language in particular places with particular actors creates performance. Speaking is material; it is to act in one's place with others (including those of the past). The process and exchange of which is creative; it is place-giving. The linguistic representative—one who performs acts of linguistic representation—can formulate and generate indeterminable and uninhabited *Stellen*, which in turn create further possibilities and meaning for the *Wesen* who participate in them.

Now that I have described the dramatic nature of language and its relation to linguistic representation and linguistic representatives, I show how the dramatic nature of language suggests the irreplaceability of linguistic representatives and is directly related to emplaced *theosis*. Balthasar's early work on Gregory of Nyssa, *Presence and Thought*, foreshadows his understanding of the dramatic task (the theotic role), suggesting what is here understood as a linguistic representative. Each epoch requires witnesses, whose goal is not to be a surrogate for the past data of scripture and tradition, but to embody God in their own particular time and language. Balthasar states, "No one, absolutely no one, will discover [the needs of the present] in our stead [or place]."[139] Situated in this performance of time (past and present of divine agency) is the linguistic representative—in Balthasar's terms the "apostolic witness"[140] or Hegel's the "acting subject"[141]—whose language is a movement toward its existence in Christ through contact with God's event in Christ via the sacraments, the lives and teachings of the *communio sanctorum*, and the present social context. Acts of language are unsubstitutable and irreplaceable. To represent, to act in one's place that invariably includes others, demands one moves forward with language.

Balthasar's patristic studies (Origen, Gregory of Nyssa, Maximus the Confessor) are examples of how a linguistic representative dramatically exchanges with its historical linguistic partners. Similarly, his narratives of the saints (Thérèse de Lisieux, Elisabeth de Dijon) parabolically exhibit the dramatic existence of the Christian life. In these, Balthasar witnesses to the present through his synthetic method with the past. Part of one's place is not simply its immediate context, but the church's tradition. Balthasar's patristic studies and narratives of the saints re-present tradition by moving forward with it; a shared place between the tradition and a linguistic representative is inhabited in the present.[142] Bieler says it this way: "This philosophy [metaphysics as reenactment] makes clear that the goal of such a metaphysics is not to cancel out the others' thoughts; instead, it represents the charge given to each of us to carry the burdens of others (Gal. 6:2), interpreted even and precisely as the philosophical task."[143] This is why I am suggesting that one cannot receive Balthasar without understanding his dynamic relation to the tradition and his mentors and friends.

Furthermore, D. C. Schindler describes the importance that Balthasar gave to his present social context in his theological formation and how it challenges Kilby's critique of Balthasar, which we noted in chapter 3:

> But Kilby has clearly not been to visit the archives in Basel, where decades have been spent trying to bring order and accessibility to the mountains of substantial correspondence Balthasar wrote in his lifetime. Rather than being narrowly obsessed with his own writing, Balthasar occupied the first hours of every day—the most important time for work—with the task of writing letters and responding to requests from others, whether those were famous theologians or first-year graduate students. The "colleagues" with whom he discussed not just his work but the problems facing the Church and the world, the great figures of literature and art, and the central questions of philosophy and theology, were some of the greatest minds and spirits of his time. The notion of truth as fruitfulness grew not only out of his long study of the tradition, but also out of his constant dialogue with others.[144]

Balthasar's linguistic acts are not done in isolation, but in encounters with others from the past and in the present. Even his writing was a means to the formation of place and actors, as explicitly stated in *My Work*:

> The activity of being a writer remains and will always remain, in the working-out of my life, a secondary function, something *faute de mieux*. At its center there is a completely different interest: the task of renewing the Church through the formation of new communities that unite the radical Christian life of conformity to the evangelical counsels of Jesus with existence in the midst of the world, whether by practicing secular professions or through the ministerial priesthood to give new life to living communities. All my activity as a writer is subordinated to this task.[145]

One can see here Balthasar's dramatic mission to act in the world through the renewal of human and ecclesial communities. The display of Balthasar's mission can be found in his formation of *Weltgemeinschaften*, also known as secular institutes, where perfection in Christ is fulfilled through engagement with the world, participating in the form of the concrete *analogia entis* by bridging the distance between the church and the world.[146]

Acts of linguistic representation are theotic because they take place in one's encounter of God in the Spirit. In such encounters, the Spirit imparts new language, proliferating in linguistic ascent. The continuation and personalization of the incarnate *Logos* is part of the activity of the Spirit to span the distance between the incomprehensibility of God's being and the limitedness of finite knowledge. Language is the horizontal, theandric dimension of God's encounter with humanity in time, yet it is theotic or vertical because the Spirit unites it with Christ.[147] Lewis Ayres notes how for Gregory of Nyssa the practice of language draws one into union with God,[148] which Martin Laird describes as the movement from "apophaticism" to "logophasis" (the word speaking): "In this instance, the bride at the zenith of an apophatic ascent, in which she has let go of concepts, images, and all manner of knowing, exhibits, paradoxically, transformed discourse."[149] A. N. Williams draws similar conclusions in regard to Aquinas's silence on the theme of *theosis* in the *Summa*: *theosis* may not occupy much space explicitly in the project, but it is embedded in the overall practice and substructure of the entire work.[150] The *Summa* is not a "system for a sake of a system. . . . The very orderly structure of the *Summa* points to a larger than systematic purpose. The import of that structure is the thesis of a mystical theology. If in its particulars the *Summa* undoubtedly belongs largely to the genres of philosophical and systematic theology, its design identifies it as a mystical theology concerned with humanity's union with God and with contemplation of God."[151] One can see why Przywara labeled Aquinas an "aporetic thinker" rather than a systematician.[152]

The resultant conclusion is that the *Theo-Drama* is Balthasar's theotic act of linguistic representation. "It might be said, then, that for Balthasar the theological task is simply to be as capacious as the Holy Spirit," Jennifer Martin states.[153] "This openness and dynamism, even playfulness, informs [his] allegiance to a *zhivoe predanie*, or 'living tradition,' which permits—nay, requires—the adoption of the same 'audacious creativity' in the mode of the Spirit that characterizes and enlivens the early Fathers."[154] This way of representing the tradition is deeply embedded in Balthasar's reconsideration of the dramatic relation between Christ and those he represents, a relation that is mediated by the Holy Spirit. However analogous and idiosyncratic it may be, the *Theo-Drama* is the linguistic and dramatic venture to move forward with language, which still unepically concludes with Augustine at the end of *The Final Act* (*TD*5): *si comprehendis non est Deus*.[155]

Thus, to read Balthasar one must enter into his contemplative posture, as Ulrich suggests of his *Homo Abyssus*.[156] One must "listen through that which has been said, in every case historically, and factically given expression, with an ear attuned to the superessentiality of the 'to be,' and in this way to get to the bottom of the thinker's movement of thought by carrying it into the ontological difference."[157] One must patiently discern the movements and countermovements of Balthasar's texts, as when reading scripture. Although there are certainly moments where Balthasar's dramatic project may ascend into the epic mode, confirming Kilby's gravamen against Balthasar, this book has also attempted to show alternative readings of problematic components by drawing on various noetic and ontic resources. Reading Balthasar in this manner does not relieve Balthasar of judgment—this would be irresponsible on the reader's part—but the *Theo-Drama* should be read in light of the dramatic and theotic form it takes.[158]

Bonhoeffer as a Social Representative: Ethics, Place, and Ordinary/Extraordinary Action

The life and teachings of Dietrich Bonhoeffer appear to display the emplaced character of Christian *theosis* and the dramatic element of Christian action. In the editorial of *Communio* published the year Balthasar died, Balthasar speaks to the "meaning of the communion of saints." Communion is not simply fellowship, but is defined "as an 'active life for each other' and, thus, as an act of 'representation.'" He concludes by momentarily highlighting two witnesses who exemplify what he means by Christian communion: Bernanos and Bonhoeffer.[159] The fact that Balthasar makes this move to acknowledge Bonhoeffer as a witness to the concept of representation and considering that other Balthasar scholars (Chau and Walatka) have begun "taking Balthasar to the street" provides us warrant to complement the invisible and spiritual nature of representative action in *TD*4 with a more social and concrete understanding of action in the place of the other.[160] Furthermore, Rowan Williams has recently shown that there is a "striking parallel" between Bonhoeffer's and Przywara's Christologies and their implications for one's active participation in historical suffering.[161]

In this subsection, I develop the inchoate political and social nature of Balthasar's dramatic project by looking at Bonhoeffer's theological ethics as a personification of what is meant by "social representative," establishing ordinary and extraordinary acts of social representation as a *Grundkategorie* of humanity's existence. I frame *ordinary* social representative action in Christian faithfulness to place and its inhabitants, furthering the theotic unity of place, action, and actors.[162] I then frame *extraordinary* representative action as liberating action for the displaced, which Bonhoeffer's assassination plans are a concrete witness to. Although I primarily focus on Bonhoeffer, I also highlight other examples that further illuminate our understanding of ordinary and extraordinary social representatives. Finally, I elucidate the relationship between representative suffering and social transformation and offer an alternative interpretation of the martyrs of Compiègne than the one I outlined above.

Written in the early years of World War II and before Bonhoeffer was imprisoned in 1943 were thirteen manuscripts, which now form the book *Ethics*. As a continuation of his doctoral dissertation-turned-book *Sanctorum Communio*, it is Bonhoeffer's crown jewel. Bonhoeffer does not define Christian ethics by personal piety or questions such as, "How can I do something good?"[163] Rather, "The *subject matter of a Christian ethic is God's reality revealed in Christ becoming real* [*Wirklichwerden*] *among God's creatures*, just as the subject matter of doctrinal theology is the truth of God's reality revealed in Christ."[164] At the center of Bonhoeffer's Christology is God's representative action for humanity, and Christians are to make this reality an actuality by living in responsible action for others.[165] Bonhoeffer's understanding of responsible action includes the particularities of one's own history. Repudiating any notion of abstract universal moral laws, a Christian ethic is the concrete and particular embodiment of Christ in an existent's social sphere.[166] Bonhoeffer states, "What confers the freedom to act responsibly toward the world and within history is to recognize Jesus Christ as God's love for the real world with its real history, politics, etc., or, in other words, to recognize real human beings, circumstances, movements, i.e., the real world as present in Jesus Christ and Jesus Christ as present in the real world."[167] Thus, Bonhoeffer locates the norm of the Christian ethical life in the common, in concrete action for the sake of others in political, familial, ecclesial, and cultural spheres.[168]

Responsibility for others is related to drama; it is part of humanity's social existence. As Quash states, "There cannot be proper drama without social life (or, to put it another way, without responsibility)."[169] By "social," I mean the bodily, not as opposed to invisible vicarious action, but as the place the spiritual is inhabited. According to Robert Jenson, the locus of one's availability to his or her neighbor is his or her body. The Spirit's presence in the elements of the Eucharist is an analogy of the Spirit's presence in human bodies.[170]

Consequently, emplaced *theosis* as enacted by a social representative is first and foremost grounded in an existent's inhabitation of the place he or she occupies. Christof Gestrich states,

> Originally, the German word *Wesen* also includes a reference precisely to the *Stelle*. Etymologically, *Wesen* stems from the Germanic denotation of one's surroundings and place where one lives. The words "Haus*Wesen*" (household), "An*Wesen*" (estate), and "An*Wesen*heit" (presence) still remind us of this. Etymologically, too, the ultimate reality of *Wesen* and *Stelle* becomes visible here.[171]

Representation is social, not simply because it shows that social actions are essential to human relationality, but because one's social context frames the particularities of representative and theotic action.[172] Place is an ethical category because it is the stage where one encounters the context by which one must enact a Christian ethic of love.

The resultant framework is that representation is not simply a *Grundkategorie* for Christology, but is a basic category for the reality of human existence itself. In Bonhoeffer's own words, "*Stellvertretung* is the life principle of the new humanity."[173] We find an example of an ordinary social representative in parenting. A parent's faithful actions to educate, nurture, and provide for their children, especially the disabled who cannot always act for themselves, are a concrete witness and embodiment of God's loving action for his people.[174] In the same way that it was only befitting that Christ acted in the place of humanity because he is the place of humanity's possibility in the triune life, Christian action for others starts in its faithfulness to the familial, social, and ecclesial places it already inhabits (Luke 16:10). By framing *theosis* within the dialectical notion of conscious subject and theological personhood, the Christian ethical life is the embodiment of the reality of Christ in the historical particularities of one's place, culminating in the attunement of personhood, place, and action.

At the same time, Christ's representative agency opens out for humanity's participation in action for the displaced, action that calls for extraordinary social representatives. The displaced are those who find an egregious distance between their existence and their place. This includes both physically displaced people—those denied a place (refugees)—and spiritually displaced people—those whose essence (*Sosein*) in Christ is treacherously distant from their day-to-day existence (*Dasein*). In the same way that Christ re-placed a displaced people, traversing the unholy ontological divide between God and sinful humanity, so the church is called to preserve and create places for those who are displaced. For the spiritually displaced, the sacraments are a concrete realization of representative re-placement. The physical elements become the dramatic means that incorporates people into their place in Christ.[175] Since what concerns us here is social representative action, I focus on Bonhoeffer's attempted tyrannicide, which is a striking illustration of action for the physically and socially displaced. I also highlight other examples of Christian witnesses who embody the concept of social representation.[176]

Bonhoeffer describes responsible action for others as that which is "in accordance with the reality of Christ."[177] The reality Christians are responsible for is the humanity that was assumed and redeemed by Jesus Christ: "The attempt to understand reality apart from that action of God in and upon reality means living in an abstraction."[178] Thus, any historical place detached from its reconciled reality in Christ is what Christians are responsible for, demanding "concrete, responsible action of love for all human beings."[179] More specifically, this means the active willingness to become guilty for others, as Christ did for humanity: "Precisely because and when it is responsible, because and when it is exclusively concerned about the other human being, because and when it springs from selfless love for the real human brother or sister—vicarious responsible action cannot seek to withdraw from the community of human guilt."[180] What is more theoretical in *Ethics* is personified in Bonhoeffer's willingness to become guilty by assassinating Hitler to preserve the place of Jews from Nazi oppression.[181] Joachim von Soosten reflects:

> It is therefore no accident that in Bonhoeffer's sketches for his *Ethics*, the concept of vicarious representative action stands at the center of his reflections on responsibility. If one further considers that the *Ethics* fragments should be understood as a theological account of the journey leading to resistance against the Hitler regime, then the idea of vicarious representative

action becomes the center of Bonhoeffer's justification of his conspiratorial activities. The phrase "the church is church only if it exists for others," which Bonhoeffer uses as late as his prison letters, testifies to the continuity of this motif in his theology. . . . It [Bonhoeffer's theology of the cross] is the most radical expression of the idea that God's truth, although already real, can and even must become true only in the reality of the world through the witness of persons who in vicarious representative action mutually stand-up-for-each-other [*Füreinandereintreten*].[182]

A lacuna separates Balthasar's focus on vicarious representation in *TD*4 and Bonhoeffer's focus in his life and *Ethics*. Balthasar displays vicarious action as mystical suffering for others, which can be elusively fruitful for those on earth and in purgatory. For Bonhoeffer, vicarious action is one's active and free willingness to act for others through historical and political means.[183] In his place, it meant the willingness to incur guilt, not mystically imparted as in Balthasar, but historically imparted through his dramatic action for displaced Jews. Another person who highlights the historical embodiment of holiness is Dorothy Day. William Cavanaugh discerns that Day's interpretation of the Mystical Body led to direct and concrete action against war (protesting, refusing jobs that contributed to war, etc.), rather than using the concept of the Mystical Body to speak of a hidden unity above the battlefield: "The Mystical Body of Christ was a real, concrete communion of human bodies which directly challenged other, violent attempts to organize human bodies to do one another harm."[184]

In summary, special circumstances demand extraordinary actions for others as a means of liberation for those whose place and existence are in danger of annihilation. Active suffering and death for the displaced is an example of Christian *theosis* because it follows the path of Christianity's cruciform narrative (John 15:13). Recently, Pope Francis added death on behalf of someone else as a pathway to become sainted.[185] Contemporary examples that illuminate the meaning of extraordinary social representation include Oscar Romero, the four churchwomen murdered in El Salvador, Martin Luther King Jr., and Wang Zhiming. In the lives of each of these Christian representatives, we see deliberate action in, with, and for the oppressed and displaced. They do stand in solidarity with those who are suffering, but they also do more by actively seeking to increase the place of those they stand in for. These extraordinary social representatives became entangled with the historical and physical sufferings of those they represented by confronting the oppressive forces that worked against God.

The dispute here with Balthasar is not the mystical aspect of representation. It is that his theo-dramatic vision of representation is unrealized in his interpretation of the martyrs of Compiègne, which he uses in *TD4* as the supreme example of the dramatic dimension of the *communio sanctorum*. As a whole, Balthasar's Christology and dramatic soteriology would seem to offer a vision of concrete and historical action for others, similar to Bonhoeffer's theology of *Stellvertretung*. Derek Brown argues that Balthasar's theology forces Christians to consider their concrete place as they mediate Christ: "To be contextualized by Christ's decisive hour is to perform 'specific deeds in an active apostolate of service to neighbor.' These acts of service, as demonstrated by the lives of the saints, can call for the ultimate act of martyrdom."[186] There are certainly clear moments in the *Theo-Drama* where Balthasar is appreciative of the social and political implications of dramatic theology.[187] Furthermore, besides mentioning Bonhoeffer in the article already cited, he will also say in another article published the same year that in addition to the traditional four marks of the church (one, holy, catholic, and apostolic), another element should be added—the *communio sanctorum*—and that this category "clarifies and concretizes" the other four marks. He then states that the communion of saints is "a church sustained by ethics, good works, social consciousness, and the liberation of those who are politically and socially downtrodden."[188]

Therefore, let me offer an alternative interpretation of the martyrs of Compiègne that better encapsulates the dramatic vision of extraordinary action in the place of others by focusing on historical place and social transformation. First, the grammar of Christ's dramatic action is shared in the physical sufferings of those who suffer on behalf of others. The instigator of historical suffering is history—God does not silently lurk behind the scenes taking delight in it. Through the church's self-giving to the unholy distances that pervade this world, physical suffering and death are inevitable.[189] In the same way that Christ's oneness with the unholy distance between God and humanity inexorably led to his descent, so the church's oneness with the displaced will often lead to their historical displacement. "To enact the person of Wisdom is inevitably bound more closely with the fundamental act of self-humiliation or self-dispossession in the Word's becoming flesh," says Rowan Williams. "So to represent Wisdom is precisely to represent an agency that is displaced for the sake of another."[190] The sufferings of the nuns of Compiègne occurred because of their free self-giving to their historical place in light of their obedience to their vows. It has nothing to do with a passive suffering they mystically endure to relieve the guilt of others by recapitulating Christ's eternal suffering historically. Balthasar's apocalyptic portrayal of the dramatic struggle between the victory of Christ and the forces of evil would lead to this type of interpretation, but his actual interpretation ventures back into absolute tragedy, where God is the agent of the historical suffering of the nuns. By linking suffering to one's representation of his or her place mirroring Christ's representation of humanity, Bonhoeffer offers a better vision for dramatic action than does Balthasar. With this interpretation of the martyrs of Compiègne, representation is disassociated from the eternal appeasement of divine wrath and is associated with the expansion of Christ's representative action for the displaced.

Second, as I noted in chapter 3, Christian tragedy should lead to social transformation. Tragic drama as distinct from absolute tragedy insists that a social representative's suffering culminates in the creation of a new order. The political and structural suffering of representative action liberates others from their historical displacement. There is no need for the social representative to suffer spiritually by being abandoned by God—humanity is already fully reconciled in Christ. Using the Carmelite nuns' martyrdom as a historical parable, what we are looking for is whether their suffering changed others on their historical stage. English Benedictine nuns, who were also imprisoned at the time and were to be guillotined, credit the Carmelites with the prevention of their ensuing martyrdom and with the ending of the Reign of Terror, which occurred a few weeks later.[191] Whether this conclusion is historically accurate or not is not essential since the story is being used parabolically here and in Balthasar. What is of importance is the assiduous declaration that the nuns' suffering for others was not an event used by God to relieve the spiritual guilt of others so he could then extend his goodness to them, but rather that historical suffering creates possibilities and places for God to liberate those who were also physically suffering.

Finally, extraordinary acts of social representation are tragic, yet are subverted through Christ's ongoing recapitulating activity in the Spirit. They are therefore a place where God extends his ineffable goodness in the midst of historical pain. Martyrdom is a horrendous tragedy to God. Yet, as we become displaced in the world through sacrificial death, God in his infinite goodness accompanies us in the Spirit, not abandoning us and unconditionally displacing us, but welcoming us into our eschatological essence in Christ, where we become entirely emplaced through unity with Christ in the Spirit. In the face of humanity's egregious tragedies, the saints' deaths for others create the possibility for the disarmament of human displacement, and human bereavement is placated as the mystery of triune fellowship is imparted into human history. Eschatologically, Christ's reception of the martyrs includes the continuation of his wounds. What may feel like forsakenness in historical tragedy is assumed within an already reconciled forsakenness.[192] As members of his body, the *totus Christus* receives the tragedies that pervade his creation through his wounded side, and humanity becomes emplaced into the continual act of God's outpouring and generative grace.

Conclusion

In this chapter, we explored the relationship between representation and *theosis*, constructing a pneumatological reading of the dramatic exchange formula. The Spirit was entitled the Continual Representative, who incorporates humanity into the person and work of Christ. In this construction, I tied *theosis* to the communion of saints' missional and incorporating actions for others and emplaced humanity's eschatological essence in Christ in the particularities of human history. I then moved from the activity of *communio sanctorum* to the Spirit's agency, suggesting that the Spirit's dramatic prayer for humanity bears historical and eschatological fruit in-and-beyond human agency. The resultant framework was that the category of representation, action in, with, and for others, became a basic category of humanity's dramatic and theotic existence, as I developed concretely in linguistic and social spheres.

CONCLUSION

Das Wort, das die Existenz Jesu Christi am zentralsten kennzeichnet, heißt Stellvertretung.

The one word that most centrally characterizes the existence of Jesus Christ is representation.
  —Balthasar, "Katholizismus und Gemeinschaft der Heiligen," 3

Representation, drama, and salvation coalesce on the stage of creation; they are oriented toward place, action, freedom, and responsibility. Before the drama of creation, the performance of representation—action in, with, and for the other—is enacted in the simplicity of triune self-giving and self-receiving love. God the Father acts in, with, and for the Son by generating a place of otherness for him to act in unity with the Spirit. Within the primordial other, God acts by opening up a positive distance for finite freedom and creating creatures with the inherent capacity to act in, with, and for others. Humanity was ultimately created in and toward the other in God, who contains the otherness of creation. Representing humanity since the foundation of the world, Jesus Christ is humanity's place. Thus, when Christ acts in humanity's place of sin, self-contradiction, and privation, and tragically substitutes for its death as its representative, he liberates humanity from death by traversing the unholy distance of sin and filling the cosmos with the triune life in the Spirit. In Christ's ascension, he emplaces human nature in the infinite flow of triune love, representing humanity in God. The Spirit of God continues Christ's representation of humanity by incorporating humanity into its place in Christ. Because the ascension of the Son and the descent of the Spirit at Pentecost are tacitly paired, the distance between the triune life and creation is forever crossed over. The Continual Representative cultivates historical representative activity in the *communio sanctorum* as it awaits its final emplacement in the eternal activity of God.

In the *Epilogue* to the trilogy, Balthasar states that the foundational concept of representation is meaningless if one does not "see the sense of it."[1] The failure of many theologians to discern the meaning of vicarious action in the place of the other, including its ontological, social, and forensic components, began to concern Balthasar in the 1970s and prompted him to construct a theology of *Stellvertretung* in his trinitarian and dramatic theology of the cross. Balthasar scholars concur that *Stellvertretung* is paramount to his theological system, but they diverge from there on, disagreeing on its translation, function, and contribution. It seems, then, that a failure to perceive the meaning of "representation" persists, despite Balthasar's intention to provide an "exact elaboration."[2]

Therefore, the main task of this book has been to develop the meaning and function of representation and, in doing so, further unveil the nature of the Christ–creation relationship. My goal was not to provide a final definition of *Stellvertretung*—such an approach would be at odds with Balthasar's own practice of theologizing—but rather to proffer a theological road map that brings to light the variety of voices, logics, and dramatic movements at play in Balthasar's vision for the term. I pursued this task by examining and moving forward the *spiritual*, *constructive*, and *systematic* elements of Balthasar's theology of representation.

First and foremost, I have engaged the *spiritual* nature of Balthasar's theology of representation. Representation shapes not only the doctrines of Balthasar's dramatic soteriology but also his very practice of theology. By developing the relationship between drama, representation, and language, I have shown with Ulrich that language itself is action in, with, and for the other. This philosophy of language, mediated by the capaciousness of the Spirit, is deeply embedded in Balthasar's dramatic emplacement of scripture and the tradition. His reenactment of the tradition includes a symphony of voices and logics that are not canceled out but incorporated into his theo-dramatic portrayal of the divine life and human salvation.

Therefore, joining with other recent studies on Balthasar, I have suggested that to read Balthasar dramatically one must engage the movements of his texts with his same spirit of contemplation, discernment, and freedom. In other words, one must act in the place of Balthasar's thought with the same spirit that he represents the tradition. I have given particular attention to educe the tacit *Stellen* of Przywara, de Lubac, and Ulrich in Balthasar's theology. I also engaged other theologians (Bonhoeffer, Hoffmann, Sölle, and Williams) who also seek to rehabilitate the concept of *Stellvertretung*. By considering these two sets of voices, I reexamined key parts of the *Theo-Drama* that are relevant to representation. In doing so, my ultimate desire was to discern Balthasar's spiritual voice by entering into—acting in, with, and for—his own thought and mission, while also calling for a renewed hearing of relevant aspects of Balthasar's doctrine from their detractors.

This posture of interpreting Balthasar opened the way for me to engage Balthasar *constructively* in order to elucidate representation's place in traditional doctrine. In part 1, I developed a theology of representation and a dramatic exchange formula from a sympathetic and constructive, and in some places critical, interpretation of Balthasar's trinitarian and christological metaphysic. Balthasar's account of representation is motivated by questions about the rationality of representation. He asks, "How can someone 'represent' sinners?"[3] How can a person *act in the place of* another person without violating the other's freedom? Balthasar suggests that creaturely *Stellvertretung* is coherent and possible because there is representation and pro-existence in the triune processions. The triune Persons exist as eternal and dramatic action in the place of the other, which precedes and makes possible christological and creaturely *Stellvertretung*. The notion of pro-existence and *Stellvertretung* take interpersonal models of the Trinity one step further by elucidating a more active and concrete relation between the triune Persons. We saw, then, that the fundamental components of Balthasar's trinitarian theology are mutually involved with his theology of representation: if Christ is to *act in the place of* humanity and *make a place* for humanity in the triune life, then there must already be distance, roominess, and place-acting in the triune life. Such a spatialized account of the triune life does not need to be at odds with the simplicity and unity of the divine being, though. Rather, if interpreted through the *analogia entis* and aural space, intratrinitarian spatiality imagines divine oneness through the diversity, drama, and freedom depicted in the economy of God without being exclusively centered on a particular object, place, or person. Musical space captures the capacious, interpenetrating, and polyphonic nature of divine space, uniting God's inward and outward activities.

The divine processions, then, display the ideal form of *inkludierende Stellvertretung*, which is analogically reflected in creaturely being. Ulrich helped us to see that creaturely being reflects the grammar of triune pro-existence, making representation—action in, with, and for the other—inherent to creaturely existence. Such action is not limited to ordinary kinds of external, social, or forensic action, but extends to internal, ontological, and vicarious action. This trinitarian metaphysic of representation provides the metaphysical components for more social-oriented theologies of representation, such as Dietrich Bonhoeffer's.[4]

In chapter 2, I continued the constructive vision of this book by taking into account how Balthasar's theo-dramatic construal of Christ's two natures affects his theology of representation. Interpreters' definitions of Balthasar's theology of *Stellvertretung* often focus on its soteriological account in *TD*4, which too easily confines Balthasar's soteriology to penal substitution grammar (Brown, Coffey, and Pitstick). Such interpretations can fail to discern the other theological foundation of Balthasar's conception, one of which is his mission Christology in *TD*3. The discernment of the inherent unity of Balthasar's theology of the cross and theology of the Incarnation brings to the surface his wider set of interlocutors (Maximus the Confessor, Aquinas, Buber, Przywara, and Barth) and the way they influence the function of representation in Balthasar's dramatic soteriology. By considering these voices in tandem with emerging conversations about the universal and the concrete in Balthasar's theology, it is evident that Christ's universal and objective action for humanity does not compete with the personal, historical, and concrete actions of the *dramatis personae*. Therefore, I defined Christ as the theo-dramatic representative. *Theo*-dramatic signifies his universal-vertical representation of

Conclusion 169

humanity, because his relation to creation is primary, intrinsic, and differentiated, acting in-and-beyond those he represents. At the same time, without a horizontal consideration of Christ's two natures and energies, monophysitism and monothelitism arise, replacing or absorbing human action. Therefore, Christ's representation is also theo-*dramatic*, because he acts with humanity by imparting his mission to human persons in the Spirit. In both of these universal and personalizing aspects of *Stellvertretung*, it is apparent why substitution is an inadequate translation. Substitution can be used appropriately as a subtheme of representation in *soteriological Stellvertretung*, but it cannot account for Balthasar's broader christological commitments without being attached to the concept of representation.

With these two constructive foundations in place, I then presented a *systematic* analysis of how representation functions in Balthasar's dramatic soteriology. In part 2, I defined Balthasar's theology of representation through the explication of the soteriological themes of redemption and *theosis*. Given that Balthasar does not provide the exact elaboration of the concept of representation that he promised in *TD*4, I provided a broad soteriological elaboration underneath the heading of "dramatic representation" and showed how the various biblical and theological elements of atonement function together in the drama of finite and infinite freedom. With the exception of Aidan Nichols, who rightly argues for a nondivaricated translation of *Stellvertretung*, "at once representation and vicarious substitution,"[5] Balthasar scholars often confine his soteriology to a particular model of atonement. I argued instead that Christ's representation of humanity is dramatic because it includes various movements and countermovements to grasp its meaning, resisting trite systemization. Liberation, recapitulation, exchange, penal substitution, solidarity, and tragedy all play a role in the grand drama of redemption, but my analysis displayed how they do so within Balthasar's trinitarian and christological metaphysic of representation. This account displays how the forensic and wrath-oriented logics of penal substitution and satisfaction models of atonement, which have led to widespread concerns with atonement in general, play a significantly modified role in Balthasar's dramatic soteriology. It is, therefore, incumbent on ecumenical atonement scholars to consider Balthasar's dynamic understanding of *Stellvertretung*.

The spiritual, constructive, and systematic elements of Balthasar's theology of representation came together in chapter 4, where I extended the category of representation to pneumatology, ecclesiology, and *theosis*. Christ's representation of humanity is continued and completed by the Spirit in the *communio sanctorum*. There are three contributions of this chapter. (1) Representation is now a pneumatological category, whereas it is typically confined to Christology and atonement theology. The Spirit acts in the place of the Son's humanity by expanding the boundaries of his body and incorporating its members into his activity. (2) By connecting representation to the agency of the Spirit, it became a significant way of understanding personal and ecclesial *theosis*. Representation uniquely shows how the divine mission to incorporate humanity into the place of Christ is united to humanity's places, actions, and missions. Christ's theo-dramatic representation of humanity becomes emplaced in the concrete activity of the church. This process, which I called "emplaced *theosis*," culminates in the dramatic attunement of personhood, place, and action. (3) Representation became a basic category of the theologian's task and humanity's social existence. Ulrich's metaphysics as reenactment elucidates how *Stellvertretung* is inherent to the theological task by showing how language itself is action in, with, and for the other. Theologians act in the place of the tradition by creatively reenacting its spirit in their own place, time, and history. Representation is also inherent to humanity's concrete social existence. Bonhoeffer's social-oriented theology of representation displays how action in the place of the other starts with faithful activity in one's familial, social, and ecclesial place and extends to extraordinary action for the physically and spiritually displaced. By developing the category through these linguistic and social elements, representation was conceived in a way that invokes participation, inclusion, and responsibility. Altogether, this account mollifies modern anxiety regarding substitution models of atonement that diminish humanity's moral and social responsibility through their underlying logic of replacement. Balthasar, Sölle, and Bonhoeffer shared the same concern regarding the concept of *Stellvertretung*, but they creatively retrieved the term in a way that inspires human participation.

Overall, I have moved Balthasar's theology of representation forward by elucidating, judging, amending, and developing it, and in doing so his "essential contribution" to contemporary theology is more approachable.⁶ The concept is no longer simply a devotional category (Ratzinger) that lacks color (Sölle) and a theological foundation (Balthasar). *Stellvertretung* is now a *Grundkategorie*: representation is universal, because it portrays the dramatic exchange between Christ and humanity, and it is dramatic, because it depicts how the Spirit's incorporation of humanity into the triune life is emplaced in the concrete particularities of humanity's places and activities. In fact, because this project is related to its writer's place and time, this work itself is a dramatic act of linguistic representation. That is, this project is the theotic and linguistic act of the writer to move the christological category of representation forward, while still unepically concluding with Augustine: *si comprehendis non est Deus*.

NOTES

Introduction

1. Henri de Lubac, "A Witness of Christ in the Church: Hans Urs von Balthasar," https://www.crossroadsinitiative.com/media/articles/hans-urs-von-balthasar-eulogy-de-lubac.
2. *TD*1, 18.
3. Edward T. Oakes, *Pattern of Redemption: The Theology of Hans Urs von Balthasar* (New York: Continuum, 1997), 230.
4. *TD*4, 317–423.
5. *MW*, 97.
6. *TD*4, 318 (emphasis original).
7. Quoted by Frank A. James III, "General Introduction," in *The Glory of the Atonement: Biblical, Historical, and Practical Perspectives*, ed. Charles E. Hill and Frank A. James III (Downers Grove, IL: InterVarsity, 2004), 15.
8. Thomas Chubb, *The True Gospel of Jesus Christ Asserted* (Whitefish, MT: Kessinger, 2010); John Locke, *The Reasonableness of Christianity*, ed. I. T. Ramsey (Stanford, CA: Stanford University Press, 1958).
9. Joanne Carlson Brown and Rebecca Parker, "For God So Loved the World?," in *Christianity, Patriarchy, and Abuse: A Feminist Critique*, ed. Joanne Carlson Brown and Carole R. Bohn (New York: Pilgrim Press, 1989), 1–30; Delores Williams, "Black Women's Surrogacy Experience and the Christian Notion of Redemption," in *After Patriarchy: Feminist Transformations of the World Religions*, ed. Paul M. Cooey, William R. Eakin, and Jay B. McDaniel (Maryknoll, NY: Orbis, 1991), 1–14.
10. Tony Jones, *Did God Kill Jesus? Searching for Love in History's Most Famous Execution* (New York: HarperCollins, 2015).
11. Peter Schmiechen, *Saving Power: Theories of Atonement and Forms of the Church* (Grand Rapids, MI: Eerdmans, 2005), 345.
12. For a lengthy bibliography of contemporary atonement literature, see Vic Froese, "Atonement: A Bibliography," *Direction* 41 (2012): 165–83.

13. Oliver D. Crisp and Fred Sanders, eds., *Locating Atonement: Explorations in Constructive Dogmatics* (Grand Rapids, MI: Zondervan, 2015), 13. In general, atonement models were not intended to be "self-contained theories" in either the Catholic or Protestant traditions. Yet, within specific historical systems in both traditions, models were accentuated in such a way that one model became more dominant than another. It is against such one-sided approaches that Balthasar offers his "dramatic soteriology," which seeks to hold together all the biblical and traditional models without producing a new system. See *TD4*, 240–44.

14. Rowan Williams, *On Christian Theology* (Oxford: Blackwell, 2000), 101.

15. Dorothee Sölle, *Christ the Representative: An Essay in Theology after the "Death of God,"* trans. David Lewis (Philadelphia: Fortress, 1967), 13.

16. Dietrich Bonhoeffer, *Sanctorum Communio: A Theological Study on the Sociology of the Church*, vol. 1 of *Dietrich Bonhoeffer Works*, ed. Clifford J. Green and Joachim von Soosten, trans. Reinhard Krauss and Nancy Lukens (Minneapolis: Fortress, 1998); Dietrich Bonhoeffer, *Ethics*, in *Dietrich Bonhoeffer Works— Reader's Edition*, ed. Clifford J. Green, trans. Reinhard Krauss, Charles C. West, and Douglas W. Scott (Minneapolis: Fortress, 2015), 177–206.

17. Jeannine Michele Graham, *Representation and Substitution in the Atonement Theologies of Dorothee Sölle, John Macquarrie, and Karl Barth* (Oxford: Peter Lang, 2005).

18. Balthasar, "Katholizismus und Gemeinschaft der Heiligen," *Communio Internationale Katholische Zeitschrift* 17 (1988): 3: "Das Wort, das die Existenz Jesu Christi am zentralsten kennzeichnet, heißt Stellvertretung."

19. Balthasar, "Editorial: The Meaning of the *Communion of Saints*," *Communio* 15, no. 2 (1988): 162.

20. *TD4*, 11; Sölle, *Christ the Representative*, 15.

21. Rowan Williams, *Christ the Heart of Creation* (London: Bloomsbury Continuum, 2018), 203.

22. Ibid. Other German words also translate as "representation" or "substitution": *Repräsentation, Ersatzmann, Darstellung, Vorstellung*, and *Substitution*.

23. Daniel P. Bailey, "Concepts of *Stellvertretung* in the Interpretation of Isaiah 53," in *Jesus and the Suffering Servant: Isaiah 53 and Christian Origins*, ed. William H. Bellinger Jr. and William R. Farmer (Eugene, OR.: Wipf & Stock, 1998), 225.

24. Sölle, *Christ the Representative*, 19–23.

25. Morna D. Hooker, "Did the Use of Isaiah 53 to Interpret His Mission Begin with Jesus?," in Bellinger and Farmer, eds., *Jesus and the Suffering Servant*, 96. Even so, the common English usage of "substitution" does not necessarily

need to imply an exclusive action in every case. For example, a substitute teacher acts together with the absent teacher by continuing the designated curriculum until the latter can resume his or her place. The teacher may not be physically present, but is present, one could say represented, through the substitute. The terms need not be mutually exclusive, as Sölle insists.

26. Peterson provides a comprehensive analysis of Rahner's soteriology and argues that Rahner's Christology of *das Realsymbol* lends itself to a theology of inclusive *Repräsentation*. See Brandon R. Peterson, *Being Salvation: Atonement and Soteriology in the Theology of Karl Rahner* (Minneapolis: Fortress, 2017); Peterson, "Grace in Our Place? The Concept of Representation in the Theology of Karl Rahner," *Theological Studies* 81, no. 2 (2020): 438–52.

27. Stephan Schaede, *Stellvertretung: Begriffsgeschichtliche Studien zur Soteriologie* (Tübingen: Mohr Siebeck, 2004), 2.

28. Martin Bieler, *Befreiung der Freiheit: Zur Theologie der stellvertretenden Sühne* (Freiburg: Herder, 1996); Christof Gestrich, *Christentum und Stellvertretung: Religionsphilosophische Untersuchungen zum Heilsverständnis und zur Grundlegung der Theologie* (Tübingen: Mohr Siebeck, 2001); Karl-Heinz Menke, *Stellvertretung: Schlüsselbegriff christlichen Lebens und theologische Grundkategorie* (Freiburg: Johannes Verlag Einsiedeln, 1991).

29. Aidan Nichols, "Adrienne von Speyr and the Mystery of the Atonement," *New Blackfriars* 73 (1992): 542–53.

30. Andrew Louth, "The Place of *Heart of the World* in the Theology of Hans Urs von Balthasar," in *The Analogy of Beauty: The Theology of Hans Urs von Balthasar*, ed. John Riches (Edinburgh: T&T Clark, 1986), 147–63.

31. *TKB*, 178.

32. Barth, *CD*, IV.1:vii–viii.

33. *H2/2*, 773–79.

34. *GL7*, 202–34.

35. Veronica Donnelly, *Saving Beauty: Form as the Key to Balthasar's Christology* (Oxford: Peter Lang, 2007), 185.

36. *TL2*, 345.

37. *DJ*, 35.

38. To provide further substantiation for the claim that *Stellvertretung* moves to being more central in Balthasar's soteriology in the 1970s, we find that in *GL7* (1969) Balthasar uses the German word *Ort* to describe the "place" of humanity's origination in Christ (*H3/2.2*, 418). When *Stellvertretung* becomes more overt in Balthasar's theology in the *Theo-Drama*, he uses the German word *Stelle*, making a unique connection between *Stellvertretung* and the place of humanity's existence, as we shall see in chapter 2.

39. Balthasar, "Über Stellvertretung," *Résurrection: Revue de Doctrine Chrétienne* 41 (1973): 2–9. English translation: "Vicarious Representation," in *ET*4, 415–22.

40. Balthasar, "Stellvertretung: Schlüsselwort christlichen Lebens," *Leben in Geist* 4 (1976): 3–7.

41. Ibid., 4: "Der Gedanke der Stellvertretung, so sagten wir anfangs, steht im Herzpunkt des christlichen Dogmas."

42. *HMR*, 15–42.

43. Balthasar, "Theology and Aesthetic," *Communio* 8, no. 1(1981): 65–66. That same year, he also published an article that interprets christological *pro nobis* through the lens of representation. See Balthasar, "Crucifixus etiam pro nobis," *Communio Internationale Katholische Zeitschrift* 9 (1980): 26–35.

44. *EP*, 101–6, 118–20; *TL*2, 121, 146, 230, 234, 301–6, 346, 360–61; *TL*3, 204, 283–89, 345–49.

45. *TD*3, 245.

46. Joseph Ratzinger, "Stellvertretung," in *Handbuch Theologischer Grund-Begriffe*, ed. Heinrich Fries, 2:566 (München: Kösel, 1962–63): "Stellvertretung ist eine der Grundkategorien der biblischen Offenbarung, die jedoch wohl infolge des Fehlens eines geeigneten philosophischen Modells in der Theologie nur kümmerlich entfaltet und schließlich weitgehend in die reine Erbauungsliteratur abgedrängt worden ist." For an article on Ratzinger's use of *Stellvertretung*, see Christopher Ruddy, "'For the Many': The Vicarious-Representative Heart of Joseph Ratzinger's Theology," *Theological Studies* 75, no. 3 (2014): 564–84.

47. Sölle, *Christ the Representative*, 60.

48. In *TD*4, Balthasar analyzes Rahner's soteriology and critically remarks on Rahner's aversion to the theological use of *Stellvertretung*. Therefore, the prominence and defense of *Stellvertretung* in the *Theo-Drama* may have also arisen because Balthasar is concerned about the theological implications if the term is dismissed altogether. Given that Balthasar is also critical of replacement or exclusive understandings of *Stellvertretung* and reconstructs the term in a more inclusive light, it is unfortunate that Rahner does not explicitly address Balthasar's theology of *Stellvertretung* (see Peterson, *Being Salvation*, 218). In chapter 2, I point to places where Balthasar's revised understanding of representation may satisfy some of Rahner's objections, and in chapter 3, I outline some of the key concerns Balthasar has with Rahner's soteriology.

49. *TDg*3, 11: "Ein Hauptanliegen dieses Bandes ist die exakte Herausarbeitung des Begriffs der Stellvertretung, der nach einer Periode der Vergessenheit plötzlich neu ins Licht tritt."

50. *TD*4, 11.

51. *TD*2, 54–62; *MW*, 98–99.

52. *TL*1, 8; Stephen Fields, "The Beauty of the Ugly: Balthasar, the Crucifixion, Analogy and God," *International Journal of Systematic Theology* 9, no. 2 (2007): 172–83; Thomas O'Meara, "Of Arts and Theology: Hans Urs von Balthasar's Systems," *Theological Studies* 42, no. 2 (1981): 272–76; Rowan Williams, "Balthasar and the Trinity," in *The Cambridge Companion to Hans Urs von Balthasar*, ed. Edward T. Oakes, SJ, and David Moss (Cambridge: Cambridge University Press, 2004), 49.

53. *TD*1, 9–12. Quash notes Balthasar's indebtedness to Hegel's dramatic typology; see Ben Quash, "Drama and the Ends of Modernity," in *Balthasar at the End of Modernity*, ed. Lucy Gardner et al. (Edinburgh: T&T Clark, 1999), 145–46.

54. *TD*1, 25–50.

55. *TD*1, 17–18.

56. Quash, "Drama and the Ends of Modernity," 144 (emphasis original).

57. Sölle, *Christ the Representative*, 24–29.

58. *TD*4, 231–423.

59. *TD*4, 231–316.

60. *TD*4, 318.

61. *TD*4, 317–20.

62. *TD*4, 240–44, 317.

63. *TD*4, 243, 319.

64. *TD*4, 319.

65. Aidan Nichols, "St. Thomas Aquinas on the Passion of Christ: A Reading of *Summa theologiae* IIIa., q. 46," *Scottish Journal of Theology* 43, no. 4 (1990): 447–59.

66. Eugene F. Rogers Jr., *After the Spirit: A Constructive Pneumatology from Resources outside the Modern West* (Grand Rapids, MI: Eerdmans, 2005), 56.

67. Robert A. Pesarchick, *The Trinitarian Foundation of Human Sexuality as Revealed by Christ according to Hans Urs von Balthasar: The Revelatory Significance of the Male Christ and the Male Ministerial Priesthood* (Rome: Gregorian University Press, 2000), 88.

68. Aidan Nichols, *Divine Fruitfulness: A Guide through Balthasar's Theology beyond the Trilogy* (London: T&T Clark, 2007), 177.

69. To name those not included elsewhere in this introduction: Bieler, *Befreiung der Freiheit*, 13–19; 377–87; Gilles Emery, "The Immutability of the God of Love and the Problem of Language Concerning the Suffering of God," in *Divine Impassibility and the Mystery of Human Suffering*, ed. James F. Keating and Thomas Joseph White (Grand Rapids, MI: Eerdmans, 2009), 48–52; Lucy Gardner and David Moss, "Something Like Time; Something Like the Sexes— an Essay in Reception," in Gardner et al., eds., *Balthasar at the End of Modernity*,

109–10; Norbert Hoffmann, *Sühne: Zur Theologie der Stellvertretung* (Freiburg: Johannes Verlag Einsiedeln, 1981); Mark A. McIntosh, *Christology from Within: Spirituality and the Incarnation in Hans Urs von Balthasar* (Notre Dame, IN: University of Notre Dame Press, 2000), 54; Marc Ouellet, "The Foundations of Christian Ethics according to Hans Urs von Balthasar," *Communio: International Catholic Review* 17, no. 3 (1990): 383; Todd Walatka, *Von Balthasar and the Option for the Poor: Theodramatics in the Light of Liberation Theology* (Washington, DC: Catholic University of America Press, 2017), 121; Graham Ward, "Kenosis: Death, Discourse, and Resurrection," in Gardner et al., eds., *Balthasar at the End of Modernity*, 47–49.

70. Ellero Babini, "Jesus Christ: Form and Norm of Man according to Hans Urs von Balthasar," in *Hans Urs von Balthasar: His Life and Work*, ed. David Schindler (San Francisco: Ignatius, 1991), 226.

71. Junius Johnson, *Christ and Analogy: The Christocentric Metaphysics of Hans Urs von Balthasar* (Minneapolis: Fortress, 2013), 18.

72. *EP*, 119.

73. Donnelly, *Saving Beauty*, 187.

74. Louth, "The Place of *Heart of the World*," 159–60.

75. Steffen Lösel, "A Plain Account of Christian Salvation? Balthasar on Sacrifice, Solidarity, and Substitution," *Pro Ecclesia* 13, no. 2 (2004): 165.

76. Aidan Nichols, *No Bloodless Myth: A Guide through Balthasar's Dramatics* (Edinburgh: T&T Clark, 2000), 99.

77. David Brown, "Images of Redemption in Art and Music," in *The Redemption: An Interdisciplinary Symposium on Christ as Redeemer*, ed. Stephen T. Davis, Daniel Kendall, and Gerald O'Collins (Oxford: Oxford University Press, 2006), 306; David Coffey, *Deus Trinitas: The Doctrine of the Triune God* (Oxford: Oxford University Press, 1999), 140–41; Alyssa Lyra Pitstick, *Light in Darkness: Hans Urs von Balthasar and the Catholic Doctrine of Christ's Descent into Hell* (Grand Rapids, MI: Eerdmans, 2007), 110–13.

78. Gerard F. O'Hanlon, *The Immutability of God in the Theology of Hans Urs Von Balthasar* (Cambridge: Cambridge University Press, 2007), 32.

79 Antoine Birot, "'God in Christ, Reconciled the World to Himself': Redemption in Balthasar," *Communio: International Catholic Review* 24, no. 2 (1997): 278.

80. John R. Cihak, *Balthasar and Anxiety* (London: T&T Clark, 2009), 166.

81. Pesarchick, *The Trinitarian Foundation of Human Sexuality*, 98.

82. Michele Schumacher, "The Concept of Representation in the Theology of Hans Urs von Balthasar," *Theological Studies* 60, no. 1 (1999): 54.

83. Coffey, *Deus Trinitas*, 139–41.

84. Donnelly, *Saving Beauty*, 183–234; Thomas E. Kryst, "Interpreting the Death of Jesus: A Comparison of the Theologies of Hans Urs von Balthasar and Raymund Schwager" (PhD diss., Catholic University of America, 2009); Menke, *Stellvertretung*, 266–310; David W. Nuss, "Jesus the Christ as Stellvertreter: Aspects of Dramatic Soteriology in Selected Writings of Hans Urs von Balthasar" (Licentiate in Sacred Theology, Catholic University of America, 2000).

85. Cyril O'Regan, *The Anatomy of Misremembering: Von Balthasar's Response to Philosophical Modernity*, vol. 1, *Hegel* (New York: Crossroad, 2014).

86. *PT*, 11–12.

87. O'Regan, *Anatomy of Misremembering*, 135.

88. Jennifer Newsome Martin, *Hans Urs von Balthasar and the Critical Appropriation of Russian Religious Thought* (Notre Dame, IN: University of Notre Dame Press, 2015), 2.

89. Walatka, *Von Balthasar and the Option for the Poor*, 40, 42.

90. Balthasar, "Editorial," 162; Martin, *Balthasar and the Critical Appropriation*, 203.

91. Balthasar, *Our Task: A Report and a Plan*, trans. John Saward (San Francisco: Ignatius, 1994), 38; *MW*, 19, 89.

92. *TD*4, 11.

93. Walatka, *Von Balthasar and the Option for the Poor*, 44.

94. It may seem odd to choose three Protestant theologians. My own confessional location is indeed within the Protestant tradition, but I chose these three theologians because of their engagement with the concept of *Stellvertretung*. This kind of ecumenical engagement draws out valuable nuances of Balthasar's theology of representation for two reasons: (1) the questions Balthasar was asking of his Catholic models of atonement are similar to ones being asked of Protestant soteriologies; and (2) he employs aspects of Protestant soteriologies to strengthen his Catholic soteriology.

95. Balthasar's theology of *Stellvertretung* is central to this study, but the other authors' constructions offer elements that Balthasar's does not. For example, Sölle analyzes the linguistic elements of *Stellvertretung* in detail, and Bonhoeffer develops the social and political implications, both of which are in a nascent state in Balthasar. Yet, according to Rowan Williams, Bonhoeffer's theology of representation fails to develop the necessary trinitarian and pneumatological elements of *Stellvertretung* (Williams, *Christ the Heart of Creation*, 197), which Balthasar's account does offer. Therefore, I integrate Balthasar's metaphysical and theological foundations for representation with aspects of Bonhoeffer's, Sölle's, and Williams's accounts.

96. Walatka, *Von Balthasar and the Option for the Poor*, 134.

97. See Williams's theology of language in Rowan Williams, *The Edge of Words: God and the Habits of Language* (London: Bloomsbury, 2014).

98. Peter J. Casarella, foreword to *Theo-Poetics: Hans Urs von Balthasar and the Risk of Art and Being*, by Anne Carpenter (Notre Dame, IN: University of Notre Dame Press, 2015), xi.

Chapter One

1. Nichols, *No Bloodless Myth*, 157–71; Williams, "Balthasar and the Trinity," 49.
2. *TD*4, 319.
3. Erich Przywara, *Analogia Entis, Metaphysics: Original Structure and Universal Rhythm*, trans. John R. Betz and David Bentley Hart (Grand Rapids, MI: Eerdmans, 2014), 120, 132.
4. *TD*4, 332.
5. *TDg*3, 11.
6. *TD*4, 332.
7. *EP*, 119.
8. *TD*3, 245; *TD*4, 332; Sölle, *Christ the Representative*, 60.
9. *TD*3, 245.
10. *TD*4, 332–38.
11. *TD*4, 332–34.
12. *TDg*3, 310: "Er kann es aufgrund seines topos innergöttlicher absoluter Differenz vom schenkenden Vater."
13. *TD*5, 91–95, 375–85.
14. Distance and place often receive attention by scholars studying Balthasar's doctrine of the Trinity, but representation does not, which seems puzzling since some of the most consistent critiques of Balthasar's trinitarian theology focus on passages in *TD*4 that are also about representation. For example, "place" is the same word for the *Stelle* of *Stellvertretung*, and Balthasar begins using *Stelle* consistently in his trinitarian theology in the *Theo-Drama*, where he is principally concerned with securing representation as an essential theological category.
15. Ian McFarland, "Present in Love: Rethinking Barth on the Divine Perfections," *Modern Theology* 33, no. 2 (April 2017): 249–50; Katherine Sonderegger, *The Doctrine of God*, vol. 1 of *Systematic Theology* (Minneapolis: Fortress, 2015), xxiii, 480–81.
16. *TD*4, 324. Balthasar and Rahner offer twentieth-century Catholic theology two possible orientations, symbolized in the founding of the journals:

Communio and *Concilium*. For more on their relationship, see Karen Kilby, "Balthasar and Karl Rahner," in Oakes and Moss, ed., *The Cambridge Companion to Hans Urs von Balthasar*, 256–68; Rowan Williams, "Balthasar and Rahner," in *The Analogy of Beauty: The Theology of Hans Urs von Balthasar*, ed. John Riches (Edinburgh: T&T Clark, 1986), 11–35.

17. Karl Rahner, *The Trinity* (New York: Seabury, 1974), 21–22. Rahner's Rule ("The 'economic' Trinity is the 'immanent' Trinity and the 'immanent' Trinity is the 'economic' Trinity") challenges the starting point of Augustinian and medieval Latin theology when considering the relation between the treatises *De Deo Uno* and *De Deo Trino*. According to Rahner, medieval Latin theologians started with the one God *before* they considered the triune God, taking their foundation from philosophical conceptions of God. In doing so, they divorced their speculations about the one God from the self-communication of the triune God throughout salvation history. This way of reading Western trinitarian theology is often attributed to Theodore de Régnon. Régnon split trinitarian history into Greek theology and Latin theology, with the former being more trinitarian and a superior starting point for reflections on the doctrine of God. Many scholars now question this popular way of differentiating between the Greek and Latin theology. See Michel Barnes, "De Régnon Reconsidered," *Augustinian Studies* 26, no. 2 (1995): 51–79; Sarah Coakley, "Rethinking Gregory of Nyssa: Introduction—Gender, Trinitarian Analogies, and the Pedagogy of *the Song*," in *Re-thinking Gregory of Nyssa*, ed. Sarah Coakley (Oxford: Blackwell, 2003), 431–43; Rowan Williams, *On Augustine* (London: Bloomsbury, 2016).

18. *TD*4, 321. Balthasar is critiquing the formality of trinitarian relations here, but he also questions Rahner's understanding of formal causality in other places (*TD*4, 276–81). Coffey offers a similar critique to Balthasar's, noting that the main weakness of Rahner's theology is his concept of person and his lack of an emphasis on relation in the Trinity. See David Coffey, "Trinity," in *The Cambridge Companion to Karl Rahner*, ed. Declan Marmion and Mary E. Hines (Cambridge: Cambridge University Press, 2005), 108–10. For more critiques of Rahner, see Yves Congar, *I Believe in the Holy Spirit*, trans. David Smith (New York: Seabury, 1983), 3:13–15; Stephen R. Holmes, *The Quest for the Trinity: The Doctrine of God in Scripture, History, and Modernity* (Downers Grove, IL: InterVarsity Press, 2012), 11; Bruce Marshall, *Trinity and Truth* (Cambridge: Cambridge University Press, 2000), 263–65; Randal Rauser, "Rahner's Rule: An Emperor without Clothes," *International Journal of Systematic Theology* 7, no. 1 (2005): 91–94; Thomas F. Torrance, *Trinitarian Perspectives: Toward Doctrinal Agreement* (Edinburgh: T&T Clark, 1994), 78–79.

19. Rahner, *Trinity*, 76.

20. Ibid., 106 (emphasis original). For more on Rahner's doctrine of the Trinity, see Karl Rahner, *Foundations of Christian Faith: An Introduction to the Idea of Christianity*, trans. William V. Dych (New York: Seabury Press, 1978), 116–37.

21. Jürgen Moltmann, *The Crucified God: The Cross of Christ as the Foundation and Criticism of Christian Theology*, trans. Margaret Kohl (Minneapolis: Fortress, 1993), 246.

22. *TD4*, 320–22; *TD5*, 227–29; Veli-Matti Kärkkäinen, "The Trinitarian Doctrines of Jürgen Moltmann and Wolfhart Pannenberg in the Context of Contemporary Discussion," in *The Cambridge Companion to the Trinity*, ed. Peter C. Phan (Cambridge: Cambridge University Press, 2011), 237.

23. *TD5*, 228–29. Hegelian ambivalence refers to the distinction of the God/world relation and immanent/economic Trinity.

24 *TD4*, 322–23.

25. *TD4*, 327.

26. *TD4*, 327.

27. *HW*, 54; *TD4*, 319–32; *TD5*, 66–98.

28. *MW*, 19, 89. The second influence is Adrienne von Speyr, whose spiritual visions contribute greatly to Balthasar's trinitarian depictions (see *TD5*).

29. *TD4*, 323–24, 327. Balthasar's presentation of the *analogia entis* can be found in *TL1*, which is a reissuing of *Wahrheit der Welt* (Einsiedeln: Johannes Verlag, 1947).

30. John R. Betz, translator's introduction to Przywara, *Analogia Entis*, 44. For an excellent review of the analogy of being, see Thomas Joseph White, ed., *The Analogy of Being: Invention of the Antichrist or the Wisdom of God?* (Grand Rapids, MI: Eerdmans, 2011).

31. Norman P. Tanner, ed., *Decrees of the Ecumenical Councils* (Washington, DC: Georgetown University Press, 1990), 1:232.

32. For an alternative way of interpreting the relationship between *analogia attributionis* and *analogia proportionalitatis*, see E. L. Mascall, *Existance and Analogy* (London: Longmans, Green and Co, 1949), 92–121.

33. Przywara, *Analogia Entis*, 231–35. For example, the Fourth Lateran Council decided that one must not equate ecclesial unity and the unity of the triune God. Creaturely unity is one plurality, whereas divine unity is of a different kind, which the council calls the "Incomprehensible and Ineffable One Highest Something" (see ibid., 344–55).

34. Przywara, *Analogia Entis*, 264, 268.

35. Lewis Ayres, *Nicaea and Its Legacy: An Approach to Fourth-Century Trinitarian Theology* (Oxford: Oxford University Press, 2006), 285, 300, 363.

36. Przywara, *Analogia Entis*, 362.

37. Ibid.

38. Hart, *The Experience of God*, 138–40. Aquinas, *ST* Ia.3.7.
39. Ayres, *Nicaea and Its Legacy*, 236, 278.
40. D. Stephen Long, *The Perfectly Simple Triune God: Aquinas and His Legacy* (Minneapolis: Fortress, 2016).
41. Augustine, *Confessions* 12.7.
42. Gregory of Nyssa, *The Great Catechism* 27 (emphasis original).
43. *PT*, 27–36.
44. *GL*5, 613–27; Balthasar, *Our Task*, 38.
45. Quoted by Stefan Oster, "Thinking Love at the Heart of Things: The Metaphysics of Being as Love in the Work of Ferdinand Ulrich," *Communio* 37, no. 4 (2010): 664.
46. Martin Bieler, "*Analogia Entis* as an Expression of Love according to Ferdinand Ulrich," in *The Analogy of Being: Invention of the Antichrist or the Wisdom of God*, ed. Thomas Joseph White (Grand Rapids, MI: Eerdmans, 2011), 317.
47. Ulrich, *HA*, 201, 211.
48. Ulrich, *HA*, 212.
49. Ulrich, *HA*, 211.
50. Bieler, "*Analogia Entis* as an Expression of Love," 332 (emphasis original).
51. Ulrich, *HA*, 114, 319, 372.
52. Ulrich, *HA*, 207.
53. *TD*4, 323. Balthasar also affirms Bulgakov's theology in his history of soteriology; see *TD*4, 313–14. For an understanding of Bulgakov's influence on Balthasar, see Brandon Gallaher, *Freedom and Necessity in Modern Trinitarian Theology* (Oxford: Oxford University Press, 2016), 45–116; Martin, *Balthasar and the Critical Appropriation*.
54. Sergius Bulgakov, *The Lamb of God*, trans. Boris Jakim (Grand Rapids, MI: Eerdmans, 2008), 98–99, 129, 134, 213–46.
55. *TD*4, 323–28; *TD*5, 84; *TL*2, 83, 177–78.
56. *TD*4, 323; *TDg*3, 301.
57. *TD*4, 325; *TDg*3, 302.
58. *TD*4, 323.
59. Christopher Hadley, "The All-Embracing Frame: Distance in the Trinitarian Theology of Hans Urs von Balthasar" (PhD diss., Marquette University, 2015), 23.
60. Williams, "Balthasar and the Trinity," 41. For more on Williams's interpretation of difference in Balthasar, see Rowan Williams, *Wrestling with Angels: Conversations in Modern Theology*, ed. Mike Higton (Grand Rapids, MI: Eerdmans, 2007), 77–85.
61. *TDg*3, 302, 310–11, 337; *TD*5, 91–95.

62. *TLg*2, 62, 119, 159, 165, 270, 288, 315–16.

63. For a couple examples of those who use Horner's taxonomy, see Hadley, "The All-Embracing Frame"; Randall Stephen Rosenberg, "Theory and Drama in Balthasar's and Lonergan's Theology of Christ's Consciousness and Knowledge" (PhD diss., Boston College, 2008).

64. *ET*3, 173.

65. Robyn Horner, *Jean-Luc Marion: A Theo-Logical Introduction* (Aldershot: Ashgate, 2005), 51–53.

66. *TD*5, 94.

67. *TD*2, 257–58, 262; *TD*5, 88–95, 485.

68. Ayres, *Nicaea and Its Legacy*, 280–82, 296–300.

69. Gregory of Nyssa, *Against Eunomius* 1.2; Khaled Anatolios, *Retrieving Nicaea: The Development and Meaning of Trinitarian Doctrine* (Grand Rapids, MI: Baker, 2011), 213–15; Ayres, *Nicaea and Its Legacy*, 296–97.

70. Matthew Levering, *Predestination: Biblical and Theological Paths* (Oxford: Oxford University Press, 2011), 175. Levering also critiques Balthasar's notion of trinitarian distance in other works; see Levering, *The Achievement of Hans Urs von Balthasar: An Introduction to His Trilogy* (Washington, DC: Catholic University of America Press, 2019), 214; Levering, *Scripture and Metaphysics: Aquinas and the Renewal of Trinitarian Theology* (Oxford: Blackwell, 2004), 131–32.

71. Nicholas J. Healy, *The Eschatology of Hans Urs Von Balthasar: Being as Communion* (Oxford: Oxford University Press, 2005), 133–34; Karen Kilby, *Balthasar: A (Very) Critical Introduction* (Grand Rapids, MI: Eerdmans, 2012), 107–9; Kilby, "Hans Urs von Balthasar on the Trinity," in Phan, ed., *The Cambridge Companion to the Trinity*, 211.

72. Kevin J. Vanhoozer, *Remythologizing Theology: Divine Action, Passion, and Authorship* (Cambridge: Cambridge University Press, 2010), 243.

73. *TL*1, 8, 23–33; Angela Franks, "Trinitarian *Analogia Entis* in Hans Urs von Balthasar," *Thomist* 62, no. 4 (1998): 534; Williams, "Balthasar and the Trinity," 42.

74. Balthasar does not make this connection himself, but his lifelong love for music does seem to justify this interpretation. Anne Carpenter also shows how music can provide a helpful corrective to related concerns that Kilby raises. See Carpenter, *Theo-Poetics*, 19.

75. I develop this account between spatial and musical analogies further in Jacob Lett, "Divine Roominess: Spatial and Music Analogies in Hans Urs von Balthasar and Robert Jenson," *Pro Ecclesia* 28, no. 3 (2019): 267–77.

76. Linn Marie Tonstad, *God and Difference: The Trinity, Sexuality, and the Transformation of Finitude* (New York: Routledge, 2016), 11.

77. Ibid., 11–13, 16, 48, 59, 62, 79, 82, 85–86, 99, 111, 136, 147, 156–57, 227, 231, 236, 239.

78. Ibid., 82 (emphasis original).

79. Ibid., 136.

80. Bruce D. Marshall, "The Unity of the Triune God: Reviving an Ancient Question," *Thomist* 74, no. 1 (2010): 1–32.

81. *TD*4, 324. Chapter 3 will outline Balthasar's dramatic hermeneutic.

82. *TL*1, 207–8.

83. Przywara, *Analogia Entis*, 586.

84. Ibid., 426, 584–86, 590.

85. Ibid., 589.

86. Ibid., 593–95. Such spatial-to-unspatial grammar is also employed in Gregory Nazianzen's statement regarding the "mingling" of Christ's two natures: "The Uncontained One is contained." See Aaron Riches, *Ecce Homo: On the Divine Unity of Christ* (Grand Rapids, MI: Eerdmans, 2016), 98.

87. *TD*5, 401. O'Regan argues that super-time and super-space are "metasymbols" that Balthasar uses to creatively reconceive impassibility and immutability, and he does so without "explanatory interest" (O'Regan, *Anatomy of Misremembering*, 221–44).

88. *TD*5, 77–79; *TL*2, 173–86, 315–16.

89. *TL*2, 185.

90. *TL*2, 171–86, 315–16.

91. Jeremy S. Begbie, *Theology, Music, and Time* (Cambridge: Cambridge University Press, 2000), 24–25.

92. Robert W. Jenson, "The End Is Music," in *Edwards in Our Time: Jonathan Edwards and the Shaping of American Religion*, ed. Sang Hyan Lee and Allen G. Guelzo (Grand Rapids, MI: Eerdmans, 1999), 170; Robert W. Jenson, *Systematic Theology* (Oxford: Oxford University Press, 1997–1999), 1:226.

93. Jenson, *Systematic Theology*, 1:226 (emphasis original).

94. Stephen John Wright, *Dogmatic Aesthetics: A Theology of Beauty in Dialogue with Robert W. Jenson* (Minneapolis: Fortress, 2014), 218.

95. Jenson, *Systematic Theology*, 1:236.

96. Begbie, *Theology, Music, and Time*, 24.

97. Ibid., 25.

98. Jennifer Newsome Martin has also recently offered an analogical reading of Balthasar's notion of divine distance that is compatible with divine simplicity. See Martin, "The Consubstantial Otherness of God: Divine Simplicity and the Trinity in Hans Urs von Balthasar," *Modern Theology* 35, no. 3 (2019): 542–57.

99. Bieler, "*Analogia Entis* as an Expression of Love," 332 (emphasis original). The unity of presence and separation is spelled out more clearly by Ulrich,

and Bieler suggests that Balthasar and Ulrich were corresponding about these precise issues in *TD4*, which may explain why Balthasar clarifies his accounts of divine distance in his later works.

100. *TD5*, 94.

101. *TL2*, 43, 83, 107, 152, 185.

102. O'Regan, *Anatomy of Misremembering*, 228, 239–40, 309.

103. Ibid., 228.

104. *TD2*, 262.

105. *TD2*, 257–58, 262; *TD4*, 321; *TD5*, 88–95, 485. Accounting for the way trinitarian persons relate in the economy of redemption also requires an analysis of the relationship between the wills of Christ (chapter 2).

106. *TD2*, 258–59; *TD5*, 79, 89–90, 486; *TL2*, 135–40.

107. Ayres, *Nicaea and Its Legacy*, 280–82, 296–300.

108. This clarification I am offering is similar to Brandon Gallaher's dialectical and analogical interpretation of the three types of divine freedom in Balthasar's theology. Gallaher notes that a God of absolute power (freedom 1) is without need, but within the inter-trinitarian life of free love (freedom 2), the Persons rely, need, and submit to one another (freedom 3). See Gallaher, *Freedom and Necessity*, 12–21.

109. On this point, Balthasar certainly starts with the three individual actions in the economy before proceeding to the unity of triune action. Przywara warns against thinking of divine unity this way; see Przywara, *Analogia Entis*, 355.

110. Although language of being's plentitude, excess, and surplus is scatted throughout *TL1*, my interpretation is particularly indebted in Rowan Williams's reading of difference and excess in Balthasar; see Williams, "Balthasar and the Trinity," 43; Williams, "Balthasar and Rahner," 11–35.

111. Divine distance is only fully understood if one understands Balthasar's account of divine receptivity, which I review in the next section. Receptivity is ultimately the attuning counterpart to distance in Balthasar's trinitarian grammar.

112. Horner, *Jean-Luc Marion*, 51–53.

113. The formality of Rahner's depiction does not embrace the interpersonal I/Thou relation between the Father and Son as displayed in Jesus's high priestly prayer. On the other hand, although Balthasar's and Moltmann's social/interpersonal depictions of the Trinity have similarities, the difference between Moltmann and Balthasar is that for Balthasar God's economic life is contained within the ever-greater self-giving of God, and therefore economic distance attributes no new distance to the divine being. See *TD2*, 125–26; *TD4*, 320–23; Hart, *The Beauty of the Infinite*, 322. Furthermore, Nichols and Dalzell believe that Balthasar uses a form of a "social model" of the Trinity based on Richard of

St. Victor, but they both read a more specific "interpersonal model" in Balthasar. See Thomas G. Dalzell, *The Dramatic Encounter of Divine and Human Freedom in the Theology of Hans Urs von Balthasar* (Bern: Peter Lang, 1997), 182, 186, 192; Nichols, *Pentecost*, 70. For more on Balthasar's reading of Richard of St. Victor, see *TL2*, 40–43, 62, 65, 217.

114. *TD5*, 85–91; *TL2*, 81–85.

115. Martin, *Balthasar and the Critical Appropriation*, 192–94; O'Regan, *Anatomy of Misremembering*, 237–38.

116. *TD4*, 11–12. Hoffmann's main works on *Stellvertretung* in German are Norbert Hoffmann, *Kreuz und Trinität: Zur Theologie der Sühne* (Freiburg: Johannes Verlag Einsiedeln, 1982); Hoffmann, "Stellvertretung, Grundgestalt und Mitte des Mysteriums: Ein Versuch trinitätstheologischer Begründung christlicher Sühne," *Münchener Theologische Zeitschrift* 30 (1979): 161–91; Hoffmann, *Sühne: Zur Theologie der Stellvertretung*. He has written two English summaries of these works: Hoffmann, "Atonement and the Ontological Coherence between the Trinity and the Cross," in *Towards a Civilization of Love*, ed. Mario Luigi Ciappi (San Francisco: Ignatius, 1985), 213–66; Hoffmann, "Atonement and Spirituality of the Sacred Heart: An Attempt an Elucidation by Means of the Principle of 'Representation,'" in *Faith in Christ and the Worship of Christ*, ed. Leo Scheffczyk; trans. Graham Harrison (San Francisco: Ignatius, 1986), 141–206. The first essay notes that it represents a "shortened and somewhat more clarified version of . . . *Sühne: Zur Theologie der Stellvertretung*" (263). For a good summary of Hoffmann's doctrine of atonement, see Alberto Espezel, "Inclusive Representation and Atonement in Norbert Hoffmann," *Communio* 24, no. 2 (1997): 286–96.

117. *TD5*, 244.

118. *TD5*, 244.

119. Balthasar, "Editorial," 160–62.

120. Hoffmann, "Atonement and the Ontological Coherence," 236–39: Hoffmann notes, "'Pro'-structure: In what follows the Latin prefix *pro* (as in *pro nobis*) will be used where the German original uses the Greek equivalent ὑπέρ or *hyper*, not in the sense of 'above,' 'over,' or 'beyond' (governing the accusative) but in the sense of 'for,' 'for the sake of,' and 'in the place of' (calling for the genitive). Expressions such as 'pro'-structure and 'pro'-existence are shorthand, both in the original and in this translation, for the author's idea that the very being of God, already in himself, is other-oriented, self-surrender, radically altruistic, a quality summarized by the Latin phrase *esse ad*" (264). Sölle uses ὑπέρ in a similar way in her theology of representation (see Sölle, *Christ the Representative*, 69).

121. Hoffmann, "Atonement and Spirituality," 162.

122. Ibid., 163.

123. Hoffmann, "Atonement and the Ontological Coherence," 251–52.

124. Hoffmann, "Atonement and Spirituality," 163; Hoffmann, "Atonement and the Ontological Coherence," 251–52.

125. *TD3*, 518–19; *TD5*, 82–83; *TL2*, 137.

126. *TD4*, 326.

127. Williams, *On Augustine*, 183.

128. *TD2*, 258.

129. Thomas Aquinas, "John 14: Lecture 1," in *Commentary on the Gospel of John*, https://isidore.co/aquinas/english/SSJohn.htm; Aquinas, *ST* Ia.27.1, Ia.27.2.

130. *TD5*, 81–91, 146–47; *TL2*, 135–41. Similar to his conception of distance, Balthasar's notion of divine receptivity stretches the tradition. Generally, receptivity or passive potency distinguishes creatures from God. In God, there is no potentiality because he is pure act (*actus purus*), while there is potentiality in creatures by nature of their passive potency, being by participation (Aquinas *ST* Ia.3.7, Ia.4.1, Ia.4.2, Ia.7.2, Ia.25.1, Ia.42.1.). At the same time, W. Norris Clark shows that an often unnoticed aspect of Thomistic thought is the positive feature of receptivity as a perfection of being, as is evident in the Son's procession. The Son's generation is not external, but is internal, like the act of intelligence, and is actively "accepted" by the one who proceeds (Aquinas *ST* Ia.27.1, Ia.27.2). The Son actively receives the divine being as the divine being; any other conception would be a form of Arianism. For more on divine receptivity, see W. Norris Clarke, *Person and Being* (Milwaukee: Marquette University Press, 1993), 20–24. A lengthy conversation on receptivity as a divine and creaturely attribute can be seen in *Communio*: Stephen A. Long, "Divine and Creaturely 'Receptivity': The Search for a Middle Term," *Communio* 21, no. 1 (1994): 151–61; George A. Blair, "On *Esse* and Relation," *Communio* 21, no. 1 (1994): 162–64; W. Norris Clarke, "Person, Being, and St. Thomas," *Communio* 19, no. 4 (1992): 601–18; Clarke, "Response to David Schindler's Comments," *Communio* 20, no. 3 (1993), 593–98; Clarke, "Response to Long's Comments" and "Response to Blair's Comments," *Communio* 21, no. 1 (1994): 165–71; David L. Schindler, "Norris Clarke on Person, Being, and St. Thomas," *Communio* 20, no. 3 (1993): 580–92; Schindler, "The Person: Philosophy, Theology, and Receptivity," *Communio* 21, no. 1 (1994): 172–90. For more on Balthasar's conception of divine receptivity, see D. Stephen Long, *Saving Karl Barth: Hans Urs von Balthasar's Preoccupation* (Minneapolis: Fortress, 2014), 173, 235; O'Hanlon, *The Immutability of God*; David L. Schindler, *Heart of the World, Center of the Church: Communio Ecclesiology, Liberalism and Liberation* (Grand Rapids, MI: Eerdmans, 2003), 196.

131. *EP*, 93; *GL*5, 626–27; *TD*2, 261–62, 298; *TD*4, 326; *TD*5, 82–87, 254–65; *TL*2, 140. Adrienne von Speyr is clearly the basis for Balthasar's account. For a detailed study on Speyr's influence on Balthasar's doctrine of the Trinity, see Michele Schumacher, *A Trinitarian Anthropology: Adrienne von Speyr and Hans Urs von Balthasar in Dialogue with Thomas Aquinas* (Washington, DC: Catholic University of America Press, 2014).

132. *TD*5, 86.

133. *TD*5, 83–86; *TL*2, 137; Margaret M. Turek, "Towards a Theology of God the Father: Hans Urs von Balthasar's TheoDramatic Approach" (PhD diss., University of Fribourg, 1999), 208.

134. Schindler, *Heart of the World*, 196. Clark interprets Balthasar similarly, calling receptivity "a perfection—not the imperfection—of interpersonal relations" (see Clark, "Person, Being, and St. Thomas," 612).

135. *TD*2, 256–47; *TD*5, 85–86; *TL*2, 128. As in the case of trinitarian distance, Balthasar's style invites misinterpretation of his theology of receptivity and its relation to the language of participation in being. Therefore, Stephen A. Long believes receptivity, especially in Clark's formulation inspired by Balthasar, cannot be conceived without potency being ascribed to the divine (Long, "Divine and Creaturely 'Receptivity,'" 158–60), whereas Long and Schindler believe Balthasar remains within orthodoxy in his conception of trinitarian receptivity, so long as it is conceived analogically (Long, *Saving Karl Barth*, 235; Schindler, "The Person: Philosophy, Theology, and Receptivity," 173–74, 179). However, Balthasar does seem to move beyond an analogical account when he attaches the term "riskiness" to the personal freedoms of the divine Persons to give and receive (*TD*4, 327–28; *TD*5, 88, 245). This seems to suggest that the Father must receive divinity back from the Son or cease to be God and that the Son may have decided to not give or receive. By using the language of riskiness, Balthasar undermines his usual analogical grammar. Riskiness suggests a deficiency in being and the autonomous freedom of the divine Persons, conflicting with the *analogia entis* and the doctrine of simplicity.

136. *TD*3, 518–19; *GL*5, 625–27.

137. *TD*2, 258.

138. Balthasar specifically locates activity and receptivity within sexual differences and projects them onto the divine, with activity mirroring the masculine and passivity the feminine. By doing so, Balthasar seems to absolutize gender binaries and norms. Although Balthasar does maintain that a woman's receptivity is an active one and asserts the equality between male and female, he locates receptivity as a distinctively feminine characteristic. Her activity is a response, as she is man's answer, fruitfulness, and completion; see Michelle A. Gonzalez,

"Hans Urs von Balthasar and Contemporary Feminist Theology," *Theological Studies* 65, no. 3 (2004): 570–72.

139. *TD*3, 519.

140. *TL*2, 153.

141. This description of how representation functions in the triune life and in the economy of redemption seems compatible with Gregory of Nyssa's theology. Ayres notes, "Different human persons may undertake the same task but they do not directly participate in the action of others and each one possesses his or her own special sphere of activity. . . . However, in the case of the Father we find no activity in which the Son does not also work. Similarly, the Son has no 'special activity' without the Spirit. . . . The divine persons, thus, do not simply act together, they function inseparably to constitute any and every activity towards creation"; see Lewis Ayres, "On Not Three People: The Fundamental Themes of Gregory of Nyssa's Trinitarian Theology as Seen in *To Ablabius: On Not Three Gods*," in *Re-thinking Gregory of Nyssa*, ed. Sarah Coakley (Oxford: Blackwell, 2003), 461.

142. *TD*2, 83, 136–37; Hart, "The Mirror of the Infinite," 546.

143. *TD*5, 90 (emphasis original).

144. *TD*1, 34–37; *TD*2, 258–59; *TD*5, 79, 89–90, 486; *TL*2, 135–40; *YC*, 143–44.

145. Balthasar, "Editorial," 160–62.

146. Balthasar, *Elucidations*, 92.

147. *TL*2, 169.

148. *GL*5, 627; *TD*2, 173, 203–10, 223, 316–34; *TD*3, 525–35; *TD*5, 61–110; *TL*2, 81–85, 173.

149. *TL*2, 169.

150. *TL*2, 173.

151. Balthasar, "On the Concept of Person," *Communio* 13, no. 1 (1986): 24.

152. *EP*, 43–88; *GL*5, 613–27; *TD*2, 207–42; *TD*3, 525–35; *TD*5, 68; *TL*1, 167–88.

153. Gallaher, *Freedom and Necessity*, 9.

154. Nicholas Adams, *Eclipse of Grace: Divine and Human Action in Hegel* (Oxford: Wiley-Blackwell, 2013), 49, 57–58. Hegel

155. Martin Bieler, introduction to Ulrich, *HA*, xlvi–xlix.

156. *EP*, 51.

157. Bieler, introduction to Ulrich, *HA*, xlviii (emphasis original).

158. *EP*, 51.

159. *TL*1, 45.

160. *TL*1, 47.

161. *TL*2, 184.

162. Balthasar, *Elucidations*, 92–94; *TD*2, 405–11; *TD*3, 271–82, 525–29.

163. Bieler, introduction to Ulrich, *HA*, xxxviii, xl. Ulrich regularly speaks of being as "pure mediation" (*HA*, 26, 67, 83), which could be further developed with nuance as *Stellvertretung*.

164. Ferdinand Ulrich, *Leben in Der Einheit von Leben und Tod* (Einsiedeln: Johannes Verlag, 1999), 147–99.

165. Adrian J. Walker, "Personal Singularity and the *Communio Personarum*: A Creative Development of Thomas Aquinas's Doctrine of *Esse Commune*," *Communio* 31, no. 3 (2004): 469.

166. *TL*1, 156; Ulrich, *HA*, 373–74.

167. *EP*, 57, 109–10; *TD*3, 526; *TD*5, 66–81, 90–91.

168. *TL*2, 180–81.

169. *TD*4, 254. Despite some confusion surrounding the theopaschite formula, Aaron Riches notes that it was also operative in the Chalcedonian Creed (see Riches, *Ecce Homo*, 86).

170. "Stellvertretung," 3: "Alles im christlichen Glauben hängt an den zwei kleinen Wörtchen 'pro nobis.'"

171. Barth, *CD*, IV.1:211–82.

172. Barth, *CD*, IV.1:273.

173. *TL*2, 85.

174. *TD*2, 407–8 (emphasis and brackets original).

175. *TL*2, 231–32.

176. Anatolios, *Retrieving Nicaea*, 93–95, 290.

177. Ibid., 119–21.

178. Catherine Mowry LaCugna, "Philosophers and Theologians on the Trinity," *Modern Theology* 2, no. 3 (1986): 180.

179. *TD*3, 233–34, 257; *TD*5, 76.

180. *TD*2, 261–62.

181. *EP*, 73–77; *TL*2, 84.

182. *TD*4, 261–62.

183. Clarke, *Explorations in Metaphysics*, 61–62 (emphasis original).

184. *TD*4, 273–84.

185. Noel O'Sullivan, "An Emerging Christology," in *T&T Clark Companion to Henri De Lubac*, ed. Jordan Hillebert (London: T&T Clark, 2017), 343.

186. *TD*5, 272.

187. Schindler, *Heart of the World*, 315.

188. *TL*2, 232.

189. Bailey, "Concepts of *Stellvertretung*," 225.

190. *TD*4, 419 (emphasis original).

191. *TD*4, 239.

192. *TD3*, 237. The patristic exchange formula is reflected in Paul's writings, "For you know the grace of our Lord Jesus Christ, that though he was rich, yet for your sake he became poor, so that you by his poverty might become rich" (2 Cor. 8:9), and can be summarized by Irenaeus's formulation in *Against Heresies*: "The Word of God, our Lord Jesus Christ, through his transcendent love, became what we are that he might bring us to be even what he himself is"; see Irenaeus, *Against Heresies*, 5, pref. For an overview of how this theme shows up in various church fathers, see Matthias Joseph Scheeben, *The Mysteries of Christianity*, trans. Cyril Vollert (St. Louis: Herder, 1951), 378–82. In fact, John Behr notes that the exchange formula "led inexorably" to the Council of Chalcedon; see Behr, *The Formation of Christian Theology* (Crestwood, NY: St. Vladimir's Seminary Press, 2001–2004), 1:75–76.

193. *TD4*, 333.
194. *TD4*, 253–54, 317.
195. *TDg3*, 222, 224, 242, 246, 295, 309–10.
196. *TD4*, 332 (emphasis original).
197. Przywara, *Analogia Entis*, 593.
198. Ibid., 593–95.
199. *TD5*, 482–83.
200. *TD4*, 290; *TD5*, 428. The Finnish school of Lutheran studies disputes this reading of Luther's theology; see Tuomo Mannermaa, *Christ Present in Faith: Luther's View of Justification* (Minneapolis: Fortress, 2005).
201. *TD3*, 522–23; *TD5*, 473–85.
202. Hoffmann, "Atonement and Spirituality," 163.
203. *TD4*, 370, 381; *TD5*, 105–9, 482–86; *YC*, 144.
204. *TD5*, 394–410.
205. *TL2*, 180–81; Williams, "Balthasar and Rahner," 22–23.
206. Nichols, *Divine Fruitfulness*, 177.

Chapter Two

1. Sölle, *Christ the Representative*, 60.
2. Martin, *Balthasar and the Critical Appropriation*, 95.
3. Carpenter, *Theo-Poetics*, 52.
4. Ibid., 95–116.
5. Riches, *Ecce Homo*, 8–12, 33.
6. Ibid., 33.
7. Ibid., 8–9.

8. David L. Schindler, "The Embodied Person as Gift and the Cultural Task in America: *Status Quaestionis*," *Communio* 35, no. 3 (2008): 411–12.

9. *TD3*, 221.

10. Cyril O'Regan, *The Heterodox Hegel* (New York: State University of New York Press, 1994).

11. Adams, *Eclipse of Grace*, xviii.

12. Ibid., 7, 22.

13. Ibid., 158–63.

14. O'Regan, *Anatomy of Misremembering*, 171, 193–95.

15. Balthasar began engaging with Hegel in the 1930s, a practice that carried on to the last two volumes of the *Theo-Logic* (see O'Regan, *The Anatomy of Misremembering*, 35). Balthasar is deeply indebted to both Barth's and Przywara's interpretations of Hegel. Balthasar recommends reading the following work to distinguish his theo-dramatic approach to Christology from Hegel's (*TD3*, 137): Emilio Brito, *La Christologie de Hegel: Verbum Crucis*, trans. B. Pottier (Paris: Beauchesne, 1983).

16. Levering, *The Achievement of Balthasar*, 114.

17. *CL*, 157–59.

18. Gallaher, *Freedom and Necessity*, 6–7, 227–28.

19. Przywara, *Analogia Entis*, 119–24. If Przywara is correct, then Adams's reading of Hegel's philosophy as strictly related to logic is problematic. Although Adams is offering a corrective to those who read Hegel as primarily revising Christian ontology, it is also ironic that as Adams argues for a participatory logic, he bifurcates logic and ontology, philosophy and theology. If the logic of Hegel is built upon the theology of Chalcedon, a Christology Hegel ultimately revises (see O'Regan, *The Heterodox Hegel*), then is not Hegel's logic nullified? Thus, my task in this chapter is to show the fluidity between ontology and logic in Balthasar's Christology.

20. Rowan Williams, "Dialectic and Analogy: A Theological Legacy," in *The Impact of Idealism: The Legacy of Post-Kantian German Thought*, ed. Nicholas Adams, vol. 4 of *Religion*, ed. Nicholas Boyle and Liz Disley (Cambridge: Cambridge University Press, 2013), 287–88.

21. O'Regan, *Anatomy of Misremembering*, 123.

22. Gallaher, *Freedom and Necessity*, 40, 90, 145, 161, 165, 198–99, 227–38; Andrew L. Prevot, "Dialectic and Analogy in Balthasar's 'The Metaphysics of the Saints,'" *Pro Ecclesia* 26, no. 3 (2017): 262, 272.

23. Other Balthasar scholars (Carpenter, O'Regan, and Walatka) also distinguish between the vertical and horizontal dimensions of Balthasar's theology.

24. *TD3*, 202–20; Ayres, *Nicaea and Its Legacy*, 280, 296, 313.

25. A simpler presentation of Balthasar's understanding of drama, roles, personhood, and freedom can be found in Balthasar, *Engagement with God: The Drama of Christian Discipleship*, trans. R. John Halliburton (London: SPCK, 1975).

26. *TD*3, 203.

27. See *TD*1 for an overview of the categories from drama that Balthasar incorporates.

28. *TD*3, 207.

29. *TD*3, 207–8. Balthasar shows how the difference between a conscious subject and a person can be seen in the difference between "image" (*Abbild*) of God and progress toward "likeness" or "archetype" (*Urbild*).

30. Walatka, *Von Balthasar and the Option for the Poor*, 85–90.

31. *TD*1, 645. Buber's influence on Balthasar began around the same time his patristic and Barth studies were underway in the 1940s and 1950s, making Buber one of Balthasar's key interlocutors, as is evident in Balthasar's doctrine of the Trinity, Christology, and anthropology.

32. *TD*1, 645. The focus on the "I" in dialogical philosophy is for Balthasar's mission Christology what the focus on the particular and unique in G. M. Hopkins's poetry is for Balthasar's theological aesthetics. See Carpenter, *Theo-Poetics*, 162–70.

33. Carpenter, *Theo-Poetics*, 175–76.

34. *TD*1, 636, 645.

35. This same theological problem is a concern of Ulrich's metaphysics. Ulrich distinguishes between physical spatiotemporality and ontological spatiotemporality, insisting that one must avoid the dangers of both pure spirit and pure historicity (*HA*, 321–29). Whereas Ulrich's study primarily focuses on metaphysical distinctions, I am attempting to keep the same distinctions using Balthasar's christological anthropology.

36. Levering, *The Achievement of Balthasar*, 126, 140; O'Regan, *Anatomy of Misremembering*, 152, 155–66. O'Regan notes, "Balthasar underscores the importance of a dialogical philosophy for an adequate theology. It is no accident that this occurs in the very same volume in which he announces the necessity of overcoming Hegel both on the methodological and substantive levels" (563).

37. Adams, *Eclipse of Grace*, 41.

38. *TD*1, 481.

39. *TD*3, 263–70.

40. O'Regan, *Anatomy of Misremembering*, 194.

41. *TD*3, 149–150, 156–57, 511.

42. *TH*, 29–32.

43. Marshall, "The Unity of the Triune God," 29–30.

44. Aquinas, *ST* Ia.43.1–8. For an overview of Aquinas's procession/mission distinction, see Gilles Emery, *The Trinitarian Theology of St. Thomas Aquinas*, trans. Francesca Aran Murphy (Oxford: Oxford University Press, 2007), 360–412.

45. Aquinas, *ST* Ia.43.1; Ia.43.5.

46. Aquinas, *ST* Ia.43.2.

47. Aquinas, *ST* Ia.43.3.

48. Aquinas, *ST* Ia.43.2. This is not as clear in the Blackfriars edition, but it is in Alfred J. Freddoso's new translation (not yet published). See Alfred J. Freddoso, "New English Translation of St. Thomas Aquinas's *Summa Theologiae*," https://www3.nd.edu/~afreddos/summa-translation/TOC.htm.

49. Aquinas, *ST* Ia.43.2.

50. Marshall, "The Unity of the Triune God," 20.

51. Kilby, *Balthasar: A (Very) Critical Introduction*, 98; Mackinnon, "Some Reflections on Hans Urs von Balthasar's Christology," in *The Analogy of Beauty: The Theology of Hans Urs von Balthasar*, ed. John Riches (Edinburgh: T&T Clark, 1986), 171–72; Pitstick, *Light in Darkness*, 154–57.

52. O'Regan, *Anatomy of Misremembering*, 205–21. Adams provides a strong examination of this often asserted claim. Hegel's famous phrase "God existing as community" is not entirely concerned with doctrine, but with a nonoppositional logic between God and community (Adams, *Eclipse of Grace*, 207–9).

53. Nichols, *No Bloodless Myth*, 100.

54. *MP*, vii–ix; *TD1*, 67; *TD3*, 157, 226; *TD4*, 320–26, 330–31, 362; *TD5*, 265; *TH*, 29–32; *TL3*, 42–43.

55. *TH*, 29–32.

56. *TD3*, 157–59 (emphasis original).

57. *TD4*, 334; *TDg3*, 310.

58. *TD2*, 260–71; *TD4*, 326; *TD5*, 106. For three articles by Balthasar on how Christ is the foundation of the world, see "Christ: Alpha and Omega," *Communio* 23, no. 3 (1996): 465–71; "God Is His Own Exegete," *Communio* 4, no. 4 (1986): 280–87; "The Meaning of Christ's Saying, 'I Am the Truth,'" *Communio* 14, no. 2 (1987): 158–60.

59. Riches, *Ecce Homo*, 132–33.

60. International Theological Commission, "Select Questions on Christology," http://www.vatican.va/roman_curia/congregations/cfaith/cti_documents/rc_cti_1979_cristologia_en.html.

61. *TD2*, 201.

62. Maximus the Confessor, *Ambiguum* 5, in *Maximus the Confessor*, ed. and trans. Andrew Louth (London: Routledge, 1996), 175.

63. Ibid., 170.

64. Ibid., 172–73, 176. For more on Maximus's christological terminology, see Louth, *Maximus*, 49, 212–13; Riches, *Ecce Homo*, 135.

65. Maximus the Confessor, *Ambiguum* 5, 173.

66. *CL*, 261–62. Ulrich frames this similarly; see *HA*, 323–24.

67. Maximus the Confessor, *Ambiguum* 5, 175–77.

68. Maximus the Confessor, *Opusculum* 64.

69. Maximus the Confessor, *Opuscule* 3, in Louth, ed., *Maximus the Confessor*, 191–96. Maximus distinguishes between natural and gnomic wills. A natural will simply wills the good, whereas the post-fall gnomic will can only will the good deliberately and episodically. Christ must not be thought to have two gnomic wills, but two natural wills that are unified in the divine Son incarnate.

70. *CL*, 262.

71. Joseph Ratzinger, *Behold the Pierced One: An Approach to a Spiritual Christology*, trans. Graham Harrison (San Francisco: Ignatius, 1986), 39 (emphasis original).

72. *TD3*, 165, 191–202.

73. *TD5*, 257–59.

74. Balthasar, "Die Neue Theorie von Jesus als dem 'Sündenbock,'" *Communio Internationale Katholische Zeitschrift* 9 (1980): 184–85; *TD3*, 166–67.

75. *Credo*, 45–46; *ET2*, 165; *TD3*, 149–63, 182–83, 196–97; *TH*, 36–39.

76. O'Regan, *Anatomy of Misremembering*, 193–94.

77. *TD3*, 197–98.

78. *CL*, 262.

79. *TD3*, 175–79.

80. *TD3*, 175–82.

81. O'Regan, *Anatomy of Misremembering*, 343.

82. *TD3*, 154–65, 227–28.

83. *TD3*, 202–29.

84. *TD3*, 202, 220–21; *TL2*, 311–12.

85. *MW*, 28, 35–37.

86. *MW*, 22–23.

87. Barth, *CD*, I.1:xiii. Balthasar published a short article in 1949 that names Christ as "the *analogia entis* in concrete form." See Balthasar, "Drei Merkmale des Christlichen," *Wort und Wahrheit* 4 (1949): 401–15.

88. *TKB*, 55, 110, 376–77, 383–84.

89. *TH*, 24.

90. *TD3*, 223. Thomas Joseph White provides a detailed treatment of the implicit *analogia entis* in a theology of the Incarnation; see White, "'Through him all things were made' (John 1:3): The Analogy of the Word Incarnate according to St. Thomas Aquinas and Its Ontological Presuppositions," in *The*

Analogy of Being, ed. Thomas Joseph White (Grand Rapids, MI: Eerdmans, 2011), 246–79.

91. *TL2*, 84.

92. *TKB*, 114–20, 161–67. For more on Barth's version of an analogy of being, see Bruce L. McCormack, "Karl Barth's Version of 'Analogy of Being,'" in *The Analogy of Being*, ed. Thomas Joseph White (Grand Rapids, MI: Eerdmans, 2011), 88–144.

93. Walatka, *Von Balthasar and the Option for the Poor*, 132.

94. O'Regan, *Anatomy of Remembering*, 556.

95. *TKB*, 401; *TD3*, 213–15. Frances Young notes that many incorrectly associate Cyril with an Alexandrian Logos-sarx Christology and, as a result, believe that "Cyril is incapable of doing real justice to the humanity of Christ, and his rejection of Apollinarianism is merely superficial." Young suggests that Cyril's adversaries misinterpret his appropriation of monophysite formulae, as if it were used to combat the two-nature position. Cyril clearly believed that Jesus's "human existence is entirely genuine"; see Frances Young and Andrew Teal, *From Nicaea to Chalcedon: A Guide to the Literature and Its Background* (Grand Rapid, MI: Baker, 2010), 316, 319.

96. Louth, *St John Damascene*, 40, 49–50, 160–61.

97. Ibid., 50.

98. Riches, *Ecce Homo*, 114–17.

99. John of Damascus, *Exposition of the Orthodox Faith* 3.9.

100. U. M. Lang, "Anhypostatos-Enhypostatos: Church Fathers, Protestant Orthodoxy, and Karl Barth," *Journal of Theological Studies* 49, no. 2 (1998): 654.

101. Lang, "Anhypostatos-Enhypostatos," 654 (emphasis original).

102. Riches, *Ecce Homo*, 114 (emphasis original).

103. John Behr, *The Case against Diodore and Theodore* (Oxford: Oxford University Press, 2011), 3–47.

104. *TD3*, 229; *TKB*, 107; *TL2*, 280, 316.

105. *TD4*, 373–74.

106. Nichols, *No Bloodless Myth*, 224; Gallaher, *Freedom and Necessity*, 210.

107. *TD3*, 235. Though Balthasar promotes the "from above" approach of Alexandrian Logos-sarx Christology, he also associates it with Apollinarius's denial of Jesus's human soul (*TD3*, 234; *TL2*, 303). Grillmeier's influence can be misleading. Athanasius's emphasis on the flesh (*sarx*) of Christ did not make him Apollinarian. See Peter J. Leithart, *Athanasius* (Grand Rapids, MI: Baker Academic, 2011), 120–21.

108. Oliver Crisp, *Divinity and Humanity: The Incarnation Reconsidered* (Cambridge: Cambridge University Press, 2007), 75.

109. Aquinas, *ST* IIIa.4.1–6.

110. Aquinas, *ST* IIIa.4.4. It should be noted that Balthasar may be following Barth also, given that Barth is also quite clear on this same notion; see Barth, *CD*, I.2:149–64.

111. John of Damascus, *Exposition of the Orthodox Faith* 3.7, 3.11, 4.4.

112. Ibid.

113. *TD3*, 236–237. Wolfhart Pannenberg also critiques the "central individual" concept of post-Hegelian theologians for eschatological reasons. Though the concept of a "central individual" can be found in Hegel and in Schleiermacher's "prototype," it is not until Göschel and Dorner that it is developed in Christology, coming to its fullest realization in Richard Rothe. See Wolfhart Pannenberg, *Jesus, God and Man*, trans. Lewis L. Wilkins and Duane A. Priebe (Philadelphia: Westminster, 1977), 388–90.

114. *TDg2*.2, 217: "dass die Bestimmtheit der göttlichen Sohnschaft Jesus ihn gerade zu einem sehr bestimmten einzelnen Menschen zu machen vermag."

115. *TD3*, 212–14, 236.

116. *CL*, 160–62, 261–63.

117. *CL*, 161.

118. *CL*, 208; *TKB*, 271; Riches, *Ecce Homo*, 148.

119. Bruce L. McCormack, "Atonement and Human Suffering," in *Locating Atonement: Explorations in Constructive Dogmatics*, ed. Oliver D. Crisp and Fred Sanders (Grand Rapids, MI: Zondervan, 2015), 202–3.

120. *TH*, 69–70.

121. *TD3*, 222; *TH*, 68–71; *TL2*, 316.

122. *CL*, 202, 207–8, 235–55.

123. Przywara, *Analogia Entis*, 305–6.

124. Williams, "Dialectic and Analogy," 280.

125. Ibid., 288.

126. Ibid., 288–89; O'Regan, *Anatomy of Misremembering*, 201, 203.

127. *TD4*, 332–33.

128. Menke, *Stellvertretung*, 270.

129. Schumacher, "The Concept of Representation," 54.

130. *TD3*, 233–35.

131. *TL2*, 228–29; *GL7*, 143–44.

132. *EP*, 99–101; *TL2*, 229–32.

133. *EP*, 101; *PT*, 134–35; *TD2*, 407–8; *TD3*, 234, 241; *TD4*, 332–34; *TL2*, 229–32. Balthasar acknowledges that he adopts this understanding of the human nature from L. Malevez. See L. Malevez, "L'Eglise dans le Christ: Etude de theologie historique et theorique," *Recherches de Science Religieuse* 25 (1935): 257–91, 418–40.

134. *TD3*, 241.

135. *TD3*, 234.
136. *TD3*, 233–34; *TL2*, 301–6.
137. *TDg2.2*, 212–13; *TD3*, 232.
138. *TD4*, 262–63.
139. *TD3*, 241.
140. Peterson, "Grace in Our Place?," 440. According to Peterson, Rahner's theology of *Repräsentation* and *Realsymbol* upholds an inclusive relation between the trinitarian persons and Christ and humanity. *Stellvertertung* is not possible for the Trinity because the Father and Son "are not independent, self-constituted realities, that artificially join forces, nor does the one 'step in' as a proxy for the other." Once again, it seems the problem is not the term *Stellvertretung* but certain theologies of *Stellvertretung*. Balthasar's trinitarian and christological understanding of *Stellvertretung* also seeks to uphold inclusive relations between the triune Persons and Christ and creation.
141. *TD3*, 241–43.
142. Sölle, *Christ the Representative*, 24–30, 65–66.
143. *GL7*, 464.
144. Tanner, *Christ the Key*, 101–2.
145. Sölle, *Christ the Representative*, 89–92.
146. *TD3*, 306.
147. *TD1*, 62, 558–61; *TH*, 9–27, 70–79.
148. *TH*, 68; McIntosh, *Christology from Within*.
149. *TD3*, 246.
150. *TD3*, 244–50; *TDg2.2*, 225–29; Adolf Deissmann, *Paul: A Study in Social and Religion History*, trans. William E. Wilson (London: Hodder & Stoughton, 1926), 149–53.
151. *TD3*, 121, 246–49.
152. *TD3*, 246–47.
153. *TKB*, 372–77.
154. *TD1*, 634–36.
155. O'Regan, *Anatomy of Misremembering*, 201.
156. *TD3*, 230–31.
157. Gallaher, *Freedom and Necessity*, 211.
158. Sölle, *Christ the Representative*, 89.
159. Ibid., 106–12.
160. Peterson, "Grace in Our Place?," 442.
161. Which I have clarified through dialogue with Hegel according to Adams, *Eclipse of Grace*, 20–23.
162. As Adams says of Hegel, "The false opposition between subject and object is overcome. He takes a familiar example from the structure of drama, and his

reference to the chorus is a sign that he has in mind classical Greek drama. The audience in a Greek drama are not mere spectators. Their own agency is presented to them, objectively, in the action of the chorus. The chorus is a device for drawing the audience into the drama as participants with, quite literally, a voice" (Adams, *Eclipse of Grace*, 197).

163. *TD3*, 54–55.
164. *TL1*, 13.
165. Nicholas Lash, *Believing Three Ways in One God: A Reading of the Apostle's Creed* (Notre Dame, IN: University of Notre Dame Press, 1993), 5.
166. *TD3*, 232.
167. Balthasar believes that Rahner's Christology lacks this decisive objective component, which is at least partly why he defends the importance of the term *Stellvertretung*, but Peterson argues that Rahner upholds the centrality of Christ's action *pro nobis* through his use of the term *Repräsentation*. As a subcomponent of this category, Rahner does use a revised understanding of *Stellvertretung*. See Peterson, *Being Salvation*, 224; Peterson, "Grace in Our Place?," 444–47.
168. *TD3*, 245–46, 248; *TD4*, 394–95.
169. *TD3*, 247 (emphasis original).
170. See *GL7*, 399–415.

Chapter Three

1. *MP*, 11.
2. *TD5*, 477.
3. Karl Barth's hidden influence should not be underestimated, as *Stellvertretung* is also essential to his soteriology (*CD*, IV.1:273–74). Throughout this chapter, I will show places where his influence seems most evident.
4. Pitstick, *Light in Darkness*, 110–13.
5. *HMR*, 34. Balthasar will later pick the term back up in a heavily qualified sense.
6. *TD4*, 318.
7. *TD4*, 11–12, 332–38.
8. The term "dramatic" was not chosen arbitrarily or simply because of the overall project of *Theo-Drama*, but because Balthasar often critiques other atonement theories for not being dramatic enough. Referring back to his critique of various soteriologies, Balthasar asks, "Are the systems hitherto attempted sufficiently dramatic?" (*TD4*, 318). In another place, he states, "An examination of the major attempts to construct a doctrine of redemption will reveal a number

of these one-sided approaches. In each case, they infallibly result in a loss of theodramatic tension in the whole" (*TD4*, 244).

9. Balthasar, "Theology and Aesthetic," 65.

10. Williams, *On Christian Theology*, 29–43.

11. Levering, *The Achievement of Balthasar*, 212–15; Walatka, *Von Balthasar and the Option for the Poor*, 213.

12. *MW*, 48.

13. Balthasar, *Our Task*, 38.

14. Henri de Lubac, *Medieval Exegesis: The Four Senses of Scripture*, trans. Mark Sebanc and E. M. Macierowski, 3 vols. (Grand Rapids, MI: Eerdmans, 1998–2009). The fourth volume has not been published in English yet.

15. *TD2*, 91–169.

16. For a more detailed examination of Balthasar's hermeneutical method, see W. T. Dickens, *Hans Urs Von Balthasar's Theological Aesthetics: A Model for Post-Critical Biblical Interpretation* (Notre Dame, IN: University of Notre Dame Press, 2004).

17. *TD2*, 124.

18. *TD2*, 115.

19. *TD2*, 113.

20. *TD2*, 115 (emphasis original).

21. *TD2*, 116.

22. *TD2*, 108.

23. *TD2*, 112.

24. *GL7*, 203–5.

25. *TD2*, 115–30.

26. Anselm of Canterbury, "Why God Became Man," in *Anselm of Canterbury: The Major Works*, ed. Brian Davies and G. R. Evans (Oxford: Oxford University Press, 2008), 267.

27. *TD1*, 22, 43–46, 50, 119–31; *TD2*, 116; *TD3*, 101–9, 466; *TD4*, 18, 103, 237, 243, 266, 319; *TD5*, 13–14.

28. Balthasar, "Theology and Aesthetic," 67.

29. *TD2*, 130.

30. *PT*, 79.

31. *TD2*, 56–62; Quash, "Drama and the Ends of Modernity," 145–46.

32. Kilby, *Balthasar*, 93. D. C. Schindler offers a compelling alternative reading of Balthasar; see Schindler, "A Very Critical Response to Karen Kilby: On Failing to See the Form," *Radical Orthodoxy* 3, no. 1 (2015): 68–87.

33. Quash, *Theology and the Drama of History*, 148.

34. *TD4*, 231–319.

35. Williams, *On Christian Theology*, 45.
36. Adams, *Eclipse of Grace*, 13.
37. *TD4*, 297.
38. *TD4*, 345.
39. *TD4*, 318.
40. *HMR*, 34; *TD4*, 495.
41. *TD4*, 317.
42. *TD4*, 211.
43. *TD2*, 189–334.
44. *TD4*, 137–201.
45. *TD4*, 79.
46. *EP*, 43–88; *GL5*, 613–27; *TD2*, 207–42; *TD3*, 525–35; *TD5*, 68; *TL1*, 167–88.
47. *TD2*, 213–16.
48. *TD4*, 148.
49. *TD4*, 148.
50. *TD4*, 147, 151.
51. *TD2*, 285–92.
52. *TD4*, 139.
53. *TD2*, 227–42; *TD4*, 139.
54. *GL7*, 132; *TD4*, 140, 146, 328.
55. *GL7*, 134; *TD4*, 142–46, 159.
56. *TD4*, 160.
57. *TD2*, 227–29, 284–85; *TD4*, 162–64, 370–71.
58. *TD4*, 370 (emphasis original).
59. *TD4*, 63; *TD5*, 193, 202–3, 212.
60. *ET3*, 175–76.
61. *TD4*, 362; *TDg3*, 337.
62. *PT*, 27.
63. *TD4*, 328–29.
64. *TD4*, 324.
65. *PT*, 31; *TD4*, 371.
66. *TD4*, 371. Similarly, Ulrich states, "In clinging to itself, being falls prey to absolute finitude" (*HA*, 206).
67. Rahner, *Foundations of Christian Faith*, 282–88, 296–97.
68. Ibid., 254–56, 265.
69. Ibid., 55, 211, 282–83, 305, 317.
70. Ibid., 282–83, 317.
71. Ibid., 283–84.
72. *TD4*, 275.

73. *TD*4, 283. As we have explored in the introduction and in chapter 2, Rahner's and Balthasar's theologies of representation have much in common. They are both critical of penal substitution logic, seeking instead to depict an inclusive and participatory understanding of representation. However, as it pertains to the means of salvation, Rahner and Balthasar clearly diverge. Whereas Rahner focuses on salvation through the *personhood* of Christ (see Peterson, *Being Salvation*), Balthasar focuses on the dramatic *action* of Christ. More details on this divergence are included in the subsection below titled "Dramatic Representation: Forsakenness, Death, and Hell."

74. Kevin J. Vanhoozer, *The Drama of Doctrine: A Canonical Linguistic Approach to Christian Theology* (Louisville, KY: Westminster John Knox Press, 2005), 383–85.

75. Williams, *Tragic Imagination*, 4–27.

76. *TD*4, 257. Ulrich also seems to influence the dramatic shape of Balthasar's Christology (*HA*, 111).

77. *TD*2, 152–53.

78. *GL*2, 211–59; *GL*5, 18, 107, 235; *GL*6, 20, 147–60; *GL*7, 205, 318, 326–27; *MP*, 89, 120, 140; *TD*2, 152–59, 160–62, 211, 223, 226, 276, 296; *TD*3, 117, 120, 242, 245; *TD*4, 255–66.

79. Anselm, "Why God Became Man," 284–90.

80. *TD*4, 339.

81. *GL*6, 151–65.

82. For more on the these biblical words, see Darrin W. Snyder Belousek, *Atonement, Justice, and Peace: The Message of the Cross and the Mission of the Church* (Grand Rapids, MI: Eerdmans, 2012), 59–67.

83. Anthony W. Bartlett, *Cross Purposes: The Violent Grammar of Christian Atonement* (Harrisburg, PA: Trinity Press International, 2011).

84. Belousek, *Atonement, Justice, and Peace*, 22, 48, 79.

85. *GL*7, 204–7.

86. *GL*6, 152; *TD*4, 256–58.

87. *GL*7, 202–10; *TD*2, 151–58; *TD*3, 339–51; *TD*4, 328–51.

88. *TD*4, 340.

89. *TD*4, 212, 228, 339.

90. *TD*4, 228, 341–44.

91. *TD*4, 339. For more on Lactantius, see Lactantius, *Treatise on the Anger of God*.

92. *TD*4, 343–44. For more on Heschel's understanding of God's anger, see Abraham J. Heschel, *The Prophets* (New York: Harper & Row, 1962), 279–306.

93. *TD*2, 154.

94. *TD*4, 140.

95. *GL*6, 153–54; *TD*4, 212, 252–54, 331.

96. *TD*4, 242–43.

97. *TD*4, 242. Balthasar asks, How else can one "do justice to the numerous passages in Paul, in Hebrews, the First Letter of Peter and the two passages in Mark on the 'ransom for many' (10:45) and the blood 'poured out for many' (14:24, as in the other three Last Supper passages, cf. also Jn 6:51)"? (*TD*3, 113). Martin Hengel, who Balthasar believes offers an "astonishing contribution" to understanding Christ's representation (*TD*4, 11–12), shows how the vicarious and atoning aspects of Jesus's death trace back from Paul to the words of Jesus himself. See Hengel, *The Atonement: The Origins of the Doctrine in the New Testament*, trans. John Bowden (Eugene, OR: Wipf & Stock, 2007).

98. *TD*4, 244, 274, 338, 361.

99. *TD*4, 117, 228. Christopher D. Marshall demonstrates the Hebrew usage of "righteousness" or "justice" is primarily that of *action* and *power*: "Biblical justice is thus not a static state, but, says Abraham J. Heschel, 'a power that will strike and change, heal and restore, like a mighty stream bringing life to the parched land' . . . the justice of God is not primarily or normatively a retributive justice or a distributive justice but a restorative or reconstructive justice, an action by God that recreates *shalom* and makes things right." See Marshall, *Beyond Retribution: A New Testament Vision for Crime, Vision, and Punishment* (Grand Rapids, MI: Eerdmans, 2001), 53.

100. *TD*3, 118–20.

101. See Belousek, *Atonement, Justice, and Peace*, 90, 118.

102. Expiation: *TD*3, 113, 119, 408; *TD*4, 217, 241, 271, 274, 338, 347–48. Propitiation: *TD*4, 242. For an examination of Romans 3:25, see Belousek, *Atonement, Justice, and Peace*, 244–64; J. M. Gundry-Volf, "Expiation, Propitiation, Mercy Seat," in *Dictionary of Paul and His Letters*, ed. Gerald F. Hawthorne, Ralph P. Martin, and Daniel G. Reid (Downers Grove, IL: Intervarsity Press, 1993), 279–84.

103. George Hunsinger, *The Eucharist and Ecumenism: Let Us Keep the Feast* (Cambridge: Cambridge University Press, 2008), 174.

104. *HMR*, 23–24; *TD*4, 240–41, 338. Barth may be an underlying influence here; he formulates it similarly (*CD*, IV.1:251–52).

105. *GL*7, 204–5; *TD*3, 109–17.

106. Irenaeus, *Against Heresies* 3.16.6; 3.18.7; 3.20.2–3; 3.21.9–10; 3.22.3; 5.2.1; 5.14.1–4, 5.21.1; 5.23.2; 5.31.2. For a broad overview of Balthasar's relation to Irenaeus, see Kevin Mongrain, *The Systematic Thought of Hans Urs von Balthasar: An Irenaean Retrieval* (New York: Crossroad, 2002); O'Regan, *Anatomy of Misremembering*, 290–95.

107. *TD1*, 347–48, 363; *TD2*, 49–50, 144–45, 148, 195, 202, 266–71, 409; *TD3*, 220, 252, 341; *TD4*, 118, 326, 365–66, 384–86, 407, 498; *TD5*, 30, 128, 153–68.

108. Balthasar, *The Scandal of the Incarnation: Irenaeus "Against the Heresies,"* selected with an introduction by Hans Urs von Balthasar; trans. John Saward (San Francisco: Ignatius, 1981), 53–93.

109. *TD4*, 326.

110. Ulrich, *HA*, 176.

111. Pitstick, *Light in Darkness*, 110 (emphasis original).

112. Ibid., 112–13.

113. *GL7*, 202–11, 230–33; *MP*, 97–124.

114. *GL7*, 124, 230.

115. Pitstick, *Light in Darkness*, 96–97, 175–82, 339–40, 390.

116. *GL7*, 205.

117. *TD4*, 297–300, 303–13, 317, 334, 343; René Girard, *Things Hidden since the Foundation of the World*, trans. Stephen Bann and Michael Metteer (Stanford, CA: Stanford University Press, 1987); Girard, *Violence and the Sacred*, trans. Patrick Gregory (Baltimore: Johns Hopkins University Press, 1977).

118. Balthasar, "Die Neue Theorie," 184–85.

119. Girard, *Things Hidden*, 180–82, 229–30.

120. Ibid., 182, 226.

121. Ibid., 184–89, 195, 213, 231.

122. Girard, *Violence and the Sacred*.

123. *TD4*, 334–38.

124. *MP*, 89, 111; *TD4*, 237–38, 240–43, 315, 323, 326, 330, 334–35, 396, 501.

125. *TD4*, 330.

126. *TD4*, 297, 313.

127. Belousek, *Atonement, Justice, and Peace*, 296.

128. *TL2*, 148.

129. Balthasar, "Die Neue Theorie," 184–85; *TD4*, 240, 317, 337–38, 499–501; *TD5*, 247–56; Balthasar, "The Work and Suffering of Jesus: Continuity and Discontinuity," in *Faith in Christ and the Worship of Christ*, ed. Leo Scheffczyk, trans. Graham Harrison (San Francisco: Ignatius, 1982), 18.

130. Riches, *Ecce Homo*, 100–101.

131. Ibid., 196.

132. Of the secondary sources on Balthasar's theology of *Stellvertretung*, Aidan Nichols is one of the few that observes the kind of nuances that I attempt to bring to light: "A Catholic employment of the notion of representation has

taken into itself that of humankind's incorporation into Christ, since the action and suffering of our representative must have an inner, ontic effect—and not merely an external, forensic one—on those human persons involved in theodrama, in whose place he stands" (see Nichols, *No Bloodless Myth*, 100).

133. Andrew P. Klager, "Retaining and Reclaiming the Divine: Identification and the Recapitulation of Peace in St. Irenaeus of Lyons's Atonement Narrative," in *Stricken by God? Nonviolent Identification and the Victory of Christ*, ed. Brad Jersak and Michael Hardin (Grand Rapids, MI: Eerdmans, 2007), 440–52.

134. *TD4*, 242.

135. Balthasar, "Theology and Aesthetic," 65–66 (emphasis mine).

136. *DJ*, 32–33; *TD4*, 317, 335–36; Balthasar, "Theology and Aesthetic," 65–66.

137. *TD4*, 237.

138. *TD3*, 120–21.

139. *GL7*, 222–23, 244–50; *MP*, 91–94; *TD4*, 231–40, 334.

140. Balthasar, "Die Neue Theorie," 185: "Die 'Stunde,' auf die Jesus so bewußt zulebt, ist gewiß die Stunde und 'die Macht der Finsternis,' aber wesentlicher die Stunde, die der Vater ihm gesetzt hat und die er in seiner Kenntnis und Verwaltung behält."

141. *TD4*, 334.

142. *TD4*, 240, 337–38, 499–501; *TD5*, 247–56; Balthasar, "The Work and Suffering of Jesus," 18.

143. *TD4*, 245.

144. "Fallen" and "sinful" are interchangeable in Balthasar.

145. Kelly M. Kapic, "The Son's Assumption of a Human Nature: A Call for Clarity," *International Journal of Systematic Theology* 3, no. 2 (2001): 155. To understand Irving's view, see Edward Irving, *The Collected Writings of Edward Irving*, 5 vols., ed. G. Carlyle (London: Alexander Strahan, 1865); Colin E. Gunton, "Two Dogmas Revisited: Edward Irving's Christology," *Scottish Journal of Theology* 41, no. 3 (1988): 359–76; Graham McFarlane, *Christ and the Spirit: The Doctrine of the Incarnation according to Edward Irving* (Carlisle: Paternoster, 1996).

146. Barth, *CD*, I.2:151–56; Kapic, "The Son's Assumption," 156.

147. E. Jerome Van Kuiken, *Christ's Humanity in Current and Ancient Controversy: Fallen or Not?* (London: Bloomsbury T&T Clark, 2017).

148. *TD4*, 248.

149. Van Kuiken, *Christ's Humanity*.

150. T. A. Noble, "The Hallowing of the Flesh in Biblical and Patristic Christology," in *Whistling in the Dark: Of the Theology of Craig Keen*, ed. Janice McRandal and Stephen John Wright (Eugene, OR: Cascade Books, forthcoming).

151. Cyril of Alexandria, *Commentary on John*, ed. Joel C. Elowsky, trans. David R Maxwell (Downers Grove, IL: InterVarsity Press, 2015), 2:251.
152. Gregory of Nazianzus, *On God and Christ*, Oration 30.3.
153. Ibid.
154. Ibid., Letter 101.12.
155. Ibid., Oration 30.6.
156. Ibid., Oration 30.6.
157. *TD*4, 253 (emphasis original). Van Kuiken notes that though the sin Christ assumed is primarily *counterfactual*, there is some evidence of *factual* sin. See Van Kuiken, *Christ's Humanity*, 115–16.
158. John Damascene, *Exposition of the Orthodox Faith* 3.25.
159. *TD*4, 250, 253–54, 317.
160. Gregory of Nazianzus, *On God and Christ*, Letter 101.9, 101.12; Gregory of Nyssa, *The Life of Moses* (New York: Paulist Press, 1978), 62.
161. *TD*4, 284. For more on Balthasar's relationship to Luther, see Rodney Howsare, *Hans Urs von Balthasar and Protestantism* (London: T&T Clark, 2005), 42–76.
162. *TD*4, 284. The Finnish school of Lutheran studies disputes this reading of Luther's theology; see Mannermaa, *Christ Present in Faith*.
163. Martin Luther, *Lectures on Galatians 1535: Chapters 1–4*, vol. 26 of *Luther's Works*, ed. Jaroslav Pelikan and Walter Hansen (St. Louis: Concordia, 1963), 276–91.
164. Barth, *CD*, IV.1:215, 238, 254.
165. *TD*4, 267–73.
166. *TD*4, 273.
167. *CA*, 71–83; *GL*7, 148–49, 204–8, 298–304, 363, 396; *MP*, 100–104; *TL*2, 224–41.
168. *TDg*3, 310–11. The distance concept comes up more clearly later in the volume when Balthasar uses *heilige Distanz* and *unheilige Distanz* (*TDg*3, 337).
169. *TD*4, 333–35.
170. *TDg*3, 312.
171. *TDg*3, 310.
172. *TDg*3, 310: "Er kann es aufgrund seines topos innergöttlicher absoluter Differenz vom sch enkenden Vater."
173. *TD*4, 250.
174. *GL*7, 149, 207; *TD*4, 314, 324, 336, 349; *TL*2, 235–36.
175. For example, David Bentley Hart shows how the miracles are a sign of God's restoration of creation (Hart, *The Beauty of the Infinite*, 327–28). Barth also notes the sanctifying elements involved in Christ's assumption of the flesh (*CD*, IV.1:258–59).

176. Behr, *The Formation of Christian Theology*, 2.1:226–29.

177. There is an emphasis on the "pre-arranged death" in Gregory of Nyssa's teaching on the deification of the flesh, but it still includes the Incarnation: "Instead of the death occurring in the consequence of the birth, the birth on the contrary was accepted by him for the sake of the death" (Gregory of Nyssa, *The Great Catechism* 32, 35).

178. *TD3*, 240–41; *TD4*, 267, 272–73, 317.

179. *TD4*, 313–14, 337–38, 496.

180. *TD4*, 336.

181. *HMR*, 35; *TD4*, 489, 495–96.

182. *TD4*, 335–36.

183. *TD4*, 348.

184. *TD4*, 320, 349, 496.

185. *TD4*, 349.

186. *TD4*, 496.

187. *MP*, 79; *TD4*, 325, 338, 495; *TD5*, 256–65.

188. *GL6*, 214–16; *TD4*, 349, 495–96, 501; *TD5*, 256–65.

189. *TD4*, 333.

190. *TD4*, 501.

191. *ET4*, 408; *TD4*, 496; *TD5*, 300–304.

192. *TD4*, 496.

193. *MP*, 149.

194. *ET4*, 401–14; *GL7*, 228–35; *MP*, 148–81; *TD4*, 332–51; *TL2*, 345–61; *TD5*, 300–321.

195. *ET4*, 407–8; *GL7*, 230; *MP*, 150. Edward Oakes believes Balthasar is developing the tradition, but Pitstick argues that Balthasar departs from the tradition; see Edward T. Oakes, "The Internal Logic of Holy Saturday in the Theology of Hans Urs von Balthasar," *International Journal of Systematic Theology* 9, no. 2 (2007): 184–99; Oakes, "*Descensus* and Development: A Response to Recent Rejoinders," *International Journal of Systematic Theology* 13, no. 1 (2001): 3–24; Pitstick, *Light in the Darkness*. A direct exchange between the two writers has also appeared in *First Things*: Alyssa Lyra Pitstick and Edward T. Oakes, "Balthasar, Hell, and Heresy: An Exchange," *First Things*, December 2006, 25–29; Pitstick and Oakes, "More on Balthasar, Hell, and Heresy," *First Things*, January 2007, 16–18.

196. *ET4*, 407–8.

197. *ET4*, 408 (emphasis original).

198. *GL7*, 229.

199. *ET4*, 408–9; *GL7*, 229–32; *MP*, 161–67; *TD4*, 297.

200. *ET4*, 408.

201. *MP*, 160–68.

202. *TL2*, 345.

203. Ben Blackwell affirms the close relationship between substitution and representation in Pauline theology. See Blackwell, *Christosis: Engaging Paul's Soteriology with His Patristic Interpreters* (Grand Rapids, MI: Eerdmans, 2016), 227. In contrast, Moltmann (*The Crucified God*, 263) recommends speaking of Christ's representation without substitution language.

204. *TD5*, 272.

205. *HMR*, 15–16.

206. *TD4*, 351; *TD5*, 272, 277, 285, 312.

207. *TD4*, 348.

208. For Rahner's precise interpretation of *Repräsentation*, see Peterson, *Being Salvation*, 222–25.

209. For more on Balthasar's disagreement with Rahner's soteriology, see *TD4*, 273–84.

210. *TD4*, 350; *TD5*, 193, 202–3, 285–90.

211. *TD2*, 123.

212. *TD5*, 271.

213. *TD5*, 212–46; O'Regan, *Anatomy of Misremembering*, 221–44.

214. Heschel, *The Prophets*; Thomas R. Krenski, *Passio caritatis: Trinitarische Passiologie im Werk Hans Urs von Balthasar* (Einsiedeln: Johannes Werlag, 1990); O'Hanlon, *The Immutability of God*; Thomas Weinandy, *Does God Suffer?* (Notre Dame, IN: University of Notre Dame, 2000).

215. *TD4*, 336.

216. *GL7*, 232; *TD4*, 333, 336, 338, 348–49, 496, 499–500; *TD5*, 305–11. In the *Epilogue* (120) to the trilogy, Balthasar is more cautious, linking Christ's alienation on the cross to his assumption of human nature in the Incarnation, but he says that since the assumption is by a divine person, then the alienation Christ experiences must extend into the triune life. However, here the subject that causes the Father and Son to experience separation is the unholy alienation, not the Father's direct action against the Son.

217. Albeit for different reasons, Ben Quash also notices the epic qualities of Balthasar's theology (Quash, *Theology and the Drama of History*, 131–64).

218. Weinandy, *Does God Suffer?*, 218.

219. Williams, *Tragic Imagination*, 122.

220. O'Regan, *Anatomy of Misremembering*, 226.

221. *TD1*, 343–412; *TD4*, 95–135; *TD5*, 323–69. Barth also links Christ's representation to liberation, but more specifically to liberation from judgment (*CD*, IV.1:233–35). Moltmann (*The Crucified God*, 263) believes Christ's representation leads to liberation from suffering in isolation.

222. *TD*1, 369; *TD*4, 121.

223. Donald MacKinnon, "Atonement and Tragedy," in *Borderlands of Theology and Other Essays*, ed. George W. Roberts and Donovan E. Smucker (Eugene, OR: Wipf and Stock, 2011), 97–104.

224. Hart, *The Beauty of the Infinite*, 380–87.

225. Jennifer Wallace, "Tragic Sacrifice and Faith: Abraham and Agamemnon Again," in *Christian Theology and Tragedy*, ed. Kevin Taylor and Giles Waller (Burlington, VT: Ashgate, 2011), 38–39.

226. David Bentley Hart, "No Shadow of Turning: On Divine Impassibility," *Pro Ecclesia* 11, no. 2 (2002): 192.

227. Francesca Murphy, review of *The Beauty of the Infinite*, by David Bentley Hart, *Scottish Journal of Theology* 60, no. 1 (2007): 80–89.

228. Ben Quash, "Four Biblical Characters: In Search of Tragedy," in *Christian Theology and Tragedy*, ed. Kevin Taylor and Giles Waller (Burlington, VT: Ashgate, 2011), 15–34.

229. Hart, *The Beauty of the Infinite*, 29.

230. *ET*3, 400.

231. Quash, "Four Biblical Characters," 21. For a prime example of how tragedy is conceptualized differently, see Hart's review of Williams's *The Tragic Imagination*: David Bentley Hart, "The Gospel according to Melpomene: Reflections on Rowan Williams's *The Tragic Imagination*," *Modern Theology* 34, no. 2 (2018): 226.

232. Quash, "Four Biblical Characters," 15.

233. Ibid., 15 (emphasis original).

234. Ibid., 29–31.

235. *TD*1, 424–26.

236. *TD*1, 426–27 (emphasis original).

237. Hart, *The Beauty of the Infinite*, 383.

238. Murphy, review of *The Beauty of the Infinite*, by David Bentley Hart, 86 (emphasis original). Rowan Williams also makes this same distinction between a tragic hero and melodrama's victim (Williams, *Tragic Imagination*, 87).

239. *TD*1, 433.

240. *TD*1, 431–32.

241. *TD*1, 427.

242. *TD*4, 327–28.

243. Williams, *Tragic Imagination*, 18, 25.

244. Quash, "Four Biblical Characters," 31.

245. Cited by Belousek, *Atonement, Justice, and Peace*, 298. For more on the relationship between goats and gifts in postmodernity, see Kevin J. Vanhoozer, "The Atonement in Postmodernity: Guilt, Goats, and Gifts," in *The Glory of*

the Atonement, ed. Charles E Hill and Frank A. James III (Downers Grove, IL: InterVarsity Press, 2004), 367–407.

246. Barth, *CD*, IV.1:256.
247. Behr, *The Formation of Christian Theology*, 2.1:228.
248. *HMR*, 37.
249. Quash, *Theology and the Drama of History*, 114–18.
250. *TD4*, 237–38.
251. *TD5*, 213.
252. David F. Ford, "Tragedy and Atonement," in *Christ, Ethics, and Tragedy: Essays in Honour of Donald MacKinnon*, ed. Kenneth Surin (Cambridge: Cambridge University Press, 1989), 117–30.
253. Ford, "Tragedy and Atonement," 122.
254. Kevin Taylor, "Hans Urs von Balthasar and Christ the Tragic Hero," in *Christian Theology and Tragedy*, ed. Kevin Taylor and Giles Waller (Burlington, VT: Ashgate, 2011), 134.
255. Taylor "Balthasar and Christ the Tragic Hero," 142–48.
256. *TD5*, 252–69, 323–39, 498–507.
257. *TD5*, 100–102.
258. *TD1*, 433. There is a resemblance between Balthasar's Christ and Hegel's tragic hero; see Mark R. Roche, "The Greatness and Limits of Hegel's Theory of Tragedy," in *A Companion to Tragedy*, ed. Rebecca Bushnell (Oxford: Blackwell, 2005), 51–67; Robert R. Williams, *Tragedy, Recognition, and the Death of God: Studies in Hegel and Nietzsche* (Oxford: Oxford University Press, 2012).
259. Williams, *Tragic Imagination*, 123.
260. Carpenter, *Theo-Poetics*, 21–22.
261. *TD1*, 370.
262. Williams, *Tragic Imagination*, 82–105.
263. *TD4*, 367–83, 476–87; *TD5*, 323–29.
264. Quash, *Theology and the Drama of History*, 216; Walatka, *Von Balthasar and the Option for the Poor*, 4, 18.
265. *TD4*, 483.
266. *TD4*, 476–87.
267. *TD5*, 325.
268. *TD5*, 83, 105, 112.
269. *TD5*, 251.
270. *TD4*, 499–500.
271. *TD5*, 429.
272. Rowan Williams, "Trinity and Ontology," in *Christ, Ethics, and Tragedy: Essays in Honour of Donald MacKinnon*, ed. Kenneth Surin (Cambridge: Cambridge University Press, 1989), 71–92.

273. Williams, *Tragic Imagination*, 18.
274. *TD*5, 251–52, 265, 327.
275. *TD*5, 251.
276. Hart, *The Beauty of the Infinite*, 380–87.
277. *TD*5, 245.
278. *TD*4, 326.
279. Walatka also distinguishes between the vertical and horizontal dimensions of Balthasar's theology of the cross. See Walatka, *Von Balthasar and the Option for the Poor*, 125–26.
280. *ET*3, 401.
281. Rogers, *After the Spirit*, 96–97.
282. Moltmann, *The Crucified God*, 145–153, 235–39.
283. Behr, *The Formation of Christian Theology*, 2.1:226–29.
284. *TD*5, 326.
285. *TD*5, 120.
286. Ulrich, *HA*, 319–20.
287. It should be mentioned that Barth provides a similar construction. He notes that any "negative form" of reconciliation is contained within a positive act of God (*CD*, IV.1:185, 257–59).
288. *TL*2, 229.
289. *TD*5, 261.
290. This amended formulation can also be found in another dramatic theology; see Vanhoozer, *The Drama of Doctrine*, 390; *Remythologizing Theology*, 461.
291. *TD*4, 349, 362.

Chapter Four

1. *TD*4, 367–88, 406–23; Bonhoeffer, *Ethics*; Sölle, *Christ the Representative*, 14–15.
2. Sarah Coakley, *God, Sexuality, and Self: An Essay "On the Trinity"* (Cambridge: Cambridge University Press, 2013), 309 (emphasis original).
3. Jonathan Martin Ciraulo notes that Balthasar infrequently uses the term "divinization" throughout his corpus, but he is "obsessed" with the concept. Creaturely participation in the divine or holiness is certainly a central theme throughout Balthasar's entire project. See Ciraulo, "Hans Urs von Balthasar's Indifference to Divinization," in *Mystical Doctrines of Deification*, ed. John Arblaster and Rob Faesen (New York: Routledge, 2019), 165–85.

4. *TD*4, 367–88, 406–23.

5. Walatka, *Von Balthasar and the Option for the Poor*, 89–90.

6. *TKB*, 386–89.

7. *TD*5, 382.

8. *TD*3, 354–55; *TL*3, 327.

9. Cyril O'Regan, "Two Forms of Catholic Apocalyptic," *International Journal of Systematic Theology* 20, no. 1 (2019): 54, 60–61.

10. Both "emplaced *theosis*" and "Continual Representative" are phrases I have coined. I will explain the meaning of these two phrases in the first section of this chapter. Balthasar does not use them to my knowledge. He does, however, speak of the Spirit as the "continual re-presence" (*dauernde Re-Präsenz*) of Christ (*TDg*3, 365).

11. Williams, *Christ the Heart of Creation*, 197.

12. The dramatic nature of Mariology and the sacraments and their relation to *theosis* are not considered here; I am primarily developing the relationship between *theosis* and representation.

13. *TD*4, 406–23.

14. Balthasar closes his trilogy with a theology of the Spirit, noting in the preface of *TL*3 that all of "salvation history" should "emerge according to the fundamental trinitarian dimensions of the Spirit" (13).

15. Thomas Weinandy, *The Father's Spirit of Sonship: Reconceiving the Trinity* (Edinburgh: T&T Clark, 1995). For patristic witness to this idea, see Athanasius the Great and Didymus the Blind, *Works on the Spirit* 1.25–26, 31; Basil the Great, *On the Holy Spirit*.

16. Athanasius the Great and Didymus the Blind, *Works on the Spirit*, 1.25.

17. *TKB*, 365–67. For more on the differences between Barth and Balthasar on the topic of divinization, see Cynthia Peters Anderson, *Reclaiming Participation: Christ as God's Life for All* (Minneapolis: Fortress, 2014).

18. *TKB*, 365.

19. Barth, *CD*, IV.1:97, 105, 548, 554, 581–91, 589; IV.2:503, 514–16, 532–33.

20. Barth, *CD*, IV.1:514.

21. Bruce L. McCormack, "*Justa Aliena*: Karl Barth in Conversation with the Evangelical Doctrine of Imputed Righteousness," in *Justification in Perspective: Historical Developments and Contemporary Challenges*, ed. Bruce L. McCormack (Grand Rapids, MI: Baker, 2006), 189, 193–95.

22. John Calvin, *Institutes of the Christian Religion*, ed. John T. McNeill, trans. Ford Lewis Battles (Philadelphia: Westminster Press, 1967), 1:592–621, 684–88, 754–62; Martin Luther, *Career of the Reformer I*, in *Luther's Works*, ed.

Harold J. Grimm and Helmut T. Lehmann (Philadelphia: Fortress Press, 1957), 3:296–306, 333–77.

23. Barth, *CD*, IV.2:503, 527, 531; George Hunsinger, *Disruptive Grace: Studies in the Theology of Karl Barth* (Grand Rapids, MI: Eerdmans, 2001), 272; McCormack, "*Justa Aliena*," 192, 195.

24. *TKB*, 366.

25. *TKB*, 372–77.

26. Barth, *CD*, IV.1:768.

27. *TKB*, 398–99.

28. Joachim von Soosten, editor's afterword to *Sanctorum Communio*, by Dietrich Bonhoeffer, 293, 302–3.

29. Colin Gunton, "Salvation," in *The Cambridge Companion to Karl Barth*, ed. John Webster (Cambridge: Cambridge University Press, 2000), 156; Robert Jenson, "You Wonder Where the Spirit Went," *Pro Ecclesia* 2, no. 3 (1993): 296–304; Rogers, *After the Spirit*, 19–23; Alan Torrance, "Trinity," in *The Cambridge Companion to Karl Barth*, ed. John Webster (Cambridge: Cambridge University Press, 2000), 82–83; Williams, *On Christian Theology*, 116–18.

30. Williams, *On Christian Theology*, 117.

31. Ibid., 120. For more details on Williams's critique of Barth, see Williams, *Wrestling with Angels*, 106–49.

32. *TL3*, 18–20, 202–3.

33. *TL3*, 74.

34. *TD4*, 366–67.

35. Gregory of Nyssa, *Life of Moses*, 111–20.

36. *TL3*, 203.

37. Walatka, *Von Balthasar and the Option for the Poor*, 166.

38. Rogers, *After the Spirit*, 54.

39. Ibid., 56.

40. For more on a theology of place, see John Inge, *A Christian Theology of Place* (Aldershot: Ashgate, 2003).

41. Rogers, *After the Spirit*, 155.

42. Basil the Great, *On the Holy Spirit*, 93–97.

43. Ibid., 95.

44. Rogers, *After the Spirit*, 200–207.

45. *TL1*, 13.

46. *CSL*, 211–12; *TD4*, 377; *TL3*, 167–70.

47. *EP*, 113–14; *PT*, 149–51; *TD4*, 399; Nicholas Lash, *Holiness, Speech, and Silence: Reflections on the Question of God* (Burlington, VT: Ashgate, 2004), 41.

48. Aquinas, *ST* IIIa.60.3.

49. Vatican II, *Lumen gentium*, 1, 48; Todd Walatka, "The Church as Sacrament: Gustavo Gutierrez and John Sobrino as Interpreters of *Lumen Gentium*," *Horizons* 42, no. 1 (2015): 70–95.

50. *TD4*, 391–423.

51. *TD5*, 467; *TL3*, 247.

52. Cyril of Alexandria, *Commentary on John*, 1:96–97. For a detailed study of *theosis* in Cyril of Alexandria, see Daniel A. Keating, *The Appropriation of the Divine Life in Cyril of Alexandria* (Oxford: Oxford University Press, 2004).

53. Blackwell, *Christosis*, 96–97.

54. Cyril of Alexandria, *On the Unity of Christ*, 81–82; Cyril of Alexandria, *Commentary on John*, 1:69–72, 85.

55. Cyril of Alexandria, *Commentary on John*, 2:295–307.

56. Blackwell, *Christosis*, 88.

57. I focus primarily on the relationship between representation and the missional character of Balthasar's anthropology and ecclesiology, but Walatka provides an excellent overview of Balthasar's anthropology and mission. See Walatka, *Von Balthasar and the Option for the Poor*, 150.

58. *PT*, 15–16.

59. Martin Laird, "Under Solomon's Tutelage: The Education of Desire in the Homilies of the Song of Song," in *Re-thinking Gregory of Nyssa*, ed. Sarah Coakley (Oxford: Blackwell, 2003), 517.

60. *TD5*, 427.

61. *TD5*, 427.

62. *TD4*, 406.

63. Williams, *On Christian Theology*, 131–47.

64. Carolyn A. Chau, *Solidarity with the World: Charles Taylor and Hans Urs von Balthasar on Faith, Modernity, and Catholic Mission* (Eugene, OR: Cascade, 2016), 192; Walatka, *Von Balthasar and the Option for the Poor*, 150.

65. Ciraulo, "Balthasar's Indifference to Divinization," 175.

66. C. Paul Schroeder, introduction to *On Social Justice*, by Basil the Great, 20–25.

67. Basil the Great, *On Social Justice*, *To the Rich*, 1–9.

68. *TD4*, 406: "As members of his body, 'which is the Church,' we are equipped by the Holy Spirit with our most personal mission—and this is, as we have shown, the very core of our personal being—but this mission can be nothing other than a participation in the once-and-for-all, all-embracing mission of Christ."

69. Rogers, *After the Spirit*, 144–45 (emphasis original).

70. Basil the Great, *On the Human Condition*, *Long Rules*, 3.

71. Ibid., 7.4.
72. Ibid., 7.2.
73. *TD5*, 105–6.
74. Sölle recognizes how Christ's activity of liberation is implicit in those who act on his behalf: "Because Christ dared provisionally to represent the absent God, he is present implicitly whenever a man acts or suffers in God's stead. What does it mean to act in God's stead and to represent him? It means so to assume responsibility for the irreplaceable identity of others that it remains possible for them to attain identity" (see Sölle, *Christ the Representative*, 134).
75. *TD5*, 404.
76. Cyril of Alexandria, *Commentary on John*, 2:303.
77. *Prayer*, 76.
78. *TD4*, 388; Rogers, *After the Spirit*, 99–100, 181–83.
79. For an overview of how the "incorporative" trinitarian logic of Romans 8 is used in the church fathers, see Coakley, *God, Sexuality, and Self*, 100–151.
80. Quash, "Drama and the Ends of Modernity," 163–64.
81. Williams, *The Edge of Words*, 184.
82. Przywara, *Analogia Entis*, 265.
83. Augustine, *Confessions* 3.11.
84. Przywara, *Analogia Entis*, 124.
85. Sölle believes the individual's security lies in being represented even when he or she is detached from his or her role. Such language is grounded in the Christian idea of the soul; see Sölle, *Christ the Representative*, 24–30. Gestrich calls the Spirit a keeper of humanity's place and the Son a keeper of humanity's existence; see Christof Gestrich, "God Takes Our Place: A Religious-Philosophical Approach to the Concept of *Stellvertretung*," *Modern Theology* 17, no. 3 (2001): 328.
86. *TD3*, 201
87. Ulrich, *HA*, 112–13.
88. Ulrich, *HA*, 321–29.
89. *TD5*, 375–85.
90. *TD5*, 482–83.
91. *TD5*, 521.
92. Chau, *Solidarity with the World*, 182.
93. *EP*, 102; Sölle, *Christ the Representative*, 15.
94. *TD1*, 392.
95. Donnelly, *Saving Beauty*, 208.
96. *TD1*, 397.
97. *TD4*, 421–22; Balthasar, *Bernanos: An Ecclesial Existence*, trans. Erasmo Leiva-Merikakis (San Francisco: Ignatius, 1996).

98. *TD*1, 399–400.
99. *TD*5, 339.
100. *TD*1, 400.
101. *TD*4, 421–23.
102. *TD*4, 423.
103. Balthasar, *First Glance at Adrienne von Speyr* (San Francisco: Ignatius, 1981); *GL*7, 458–70; *TD*5, 498–506; *TL*2, 360–61; *TL*3, 193.
104. Walatka, *Von Balthasar and the Option for the Poor*, 73–78.
105. Quash, *Theology and the Drama of History*, 216.
106. Williams, *Wrestling with Angels*, 84–85.
107. Walatka, *Von Balthasar and the Option for the Poor*, 75.
108. *TD*5, 382, 417.
109. Sölle, *Christ the Representative*, 61–62.
110. Far be it from the theological enterprise to say quantum entanglement means vicarious representation, yet there may be some form of analogy between Einstein's infamous phrase "spooky action at a distance," describing the interaction between two nonlocal particles, and vicarious action. For more information on quantum physics, the God-creation relationship, and divine action, see Jacob Lett, "Jürgen Moltmann's Doctrine of Divine Action: Towards a More Integrative Approach to His Doctrine of Creation," *Wesleyan Theological Journal* 49, no. 2 (2014): 204–42; John Polkinghorne, *The Trinity and an Entangled World: Relationality in Physical Science and Theology* (Grand Rapids, MI: Eerdmans, 2010); Ernest L. Simmons, *The Entangled Trinity: Quantum Physics and Theology* (Minneapolis: Fortress Press, 2014).
111. For Balthasar, the Marian nature of the church's participation in Christ is vital, but beyond the scope of this chapter; see Balthasar, *Mary for Today* (San Francisco: Ignatius, 1988); *TD*4, 405–6; *TD*5, 462. Also, a good overview and critique of Balthasar's Mariology can be found in Lucy Gardner, "Balthasar and the Figure of Mary," in Oakes and Moss, eds., *The Cambridge Companion to Hans Urs von Balthasar*, 64–78; Corinne Crammer, "One Sex or Two? Balthasar's Theology of the Sexes," in Oakes and Moss, eds., *The Cambridge Companion to Hans Urs von Balthasar*, 93–112.
112. O'Regan, *Anatomy of Misremembering*, 120.
113. *TD*2, 54–62.
114. Quash, "Drama and the Ends of Modernity," 148.
115. *TD*2, 55–56.
116. *TL*1, 202: the social nature of truth is clearly already established early in Balthasar's theology, as *TL*1 is a reissuing of *Truth of the World* (1947).
117. Williams, *The Edge of Words*, 70.
118. Ibid., 69.

119. Ibid., 189.

120. Charles Taylor, *The Language Animal: The Full Shape of the Human Linguistic Capacity* (Cambridge, MA: The Belknap Press of Harvard University Press, 2016), 103–28.

121. Ibid., 21, 32–34.

122. Ibid., 264–88.

123. Brian McKinlay, "Ludwig Wittgenstein in Rowan Williams's Theological Account of Language," *New Blackfriars* 98 (2017): 329.

124. Williams, *The Edge of Words*, 186–97. For an elaboration on Hegel's understanding of description versus logic, see Adams, *Eclipse of Grace*, 24–25.

125. Williams, *The Edge of Words*, 188.

126. Anne Carpenter also positively relates Balthasar's and Taylor's philosophies of language. See Carpenter, *Theo-Poetics*, 122–25.

127. Ulrich, *HA*, 333–39.

128. Ulrich, *HA*, 333.

129. Quoted by Bieler, introduction to *HA*, xl–xli.

130. Ulrich, *HA*, 333, 337.

131. Ulrich, *HA*, 327–28, 334–39.

132. D. C. Schindler, *Hans Urs von Balthasar and the Dramatic Structure of Truth: A Philosophical Investigation* (New York: Fordham University Press, 2004), 212.

133. Ulrich, *Leben in Der Einheit von Leben und Tod*, 147–99.

134. Bieler, introduction to *HA*, xxxviii (emphasis original).

135. Ibid., xxxviii; Schindler, *Balthasar and the Dramatic Structure of Truth*, 212–13.

136. Ulrich, *Leben in Der Einheit von Leben und Tod*, 159, 188.

137. Louis Cozolino, *The Neuroscience of Human Relationships: Attachment and the Developing Social Brain* (New York: W. W. Norton, 2014); Antonio Damasio, *Self Comes to Mind: Constructing the Conscious Brain* (New York: Vintage, 2012); Russell K. Schutt, Larry J. Seidman, and Matcheri Keshavan, eds., *Social Neuroscience: Brain, Mind, and Society* (Cambridge, MA: Harvard University Press, 2015); Daniel J. Siegel, *The Developing Mind: How Relationships and the Brain Interact to Shape Who We Are* (New York: Guilford Press, 2015).

138. Siegel, *The Developing Mind*, 308.

139. *PT*, 12.

140. *TD2*, 57.

141. Quash, "Drama and the Ends of Modernity," 150.

142. On the tradition as "an argument extended through time in which certain fundamental agreements are defined and redefined," see Alasdair MacIntyre,

Whose Justice? Which Rationality? (Notre Dame, IN: University of Notre Dame Press, 1988), 12.

143. Bieler, introduction to *HA*, xl.

144. Schindler, "A Very Critical Response to Karen Kilby," 82–83.

145. *MW*, 95.

146. *ET*2, 421–457; Balthasar, *Our Task*; Juan M. Sara, "Secular Institutes according to Hans Urs von Balthasar," *Communio* 29, no. 2 (2002): 309–36.

147. Carpenter, *Theo-Poetics*, 123.

148. Lewis Ayres, "On Not Three People," 457.

149. Laird, "Under Solomon's Tutelage," 525.

150. A. N. Williams, *The Ground of Union: Deification in Aquinas and Palamas* (Oxford: Oxford University Press, 1999), 34–101, 157–75.

151. Williams, *The Ground of Union*, 167.

152. John R. Betz, introduction to *Analogia Entis*, by Przywara, 49.

153. Martin, *Balthasar and the Critical Appropriation*, 204.

154. Ibid., 197.

155. *TD*5, 489–521.

156. Ulrich, *HA*, 5.

157. Ulrich, *HA*, 334.

158. Schindler, "A Very Critical Response to Karen Kilby."

159. Balthasar, "Editorial," 162. As I mentioned in the introduction, Balthasar also describes Charles Péguy as a unique figure who simultaneously represents the world and the church. The term Balthasar uses here in *GL*3 is *Repräsentation*, which he defines as "solidarity" (*H*2/2, 773–79). Balthasar later prefers the nuances of *Stellvertretung* over "solidarity" when it pertains to Christ's action for us, but there does not seem to be a major difference between the way he uses *Repräsentation* and *Solidarität* in *GL*3 and *Stellvertretung* in the *Theo-Drama* when the reference is human or ecclesial action for others.

160. Derek Brown, "Kneeling in the Street: Recontextualizing Balthasar," *New Blackfriars* 99 (2018): 788–806.

161. Williams, *Christ the Heart of Creation*, 233–36, 245.

162. For more on the relationship between personhood and place, see Mark R. Wynn, *Faith and Place: An Essay in Embodied Religious Epistemology* (Oxford: Oxford University Press, 2009).

163. Bonhoeffer, *Ethics*, 1, 154.

164. Ibid., 3 (emphasis original).

165. Ibid., 178.

166. Ibid., 155–56, 160.

167. Ibid., 157.

168. Ibid., 146–47, 297, 309–10.

169. Quash, "Drama and the Ends of Modernity," 140.

170. Jenson, *Systematic Theology*, 1:205–6; Rogers, *After the Spirit*, 159–60.

171. Gestrich, "God Takes Our Place," 326.

172. "We have seen a further, generalized instance of this relationship in Michael Banner's proposal that a Christian ethic should be founded upon the narratively constituted identity of the place which is the world—so that the fittingness of various behaviors is to be assessed by reference to their congruence with this 'place'" (see Wynn, *Faith and Place*, 84).

173. Quoted by Clifford J. Green, *Bonhoeffer: A Theology of Sociality* (Grand Rapids, MI: Eerdmans, 1999), 56.

174. Bonhoeffer, *Ethics*, 177; Williams, *Christ the Heart of Creation*, 207.

175. For more on Balthasar's dramatic conception of the Eucharist, see *TD*4, 389–406.

176. My aim here is not to condone violence or a just war theory, but to elucidate the nature of dramatic action for others. I use Bonhoeffer because he personally integrates representation with his Christology and ethics. I also use Dorothy Day's nonviolent action for the displaced as an example. In a completely different way, Simeon the Stylite also acts bodily, socially, and dramatically for others through pillar-standing, becoming a "communicative sign" of Christian liturgy (Rogers, *After the Spirit*, 183–88).

177. Bonhoeffer, *Ethics*, 153.

178. Ibid., 148.

179. Ibid., 156.

180. Ibid., 158.

181. Green, *Bonhoeffer: A Theology of Sociality*, 304–21.

182. Soosten, editor's afterword, 305.

183. Bonhoeffer, *Ethics*, 147, 166.

184. William T. Cavanaugh, "Dorothy Day and the Mystical Body of Christ in the Second World War," in *Dorothy Day and the Catholic Worker Movement*, ed. William Thorn, Phillip Runkel, and Susan Mountin (Milwaukee: Marquette University Press, 2011), 463.

185. Pope Francis, *Maiorem hac Dilectionem: On the Offer of Life*, The Holy See, July 11, 2017, https://www.vatican.va/content/francesco/en/motu_proprio/documents/papa-francesco-motu-proprio_20170711_maiorem-hac-dilectionem.html.

186. Brown, "Kneeling in the Street: Recontextualizing Balthasar," 803–4.

187. *TD*3, 434–35; *TD*4, 482–87.

188. Balthasar, "Catholicism and the *Communion of Saints*," *Communio* 15, no. 2 (1988): 163–68.

189. Williams, *Wrestling with Angels*, 53–76. The link between representation, Christian engagement with the world, and historical suffering seems to be even more direct in Fyodor Dostoevsky's *The Idiot*. Prince Myshkin's reception of the sufferings of the key characters inevitably leads to his own mental and physical suffering.

190. Williams, *Augustine*, 152.

191. William Bush, *To Quell the Terror: The Mystery of the Vocation of the Sixteen Carmelites of Compiègne Guillotined July 17, 1794* (Washington, DC: Institute of Carmelite Studies Publications, 1999); Matthew E. Bunson, "They Sang All the Way to the Guillotine," *Catholic Answers* 18, no. 4 (2007), https://www.catholic.com/magazine/print-edition/they-sang-all-the-way-to-the-guillotine; Terrye Newkirk, *The Mantle of Elijah: The Martyrs of Compiegne as Prophets of the Modern Age* (Washington, DC: Institute of Carmelite Studies Publications, 1995).

192. *TD5*, 502.

Conclusion

1. *EP*, 119.
2. *TDg3*, 11.
3. *TD4*, 332.
4. Williams, *Christ the Heart of Creation*, 197.
5. Nichols, *No Bloodless Myth*, 99.
6. Babini, "Jesus Christ," 226.

BIBLIOGRAPHY

Selected Works by Hans Urs von Balthasar

For an exhaustive list of Balthasar's works, see Cornelia Capol and Claudia Müller, *Hans Urs von Balthasar: Bibliographie, 1925–2005* (Einsiedeln: Johannes Verlag, 2005).

"Asceticism." *Communio* 27 (2000): 14–26.
Bernanos: An Ecclesial Existence. Translated by Erasmo Leiva-Merikakis. San Francisco: Ignatius, 2011.
"Catholicism and the Communion of Saints." *Communio* 15, no. 2 (1988): 163–68.
"Christ: Alpha and Omega." *Communio* 23, no. 3 (1996): 465–71.
Christian Meditation. Translated by Mary Theresilde Skerry. San Francisco: Ignatius, 2011.
"Christian Prayer." *Communio* 5, no. 1 (1978): 15–22.
The Christian State of Life. Translated by Mary Frances McCarthy. San Francisco: Ignatius, 1983.
"Communio: A Program." *Communio* 33, no. 1 (2006): 153–69.
Convergences: To the Sources of Christian Mystery. Translated by E. A. Nelson. San Francisco: Ignatius, 1984.
Cosmic Liturgy: The Universe according to Maximus the Confessor. Translated by Brian E. Daley. San Francisco: Ignatius, 2003.
"Creation and Trinity." *Communio* 15, no. 3 (1988): 285–93.
Credo: Meditations on the Apostles' Creed. Translated by David Kipp. San Francisco: Ignatius, 1990.
"Crucifixus etiam pro nobis." *Communio Internationale Katholische Zeitschrift* 9 (1980): 26–35.
Dare We Hope That All Men Be Saved? Translated by David Kipp and Lothar Krauth. San Francisco: Ignatius, 1988.
"Death Is Swallowed Up by Life." *Communio* 14, no. 1 (1987): 49–54.

"Die neue Theorie von Jesus als dem 'Sundenbock.'" *Communio Internationale Katholische Zeitschrift* 9 (1980): 184–85.

"Die Selbstbewusstein Jesu." *Communio Internationale Katholische Zeitschrift* 8 (1979): 30–39.

Does Jesus Know Us? Do We Know Him? Translated by Graham Harrison. San Francisco: Ignatius, 1983.

"Drei Merkmale des Christlichen." *Wort und Wahrheit* 4 (1949): 401–15.

"Earthly Beauty and Divine Glory." *Communio* 10, no. 3 (1983): 202–6.

"Editorial: The Meaning of the *Communion of Saints*." *Communio* 15, no. 2 (1988): 160–62.

Elizabeth of Dijon. London: Harvill, 1956.

Elucidations. Translated by John Riches. London: SPCK, 1975.

Engagement with God: The Drama of Christian Discipleship. Translated by R. John Halliburton. London: SPCK, 1975.

Epilogue. Translated by Edward T. Oakes. San Francisco: Ignatius, 1991.

Explorations in Theology I: The Word Made Flesh. Translated by A. V. Littledale and Alexander Dru. San Francisco: Ignatius, 1989.

Explorations in Theology II: Spouse of the Word. Translated by A. V. Littledale and Alexander Dru. San Francisco: Ignatius, 1991.

Explorations in Theology III: Creator Spirit. Translated by Brian McNeil. San Francisco: Ignatius, 1993.

Explorations in Theology IV: Spirit and Institution. Translated by Edward T. Oakes. San Francisco: Ignatius, 1995.

"The Fathers, the Scholastics, and Ourselves." *Communio* 24, no. 2 (1997): 347–96.

First Glance at Adrienne von Speyr. Translated by Antje Lawry and Sergia Englund. San Francisco: Ignatius, 1981.

"From the Theology of God to Theology in the Church." *Communio* 9, no. 3 (1982): 195–223.

"Georges Bernanos on Reason: Prophetic, Free, and Catholic." *Communio* 23, no. 2 (1996): 389–418.

The Glory of the Lord: A Theological Aesthetics I: Seeing the Form. Edited by Joseph Fessio and John Riches. Translated by Erasmo Leiva-Merikakis. San Francisco: Ignatius, 2009.

The Glory of the Lord: A Theological Aesthetics II: Studies in Theological Style: Clerical Styles. Edited by John Riches. Translated by Andrew Louth, Francis McDonagh, and Brian McNeil. San Francisco: Ignatius, 1984.

The Glory of the Lord: A Theological Aesthetics III: Studies in Theological Style: Lay Styles. Edited by John Riches. Translated by Andrew Louth, John Saward, Martin Simon, and Rowan Williams. San Francisco: Ignatius, 1986.

The Glory of the Lord: A Theological Aesthetics IV: The Realm of Metaphysics in Antiquity. Edited by John Riches. Translated by Oliver Davies, Andrew Louth, Brian McNeil, John Saward, and Rowan Williams. San Francisco: Ignatius, 1989.

The Glory of the Lord: A Theological Aesthetics V: The Realm of Metaphysics in the Modern Age. Edited by John Riches. Translated by Oliver Davies, Andrew Louth, Brian McNeil, John Saward, and Rowan Williams. San Francisco: Ignatius, 1991.

The Glory of the Lord: A Theological Aesthetics VI: Theology: The Old Covenant. Edited by John Riches. Translated by Brian McNeil and Erasmo Leiva-Merikakis. San Francisco: Ignatius, 1991.

The Glory of the Lord: A Theological Aesthetics VII: Theology: The New Covenant. Edited by John Riches. Translated by Brian McNeil. San Francisco: Ignatius, 1989.

"God Is His Own Exegete." *Communio* 13, no. 4 (1986): 280–87.

The Grain of Wheat: Aphorisms. Translated by Erasmo Leiva-Merikakis. San Francisco: Ignatius, 1995.

Heart of the World. Translated by Erasmo Leiva-Merikakis. San Francisco: Ignatius, 1980.

Herrlichkeit: Eine theologische Ästhetik II/2. Einsiedeln: Johannes Verlag, 1962.

Herrlichkeit: Eine theologische Ästhetik III/2.2: Neuer Bund. Einsiedeln: Johannes Verlag, 1969.

"The Holy Church and the Eucharistic Sacrifice." *Communio* 12, no. 2 (1985): 139–45.

In the Fullness of Faith: On the Centrality of the Distinctively Catholic. Translated by Graham Harrison. San Francisco: Ignatius, 1988.

"Jesus and Forgiveness." *Communio* 11, no. 4 (1984): 322–34.

"Jesus as Child and His Praise of the Child." *Communio* 22, no. 4 (1995): 625–34.

"Joy and the Cross." *Communio* 31, no. 2 (2004): 332–44.

"Katholizismus und Gemeinschaft der Heiligen." *Communio Internationale Katholische Zeitschrift* 17 (1988): 3–8.

Life out of Death: Meditation on the Easter Mystery. Translated by Martina Stockl. Philadelphia: Fortress, 1985.

Love Alone Is Credible. Translated by D. C. Schindler. San Francisco: Ignatius, 2004.

Love Alone: The Way of Revelation. Translated by Alexander Dru. London: Sheed and Ward, 1970.

Man in History. London: Sheed and Ward, 1967.

Martin Buber and Christianity. Translated by Alexander Dru. London: Harvill Press, 1961.

"Mary-Church-Office." *Communio* 23, no. 1 (1996): 193–98.

Mary for Today. Translated by Robert Nowell. San Francisco: Ignatius, 1988.

"The Meaning of Christ's Saying: 'I Am the Truth.'" *Communio* 14, no. 2 (1987): 158–60.

The Moment of Christian Witness. Translated by Richard Beckley. New York: Newman, 1968.

Mysterium Paschale: The Mystery of Easter. Translated by Aidan Nichols. San Francisco: Ignatius, 2000.

My Work in Retrospect. Translated by Cornelia Capol. San Francisco: Ignatius, 1993.

New Elucidations. Translated by Mary Theresilde Skerry. San Francisco: Ignatius, 1986.

The Office of Peter and the Structure of the Church. Translated by Andree Emery. San Francisco: Ignatius, 1989.

"On the Concept of Person." *Communio* 13, no. 1 (1986): 18–26.

Origen, Spirit and Fire: A Thematic Anthology of His Writings. Translated by Robert J. Daly. Washington, DC: Catholic University of America Press, 1984.

Our Task: A Report and A Plan. Translated by John Saward. San Francisco: Ignatius, 1994.

"Peace and Theology." *Communio* 12, no. 4 (1985): 398–40.

"The Poverty of Christ." *Communio* 13, no. 3 (1986): 196–98.

Prayer. Translated by Graham Harrison. San Francisco: Ignatius, 1987.

Presence and Thought: An Essay on the Religious Philosophy of Gregory of Nyssa. Translated by Mark Sebanc. San Francisco: Ignatius, 1995.

Razing the Bastions: On the Church in This Age. Translated by Brian McNeil. San Francisco: Ignatius, 1993.

The Scandal of the Incarnation: Irenaeus "Against the Heresies." Selected with an introduction by Hans Urs von Balthasar. Translated by John Saward. San Francisco: Ignatius, 1981.

A Short Primer for Unsettled Laymen. Translated by Michael Waldstein. San Francisco: Ignatius, 1985.

"Stellvertretung: Schlüsselwort christlichen Lebens." *Leben in Geist* 4 (1976): 3–7.

Test Everything: Hold Fast to What Is Good. Translated by Maria Shrady. San Francisco: Ignatius, 1989.

Theo-Drama: Theological Dramatic Theory I: Prolegomena. Translated by Graham Harrison. San Francisco: Ignatius, 1988.

Theo-Drama: Theological Dramatic Theory II: The Dramatis Personae: Man in God. Translated by Graham Harrison. San Francisco: Ignatius, 1990.

Theo-Drama: Theological Dramatic Theory III: The Dramatis Personae: The Person in Christ. Translated by Graham Harrison. San Francisco: Ignatius, 1992.
Theo-Drama: Theological Dramatic Theory IV: The Action. Translated by Graham Harrison. San Francisco: Ignatius, 1994.
Theo-Drama: Theological Dramatic Theory V: The Dramatis Personae: Man in God. Translated by Graham Harrison. San Francisco: Ignatius, 1998.
Theodramatik I: Prolegomena. Einsiedeln: Johannes Verlag, 1973.
Theodramatik II/1: Die Personen des Spiels: Der Mensch in Gott. Einsiedeln: Johannes Verlag, 1976.
Theodramatik II/2: Die Personen des Spiels: Die Personen in Christus. Einsiedeln: Johannes Verlag, 1976.
Theodramatik III: Die Handlung. Einsiedeln: Johannes Verlag, 1980.
Theodramatik IV: Das Endspiel. Einsiedeln: Johannes Verlag, 1983.
Theo-Logic: Theological Logical Theory I: Truth of the World. Translated by Adrian J. Walker. San Francisco: Ignatius, 2001.
Theo-Logic: Theological Logical Theory II: Truth of God. Translated by Adrian J. Walker. San Francisco: Ignatius, 2004.
Theo-Logic: Theological Logical Theory III: The Spirit of Truth. Translated by Graham Harrison. San Francisco: Ignatius, 2005.
Theologik I: Wahrheit der Welt. Einsiedeln: Johannes Verlag, 1985.
Theologik II: Wahrheit Gottes. Einsiedeln: Johannes Verlag, 1985.
Theologik III: Der Geist Der Wahrheit. Einsiedeln: Johannes Verlag, 1987.
A Theological Anthropology. Translation by J. Patout Burns. Eugene, OR: Wipf and Stock, 2010.
"Theology and Aesthetic." *Communio* 8, no. 1 (1981): 62–71.
"Theology and Holiness." *Communio* 14, no. 4 (1987): 341–50.
The Theology of Henry de Lubac: An Overview. Translated by Joseph Fessio and Michael Waldstein. San Francisco: Ignatius, 1991.
A Theology of History. San Francisco: Ignatius, 1994.
The Theology of Karl Barth. Translated by Edward T. Oakes. San Francisco: Ignatius, 1992.
Thérèse of Lisieux: A Story of a Mission. London: Sheed and Ward, 1953.
The Threefold Garland. Translated by Erasmo Leiva-Merikakis. San Francisco: Ignatius, 1982.
To the Heart of the Mystery of Redemption. Translated by Anne Englund Nash. San Francisco: Ignatius, 2005.
"Toward a Theology of Christian Prayer." *Communio* 12, no. 3 (1985): 245–57.
Truth Is Symphonic: Aspects of Christian Pluralism. Translated by Graham Harrison. San Francisco: Ignatius, 1987.

Two Sisters in the Spirit: Thérèse of Lisieux and Elizabeth of the Trinity. Translated by Donald Nichols, Anne Elizabeth Englund, and Dennis Martin. San Francisco: Ignatius, 1992.
"Über Stellvertretung." *Résurrection: Revue de Doctrine Chrétienne* 41 (1973): 2–9.
Unless You Become Like This Child. Translated by Erasmo Leiva-Merikakis. San Francisco: Ignatius, 1991.
"Vocation." *Communio* 37, no. 1 (2010): 111–28.
Wahrheit der Welt. Einsiedeln: Johannes Verlag, 1947.
The Way of the Cross. Translated by John Drury. London: Burns and Oates, 1969.
Who Is a Christian? Translated by Frank Davidson. New York: Newman, 1968.
"Why We Need Nicholas of Cusa." *Communio* 28, no. 4 (2001): 854–59.
"The Work and Suffering of Jesus: Continuity and Discontinuity." In *Faith in Christ and the Worship of Christ*, edited by Leo Scheffczyk; translated by Graham Harrison, 13–22. San Francisco: Ignatius, 1982.
You Crown the Year with Your Goodness: Sermons through the Liturgical Year. Translated by Graham Harrison. San Francisco: Ignatius, 1989.

Other Works Consulted

For a comprehensive list of secondary literature on Balthasar, see "Hans Urs von Balthasar: Sekundärbibliographie," http://www.johannes-verlag.de/jh_huvb_sekund.htm.

Adams, Nicholas. *Eclipse of Grace: Divine and Human Action in Hegel*. Oxford: Wiley-Blackwell, 2013.
Anatolios, Khaled. *Retrieving Nicaea: The Development and Meaning of Trinitarian Doctrine*. Grand Rapids, MI: Baker, 2011.
Anderson, Cynthia Peters. *Reclaiming Participation: Christ as God's Life for All*. Minneapolis: Fortress, 2014.
Anselm of Canterbury. "Why God Became Man." In *Anselm of Canterbury: The Major Works*, edited by Brian Davies and G. R. Evans, 260–356. Oxford: Oxford University Press, 2008.
Aquinas, Thomas. *Existence and the Nature of God* (Ia. 2–11). Vol. 2 of *Summa Theologiae*. Edited by Timothy McDermott. Cambridge: Cambridge University Press, 2006.
———. *Father, Son, and Holy Ghost* (Ia. 33–43). Vol. 7 of *Summa Theologiae*. Edited by T. C. O'Brien. Cambridge: Cambridge University Press, 2006.

---. *God's Will and Providence* (Ia. 19–26). Vol. 5 of *Summa Theologiae*. Edited by Thomas Gilby. Cambridge: Cambridge University Press, 2006.

---. "John 14: Lecture 1." *Commentary on the Gospel of John*. https://isidore.co/aquinas/english/SSJohn.htm.

---. *The Incarnate Word* (IIIa. 1–6). Vol. 48 of *Summa Theologiae*. Edited by R. J. Hennessey. Cambridge: Cambridge University Press, 2006.

---. *The Sacraments* (IIIa. 60–65). Vol. 56 of *Summa Theologiae*. Edited by David Bourke. Cambridge: Cambridge University Press, 2006.

---. *The Trinity* (Ia. 27–32). Vol. 6 of *Summa Theologiae*. Edited by Ceslaus Velecky. Cambridge: Cambridge University Press, 2006.

Athanasius the Great and Didymus the Blind. *Works on the Spirit*. Popular Patristic Series 43. Translated by Mark DelCogliano, Andrew Radde-Gallwitz, and Lewis Ayres. Yonkers, NY: St Vladimir's Seminary Press, 2011.

Attfield, D. G. "Can God Be Crucified? A Discussion of J. Moltmann." *Scottish Journal of Theology* 30, no. 1 (1977): 47–57.

Augustine. *The Confessions*. Part 1, vol. 1 of *The Works of Saint Augustine*. Edited by John E. Rotelle. Translated by Maria Boulding. Hyde Park, NY: New City Press, 2015.

---. *Homilies on the First Epistle of John*. Part 3, vol. 14 of *The Works of Saint Augustine*. Edited by Daniel E. Doyle and Thomas Martin. Translated by Boniface Ramsey. Hyde Park, NY: New City Press, 2008.

---. *The Trinity*. Part 1, vol. 5 of *The Works of Saint Augustine*. Edited by John E. Rotelle. Translated by Edmund Hill. Hyde Park, NY: New City Press, 1991.

Ayres, Lewis. *Augustine and the Trinity*. Cambridge: Cambridge University Press, 2010.

---. *Nicaea and Its Legacy: An Approach to Fourth-Century Trinitarian Theology*. Oxford: Oxford University Press, 2006.

---. "On Not Three People: The Fundamental Themes of Gregory of Nyssa's Trinitarian Theology as Seen in *To Ablabius: On Not Three Gods*." In *Re-thinking Gregory of Nyssa*, edited by Sarah Coakley, 445–75. Oxford: Blackwell, 2003.

Babini, Ellero. "Jesus Christ: Form and Norm of Man according to Hans Urs von Balthasar." In *Hans Urs von Balthasar: His Life and Work*, edited by David Schindler, 221–30. San Francisco: Ignatius, 1991.

Bailey, Daniel P. "Concepts of *Stellvertretung* in the Interpretation of Isaiah 53." In *Jesus and the Suffering Servant: Isaiah 53 and Christian Origins*, edited by William H Bellinger Jr. and William R. Farmer, 223–50. Eugene, OR: Wipf & Stock, 1998.

Barnes, Michel. "De Régnon Reconsidered." *Augustinian Studies* 26, no. 2 (1995): 51–79.
Barth, Karl. *Church Dogmatics*. 4 vols. in 14 parts. Edited by G. W. Bromiley and T. F. Torrance. Edinburgh: T&T Clark, 1936–1977.
Bartlett, Andrew W. *Cross Purposes: The Violent Grammar of Christian Atonement*. Harrisburg, PA: Trinity Press International, 2001.
Basil the Great. *On Social Justice*. Translated by C. Paul Schroeder. Popular Patristic Series 38. Crestwood, NY: St Vladimir's Seminary Press, 2009.
———. *On the Holy Spirit*. Translated by Stephen Hildebrand. Popular Patristic Series 42. Yonkers, NY: St Vladimir's Seminary Press, 2011.
———. *On the Human Condition*. Translated by Nonna Verna Harrison. Popular Patristic Series 30. Crestwood, NY: St Vladimir's Seminary Press, 2005.
Beckwith, Roger T., and Martin J. Selman, eds. *Sacrifice in the Bible*. Carlisle, UK: Paternoster, 1995.
Behr, John. *The Case against Diodore and Theodore*. Oxford: Oxford University Press, 2011.
———. *The Formation of Christian Theology*. 2 vols. Crestwood, NY: St. Vladimir's Seminary Press, 2001–2004.
Beilby, James, and Paul Eddy, eds. *The Nature of the Atonement: Four Views*. Downers Grove, IL: InterVarsity Press, 2006.
Bellafiore, Ignazio M. "Representation and Reconciliation: Hans Urs von Balthasar's Theological Interpretation of Shakespeare in the Light of the Theo-Drama." Licentiate in Sacred Theology thesis, Catholic University of America, 2007.
Belousek, Darrin W. Snyder. *Atonement, Justice, and Peace: The Message of the Cross and the Mission of the Church*. Grand Rapids, MI: Eerdmans, 2012.
Berkouwer, G. C. *Studies in Dogmatics: The Person of Christ*. Grand Rapids, MI: Eerdmans, 1954.
Betz, John R. Introduction to *Analogia Entis, Metaphysics: Original Structure and Universal Rhythm*, by Erich Przywara. Translated by John R. Betz and David Bentley Hart. Grand Rapids, MI: Eerdmans, 2014.
Bieler, Martin. "*Analogia Entis* as an Expression of Love according to Ferdinand Ulrich." In *The Analogy of Being: Invention of the Antichrist or the Wisdom of God*, edited by Thomas Joseph White, 314–40. Grand Rapids, MI: Eerdmans, 2011.
———. *Befreiung der Freiheit: Zur Theologie der stellvertretenden Sühne*. Freiburg: Herder, 1996.
———. "The Future of the Philosophy of Being." *Communio* 26, no. 3 (1999): 455–85.

———. Introduction to *Homo Abyssus: The Drama of the Question of Being*, by Ferdinand Ulrich. Translated by D. C. Schindler. Washington, DC: Humanum Academic Press, 2018.

———. "Meta-anthropology and Christology: On the Philosophy of Hans Urs von Balthasar." *Communio* 20, no. 1 (1993): 129–46.

Birot, Antoine. "'God in Christ, Reconciled the World to Himself': Redemption in Balthasar." *Communio* 24, no. 2 (1997): 259–85.

Blackwell, Ben C. *Christosis: Engaging Paul with His Patristic Interpreters*. Grand Rapids, MI: Eerdmans, 2016.

Blair, George A. "On Esse and Relation." *Communio* 21, no. 1 (1994): 162–64.

Boersma, Hans. *Violence, Hospitality, and the Cross*. Grand Rapids, MI: Baker, 2004.

Bonhoeffer, Dietrich. *Ethics. Dietrich Bonhoeffer Works—Reader's Edition*. Edited by Clifford J. Green. Translated by Reinhard Krauss, Charles C. West, and Douglas W. Scott. Minneapolis: Fortress, 2015.

———. *Ethics*. Vol. 6 of *Dietrich Bonhoeffer Works*. Edited by Clifford J. Green. Translated by Reinhard Krauss, Charles C. West, and Douglas W. Scott. Minneapolis: Fortress, 2015.

———. *Sanctorum Communio: A Theological Study on the Sociology of the Church*. Vol. 1 of *Dietrich Bonhoeffer Works*. Edited by Clifford J. Green and Joachim von Soosten. Translated by Reinhard Krauss and Nancy Lukens. Minneapolis: Fortress, 1998.

Brito, Emilio. *La Christologie de Hegel: Verbum Crucis*. Translated by B. Pottier. Paris: Beauchesne, 1983.

Brown, David. "Images of Redemption in Art and Music." In *The Redemption: An Interdisciplinary Symposium on Christ as Redeemer*, edited by Stephen T. Davis, Daniel Kendall, and Gerald O'Collins, 295–320. Oxford: Oxford University Press, 2006.

Brown, Derek. "Kneeling in the Street: Recontextualizing Balthasar." *New Blackfriars* 99 (2018): 788–806.

Brown, Joanne Carlson, and Rebecca Parker. "For God So Loved the World?" In *Christianity, Patriarchy, and Abuse: A Feminist Critique*, edited by Joanne Carlson Brown and Carole R. Bohn, 1–30. New York: Pilgrim Press, 1989.

Buber, Martin. *I and Thou*. Translated by Walter Kaufmann. New York: Charles Scribner's Sons, 1971.

Buckley, James J. "Balthasar's Use of the Theology of Aquinas." *Thomist* 59, no. 4 (1995): 517–45.

Bulgakov, Sergius. *The Lamb of God*. Translated by Boris Jakim. Grand Rapids, MI: Eerdmans, 2008.

Bunson, Matthew E. "They Sang All the Way to the Guillotine." *Catholic Answers* 18, no. 4 (2007). https://www.catholic.com/magazine/print-edition/they-sang-all-the-way-to-the-guillotine.

Bush, William. *To Quell the Terror: The Mystery of the Vocation of the Sixteen Carmelites of Compiègne Guillotined July 17, 1794*. Washington, DC: Institute of Carmelite Studies Publications, 1999.

Callahan, Ann. "The Concept of Person in the Theology of Hans Urs von Balthasar." PhD diss., Fordham University, 1993.

Calvin, John. *Institutes of the Christian Religion*. 2 vols. Edited by John T. McNeill. Translated by Ford Lewis Battles. Philadelphia: Westminster Press, 1967.

Campbell, Constantine R. *Paul and Union with Christ: An Exegetical and Theological Study*. Grand Rapids, MI: Zondervan, 2012.

Caputo, John D., and Michael J. Scanlon, eds. *God, the Gift, and Postmodernism*. Bloomington: Indiana University Press, 1999.

Carpenter, Anne. *Theo-Poetics: Hans Urs von Balthasar and the Risk of Art and Being*. Notre Dame, IN: University of Notre Dame Press, 2015.

Carroll, John T., and Joel B. Green. *The Death of Jesus in Early Christianity*. Peabody, MA: Hendrickson, 1995.

Cavanaugh, William T. "Dorothy Day and the Mystical Body of Christ in the Second World War." In *Dorothy Day and the Catholic Worker Movement*, edited by William Thorn, Phillip Runkel, and Susan Mountin, 457–64. Milwaukee: Marquette University Press, 2011.

Cawte, John "Karl Rahner's Conception of God's Self-Communication to Man." *The Heythrop Journal* 25 (1984): 260–71.

Chau, Carolyn A. *Solidarity with the World: Charles Taylor and Hans Urs von Balthasar on Faith, Modernity, and Catholic Mission*. Eugene, OR: Cascade, 2016.

Cihak, John R. *Balthasar and Anxiety*. London: T&T Clark, 2009.

Ciraulo, Jonathan Martin. "Hans Urs von Balthasar's Indifference to Divinization." In *Mystical Doctrines of Deification*, edited by John Arblaster and Rob Faesen, 165–85. New York: Routledge, 2019.

Chubb, Thomas. *The True Gospel of Jesus Christ Asserted*. Whitefish, MO: Kessinger, 2010.

Clark, Stephen R. L. *God, Religion, and Reality*. Peterborough, NH: Angelico, 2017.

Clarke, W. Norris. *Explorations in Metaphysics: Being, God, Person*. Notre Dame, IN: University of Notre Dame Press, 1994.

———. *Person and Being*. Milwaukee: Marquette University Press, 1993.

———. "Person, Being, and St. Thomas." *Communio* 19, no. 4 (1992): 601–18.
———. "Response to David Schindler's Comments." *Communio* 20, no. 3 (1993): 593–98.
———. "Response to Long's Comments" and "Response to Blair's Comments." *Communio* 21, no. 1 (1994): 165–71.
Coakley, Sarah. *God, Sexuality, and Self: An Essay "On the Trinity."* Cambridge: Cambridge University Press, 2013.
———. "Re-thinking Gregory of Nyssa: Introduction—Gender, Trinitarian Analogies, and the Pedagogy of *the Song*." In *Re-thinking Gregory of Nyssa*, edited by Sarah Coakley, 431–43. Oxford: Blackwell, 2003.
Coffey, David. *Deus Trinitas: The Doctrine of the Triune God*. Oxford: Oxford University Press, 1999.
———. "Trinity." In *The Cambridge Companion to Karl Rahner*, edited by Declan Marmion and Mary E. Hines, 98–111. Cambridge: Cambridge University Press, 2005.
Congar, Yves. *I Believe in the Holy Spirit*. 3 vols. Translated by David Smith. New York: Seabury, 1983.
Cozolino, Louis. *The Neuroscience of Human Relationships: Attachment and the Developing Social Brain*. New York: W. W. Norton, 2014.
Crammer, Corinne. "One Sex or Two? Balthasar's Theology of the Sexes." In Oakes and Moss, eds., *The Cambridge Companion to Hans Urs Von Balthasar*, 93–122.
Crisp, Oliver D. "Did Christ Have a Fallen Human Nature?" *International Journal of Systematic Theology* 6, no. 3 (2004): 270–88.
———. *Divinity and Humanity: The Incarnation Reconsidered*. Cambridge: Cambridge University Press, 2007.
Crisp, Oliver D., and Fred Sanders, eds. *Locating Atonement: Explorations in Constructive Dogmatics*. Grand Rapids, MI: Zondervan, 2015.
Cyril of Alexandria. *The Anathemas of Cyril in Opposition to Nestorius*. In *The Nicene and Post-Nicene Fathers*, vol. 3, series 2, edited by Philip Schaff and Henry Wace. Reprint, Peabody, MA: Hendrickson, 1994.
———. *Commentary on John*. 2 vols. Edited by Joel C. Elowsky. Translated by David R Maxwell. Ancient Christian Texts. Downers Grove, IL: InterVarsity Press, 2015.
———. *On the Unity of Christ*. Translated by John Anthony McGunkin. Popular Patristic Series 13. Crestwood, NY: St. Vladimir's Seminary Press, 1995.
Daley, Brian. "'A Richer Union': Leontius of Byzantium and the Relationship of Human and Divine in Christ." *Studia Patristica* 24 (1993): 239–65.

Dalzell, Thomas G. *The Dramatic Encounter of Divine and Human Freedom in the Theology of Hans Urs von Balthasar*. Oxford: Peter Lang, 1997.

Damasio, Antonio. *Self Comes to Mind: Constructing the Conscious Brain*. New York: Vintage, 2012.

Davis, Stephen T., Daniel Kendall, and Gerald O'Collins, eds. *The Redemption: An Interdisciplinary Symposium on Christ as Redeemer*. Oxford: Oxford University Press, 2006.

Deissmann, Adolf. *Paul: A Study in Social and Religion History*. Translated by William E. Wilson. London: Hodder & Stoughton, 1926.

de Lubac, Henri. *Medieval Exegesis: The Four Senses of Scripture*. 3 vols. Translated by Mark Sebanc and E. M. Macierowski. Grand Rapids, MI: Eerdmans, 1998–2009.

———. "A Witness of Christ in the Church: Hans Urs von Balthasar." Crossroads Initiative, April 20, 2017. https://www.crossroadsinitiative.com/media/articles/hans-urs-von-balthasar-eulogy-de-lubac.

Denzinger, Heinrich. *Enchiridion Symbolorum: A Compendium of Creeds, Definitions, and Declarations of the Catholic Church*. 43rd ed. Edited by Peter Hünermann. San Francisco: Ignatius Press, 2012.

Dickens, W. T. *Hans Urs von Balthasar's Theological Aesthetics: A Model for Post-Critical Biblical Interpretation*. Notre Dame, IN: University of Notre Dame Press, 2003.

Donnelly, Veronica. *Saving Beauty: Form as the Key to Balthasar's Christology*. Oxford: Peter Lang, 2007.

Doran, Robert M. *The Trinity in History: A Theology of the Divine Missions*. Vol. 1, *Missions and Processions*. Lonergan Studies. Toronto: University of Toronto Press, 2012.

Driver, John. *Understanding the Atonement for the Mission of the Church*. Scottdale, PA: Herald Press, 1986.

Drury, John L. "Hell and Hope in Balthasar: The Substitutionary Character of Christ's Descent into Hell and Its Implications for the Extent of the Atonement." *Koinonia* 17 (2005): 93–103.

Eberhart, Christian A. *The Sacrifice of Jesus: Understanding Atonement Biblically*. Minneapolis: Fortress, 2011.

Ebner, Ferdinand. *Das Wort und die geistigen Realitäten: Pneumatologische Fragmente*. Baden-Baden: Suhrkamp, 1980.

Ekblad, E. Robert. "God Is Not to Blame: The Servant's Atoning Suffering according to the LXX of Isaiah 53." In *Stricken by God? Nonviolent Identification and the Victory of Christ*, edited by Brad Jersak and Michael Hardin, 180–204. Grand Rapids, MI: Eerdmans, 2007.

Emery, Gilles. "The Immutability of the God of Love and the Problem of Language concerning the Suffering of God." In *Divine Impassibility and the Mystery of Human Suffering*, edited by James F. Keating and Thomas Joseph White, 27–76. Grand Rapids, MI: Eerdmans, 2009.

———. "*Theologia and Dispensatio*: The Centrality of the Divine Missions in St. Thomas's Trinitarian Theology." *Thomist* 74, no. 4 (2010): 515–61.

———. *The Trinitarian Theology of St. Thomas Aquinas*. Translated by Francesca Aran Murphy. Oxford: Oxford University Press, 2007.

Espezel, Alberto. "Inclusive Representation and Atonement in Norbert Hoffmann." *Communio* 24, no. 2 (1997): 286–96.

Feestra, Ronald, and Cornelius Plantinga, eds. *Trinity, Incarnation, and Atonement*. Notre Dame, IN: University of Notre Dame Press, 1989.

Fiddes, Paul S. *Past Event and Present Salvation: The Christian Idea of Atonement*. Louisville, KY: Westminster John Knox, 1989.

Fields, Stephen. "The Beauty of the Ugly: Balthasar, the Crucifixion, Analogy and God." *International Journal of Systematic Theology* 9, no. 2 (2007): 172–83.

Ford, David F. "Tragedy and Atonement." In *Christ, Ethics, and Tragedy: Essays in Honour of Donald MacKinnon*, edited by Kenneth Surin, 117–30. Cambridge: Cambridge University Press, 1989.

Franks, Angela. "Trinitarian *Analogia Entis* in Hans Urs von Balthasar." *Thomist* 62, no. 4 (1998): 533–59.

Freddoso, Alfred J. "New English Translation of St. Thomas Aquinas's *Summa Theologiae*." https://www3.nd.edu/~afreddos/summa-translation/TOC.htm.

Froese, Vic. "Atonement: A Bibliography." *Direction* 41 (2012): 165–83.

Gallaher, Brandon. *Freedom and Necessity in Modern Trinitarian Theology*. Oxford: Oxford University Press, 2016.

Galot, Jean. *Jesus, Our Liberator: A Theology of Redemption*. Translated by Angeline Bouchard. Rome: Gregorian University Press, 1982.

Gardner, Lucy. "Balthasar and the Figure of Mary." In Oakes and Moss, eds., *The Cambridge Companion to Hans Urs von Balthasar*, 64–78.

Gardner, Lucy, and David Moss. "Something Like Time; Something Like the Sexes—an Essay in Reception." In *Balthasar at the End of Modernity*, edited by Lucy Gardner, David Moss, Ben Quash, and Graham Ward, 69–138. Edinburgh: T&T Clark, 1999.

Gavrilyuk, Paul L. "The Kenotic Theology of Sergius Bulgakov." *Scottish Journal of Theology* 58, no. 3 (2005): 251–69.

George, Timothy. "The Atonement in Martin Luther's Theology." In *The Glory of the Atonement*, edited by Charles E. Hill and Frank A. James III, 263–78. Downers Grove, IL: InterVarsity Press, 2004.

Gestrich, Christof. *Christentum und Stellvertretung: Religionsphilosophische Untersuchungen zum Heilsverständnis und zur Grundlegung der Theologie.* Tübingen: Mohr Siebeck, 2001.

———. "God Takes Our Place: A Religious-Philosophical Approach to the Concept of *Stellvertretung.*" *Modern Theology* 17, no. 3 (2001): 313–34.

Girard, René. *Things Hidden since the Foundation of the World.* Translated by Stephen Bann and Michael Metteer. Stanford, CA: Stanford University Press, 1987.

———. *Violence and the Sacred.* Translated by Patrick Gregory. Baltimore: Johns Hopkins University Press, 1977.

Gockel, Matthias. "A Dubious Christological Formula? Leontius of Byzantium and the *Anhypostasis-Enhypostasis* Theory." *Journal of Theological Studies* 51, no. 2 (2000): 515–32.

Gonzalez, Michelle A. "Hans Urs von Balthasar and Contemporary Feminist Theology." *Theological Studies* 65, no. 3 (2004): 566–95.

Gorman, Michael J. *Becoming the Gospel: Paul, Participation, and Mission.* Grand Rapids, MI: Eerdmans, 2015.

———. *Cruciformity: Paul's Narrative Spirituality of the Cross.* Grand Rapids, MI: Eerdmans, 2001.

Graham, Jeannine Michele. *Representation and Substitution in the Atonement Theologies of Dorothee Sölle, John Macquarrie, and Karl Barth.* Oxford: Peter Lang, 2005.

Green, Clifford J. *Bonhoeffer: A Theology of Sociality.* Grand Rapids, MI: Eerdmans, 1999.

Green, Joel, and Mark Baker. *Recovering the Scandal of the Cross: Atonement in New Testament and Contemporary Contexts.* Downers Grover, IL: InterVarsity Press, 2000.

Gregory of Nazianzus. *On God and Christ: The Five Theological Orations and Two Letters to Cledonius.* Translated by Frederick Williams and Lionel Wickham. Popular Patristic Series 23. Crestwood, NY: St. Vladimir's Seminary Press, 2002.

Gregory of Nyssa. *Against Eunomius.* In *The Nicene and Post-Nicene Fathers*, vol. 5, series 2, edited by Philip Schaff and Henry Wace. Reprint, Peabody, MA: Hendrickson, 1994.

———. *The Great Catechism.* In *The Nicene and Post-Nicene Fathers*, vol. 5, series 2, edited by Philip Schaff and Henry Wace. Reprint, Peabody, MA: Hendrickson, 1994.

———. *Homilies on the Song of Sons.* Translated by Richard A. Norris Jr. Atlanta: Society of Biblical Literature, 2012.

———. *Life of Moses*. Translated by Abraham J. Malherbe and Everett Ferguson. New York: Paulist Press, 1978.

Grillmeier, Aloys. *Christ in the Christian Tradition*. Vol. 1, *From the Apostolic Age to Chalcedon* (451). Translated by John Bowden. Atlanta: John Knox Press, 1975.

Gundry-Volf, J. M. "Expiation, Propitiation, Mercy Seat." In *Dictionary of Paul and His Letters*, edited by Gerald F. Hawthorne, Ralph P. Martin, and Daniel G. Reid, 279–84. Downers Grove, IL: Intervarsity Press, 1993.

Gunton, Colin E. *The Actuality of Atonement: A Study of Metaphor, Rationality, and the Christian Tradition*. Grand Rapids, MI: Eerdmans, 1989.

———. "Salvation." In *The Cambridge Companion to Karl Barth*, edited by John Webster, 143–58. Cambridge: Cambridge University Press, 2000.

———. *The Theology of Reconciliation*. London: T&T Clark, 2003.

———. "Two Dogmas Revisited: Edward Irving's Christology." *Scottish Journal of Theology* 41, no. 3 (1988): 359–76.

Hadley, Christopher. "The All-Embracing Frame: Distance in the Trinitarian Theology of Hans Urs von Balthasar." PhD diss., Marquette University, 2015.

Hart, David Bentley. *The Beauty of the Infinite: The Aesthetics of Christian Truth*. Grand Rapids, MI: Eerdmans, 2003.

———. *The Experience of God: Being, Consciousness, Bliss*. London: Yale University Press, 2013.

———. "The Gospel according to Melpomene: Reflections on Rowan Williams's *The Tragic Imagination*." *Modern Theology* 34, no. 2 (2018): 220–34.

———. "The Mirror of the Infinite: Gregory of Nyssa on the Vestigia Trinitatis." In *Re-thinking Gregory of Nyssa*, edited by Sarah Coakley, 541–61. Oxford: Blackwell, 2003.

———. "No Shadow of Turning: On Divine Impassibility." *Pro Ecclesia* 11, no. 2 (2002): 188–93.

Healy, Nicholas J. *The Eschatology of Hans Urs von Balthasar: Being as Communion*. Oxford: Oxford University Press, 2005.

Hengel, Martin. *The Atonement: The Origins of the Doctrine in the New Testament*. Translated by John Bowden. Eugene, OR: Wipf & Stock, 2007.

Heschel, Abraham J. *The Prophets*. New York: Harper & Row, 1962.

Hill, Charles E., and Frank A. James, eds. *The Glory of the Atonement: Biblical, Historical, and Practical Perspectives*. Downers Grove, IL: InterVarsity, 2004.

Hoffmann, Norbert. "Atonement and Spirituality of the Sacred Heart: An Attempt at Elucidation by Means of the Principle of 'Representation.'" In

Faith in Christ and the Worship of Christ, edited by Leo Scheffczyk; translated by Graham Harrison, 141–206. San Francisco: Ignatius, 1986.

———. "Atonement and the Ontological Coherence between the Trinity and the Cross." In *Towards a Civilization of Love*, edited by Mario Luigi Ciappi, 213–66. San Francisco: Ignatius, 1985.

———. *Kreuz und Trinität: Zur Theologie der Sühne*. Freiburg: Johannes Verlag Einsiedeln, 1982.

———. "Stellvertretung, Grundgestalt und Mitte des Mysteriums: Ein Versuch trinitätstheologischer Begründung christlicher Sühne." *Münchener Theologische Zeitschrift* 30 (1979): 161–91.

———. *Sühne: Zur Theologie der Stellvertretung*. Freiburg: Johannes Verlag Einsiedeln, 1981.

Holmes, Stephen R. *The Quest for the Trinity: The Doctrine of God in Scripture, History, and Modernity*. Downers Grove, IL: InterVarsity Press, 2012.

———. *The Wondrous Cross: Atonement and Penal Substitution in the Bible and History*. London: Paternoster, 2007.

Hooker, Morna D. "Did the Use of Isaiah 53 to Interpret His Mission Begin with Jesus?" In *Jesus and the Suffering Servant: Isaiah 53 and Christian Origins*, edited by William H. Bellinger Jr. and William R. Farmer, 88–103. Eugene, OR: Wipf & Stock, 1998.

Horner, Robyn. *Jean-Luc Marion: A Theo-Logical Introduction*. Burlington, VT: Ashgate, 2005.

Howsare, Rodney. *Hans Urs von Balthasar and Protestantism*. London: T&T Clark, 2005.

Hughes, Philip E. *The True Image: The Origin and Destiny of Man in Christ*. Grand Rapids, MI: Eerdmans, 1989.

Hunsinger, George. *Disruptive Grace: Studies in the Theology of Karl Barth*. Grand Rapids, MI: Eerdmans, 2001.

———. *The Eucharist and Ecumenism: Let Us Keep the Feast*. Cambridge: Cambridge University Press, 2008.

Hydinger, Kristen, Peter Jankowski, Shelly Rambo, and Steven Sandage. "Penal Substitutionary Atonement and Concern for Suffering: An Empirical Study." *Journal of Psychology and Theology* 45, no. 1 (2017): 33–45.

Inge, John. *A Christian Theology of Place*. Burlington, VT: Ashgate, 2003.

International Theological Commission. "The Consciousness of Christ concerning Himself and His Mission." http://www.vatican.va/roman_curia/congregations/cfaith/cti_documents/rc_cti_1985_coscienza-gesu_en.html.

———. "Select Questions on Christology." http:// www.vatican.va/roman_curia /congregations/cfaith/cti_documents/rc_cti_1979_cristologia_en.html.

Irenaeus of Lyons. *Against Heresies*. In *The Ante-Nicene Fathers*, vol. 1, edited by Alexander Roberts and James Donaldson. Reprint, Peabody, MA: Hendrickson, 1994.

Irving, Edward. *The Collected Writings of Edward Irving*. 5 vols. Edited by G. Carlyle. London: Alexander Strahan, 1865.

James, Frank A., III. "General Introduction." In *The Glory of the Atonement: Biblical, Historical, and Practical Perspectives*, edited by Charles E. Hill and Frank A. James III, 15–20. Downers Grove, IL: InterVarsity Press, 2004.

Jeffery, Steve, Michael Ovey, and Andrew Sach. *Pierced for Our Transgressions: Rediscovering the Glory of Penal Substitution*. Wheaton, IL: Crossway, 2007.

Jenson, Robert. *Systematic Theology*. 2 vols. Oxford: Oxford University Press, 1997–1999.

———. *The Triune Identity: God according to the Gospel*. Philadelphia: Fortress, 1982.

———. "You Wonder Where the Spirit Went." *Pro Ecclesia* 2, no. 3 (1993): 296–304.

Jersak, Brad, and Michael Hardin, eds. *Stricken by God? Nonviolent Identification and the Victory of Christ*. Grand Rapids, MI: Eerdmans, 2007.

John of Damascus. *Exposition of the Orthodox Faith*. In *The Nicene and Post-Nicene Fathers*, vol. 9, series 2, edited by Philip Schaff and Henry Wace. Reprint, Peabody, MA: Hendrickson, 1994.

Johnson, Junius. *Christ and Analogy: The Christocentric Metaphysics of Hans Urs von Balthasar*. Minneapolis: Fortress, 2013.

Johnson, Keith L. *Karl Barth and the Analogia Entis*. London: T&T Clark, 2010.

Jones, Tony. *Did God Kill Jesus? Searching for Love in History's Most Famous Execution*. New York: HarperCollins, 2015.

Kapic, Kelly M. "The Son's Assumption of a Human Nature: A Call for Clarity." *International Journal of Systematic Theology* 3, no. 2 (2001): 154–66.

Karkkainen, Veli-Matti. *Christ and Reconciliation: A Constructive Christian Theology for the Pluralistic World*. Grand Rapids, MI: Eerdmans, 2003.

———. "The Trinitarian Doctrines of Jürgen Moltmann and Wolfhart Pannenberg in the Context of Contemporary Discussion." In *The Cambridge Companion to the Trinity*, edited by Peter C. Phan, 223–42. Cambridge: Cambridge University Press, 2011.

Keating, Daniel A. *The Appropriation of the Divine Life in Cyril of Alexandria*. Oxford: Oxford University Press, 2004.

Kilby, Karen. "Balthasar and Karl Rahner." In Oakes and Moss, eds., *The Cambridge Companion to Hans Urs von Balthasar*, 256–68.

———. *Balthasar: A (Very) Critical Introduction*. Grand Rapids, MI: Eerdmans, 2012.

———. "Hans Urs von Balthasar on the Trinity." In *The Cambridge Companion to the Trinity*, edited by Peter C. Phan, 208–22. Cambridge: Cambridge University Press, 2011.

———. *Karl Rahner: Theology and Philosophy*. London: Routledge, 2004.

Klager, Andrew P. "Retaining and Reclaiming the Divine: Identification and the Recapitulation of Peace in St. Irenaeus of Lyons' Atonement Narrative." In *Stricken by God? Nonviolent Identification and the Victory of Christ*, edited by Brad Jersak and Michael Hardin, 440–52. Grand Rapids, MI: Eerdmans, 2007.

Kotsko, Adam. *The Politics of Redemption: The Social Logic of Salvation*. London: T&T Clark, 2010.

Krenski, Thomas R. *Passio caritatis: Trinitarische Passiologie im Werk Hans Urs von Balthasar*. Einsiedeln: Johannes Verlag, 1990.

Kryst, Thomas E. "Interpreting the Death of Jesus: A Comparison of the Theologies of Hans Urs von Balthasar and Raymund Schwager." PhD diss., Catholic University of America, 2009.

Kušnieriková, Michaela. *Action for Others: Trinitarian Communion and Christological Agency*. Minneapolis: Fortress, 2017.

Lactantius. *Treatise on the Anger of God*. In *The Ante-Nicene Fathers*, vol. 7, edited by Alexander Roberts and James Donaldson. Reprint, Peabody, MA: Hendrickson, 1994.

LaCugna, Catherine Mowry. *God for Us: The Trinity and Christian Life*. San Francisco: HarperSanFrancisco, 1973.

———. "Philosophers and Theologians on the Trinity." *Modern Theology* 2, no. 3 (1986): 168–81.

Laird, Martin. "Under Solomon's Tutelage: The Education of Desire in the Homilies of the Song of Song." In *Re-thinking Gregory of Nyssa*, edited by Sarah Coakley, 507–25. Oxford: Blackwell, 2003.

Lang, U. M. "Anhypostatos-Enhypostatos: Church Fathers, Protestant Orthodoxy, and Karl Barth." *Scottish Journal of Theology* 49, no. 2 (1998): 630–57.

Lash, Nicholas. *Believing Three Ways in One God: A Reading of the Apostles' Creed*. Notre Dame, IN: University of Notre Dame Press, 1993.

———. *Holiness, Speech, and Silence: Reflections on the Question of God*. Burlington, VT: Ashgate, 2004.

Leahy, Brendan. *The Marian Profile in the Ecclesiology of Hans Urs von Balthasar*. New York: New City Press, 2000.

Leamy, Katy. "A Comparison of the Kenotic Trinitarian Theology of Hans Urs von Balthasar and Sergei Bulgakov." PhD diss., Marquette University, 2012.

Leithart, Peter J. *Athanasius*. Grand Rapids, MI: Baker Academic, 2011.

Lett, Jacob. "Divine Roominess: Spatial and Music Analogies in Hans Urs von Balthasar and Robert Jenson." *Pro Eccelsia* 28, no. 3 (2019): 267–77.

———. "Jürgen Moltmann's Doctrine of Divine Action: Towards a More Integrative Approach to His Doctrine of Creation." *Wesleyan Theological Journal* 49, no. 2 (2014): 204–42.

Levering, Matthew. *The Achievement of Hans Urs von Balthasar: An Introduction to His Trilogy*. Washington, DC: Catholic University of America Press, 2019.

———. "Christ, the Trinity, and Predestination: McCormack and Aquinas." In *Trinity and Election in Contemporary Theology*, edited by Michael Dempse, 254–84. Grand Rapids, MI: Eerdmans, 2011.

———. *Predestination: Biblical and Theological Paths*. Oxford: Oxford University Press, 2011.

———. *Scripture and Metaphysics: Aquinas and the Renewal of Trinitarian Theology*. Oxford: Blackwell, 2004.

Locke, John. *The Reasonableness of Christianity*. Edited by I. T. Ramsey. Stanford, CA: Stanford University Press, 1958.

Lonergan, Bernard. *The Triune God: Systematics*. Edited by Robert M. Doran and Daniel Monsour. Translated by Michael G. Shields. Toronto: University of Toronto Press, 2007.

Long, D. Stephen. *The Perfectly Simple Triune God: Aquinas and His Legacy*. Minneapolis: Fortress, 2016.

———. *Saving Karl Barth: Hans Urs von Balthasar's Preoccupation*. Minneapolis: Fortress Press, 2014.

Long, Stephen A. "Divine and Creaturely 'Receptivity': The Search for a Middle Term." *Communio* 21, no. 1 (1994): 151–61.

Lösel, Steffen. "Murder in the Cathedral: Hans Urs von Balthasar's New Dramatization of the Doctrine of the Trinity." *Pro Ecclesia* 5, no. 4 (1996): 427–39.

———. "A Plain Account of Christian Salvation: Balthasar on Sacrifice, Solidarity, and Substitution." *Pro Ecclesia* 13, no. 2 (2004): 141–71.

Louth, Andrew. "The Place of *Heart of the World* in the Theology of Hans Urs von Balthasar." In *The Analogy of Beauty: The Theology of Hans Urs von Balthasar*, edited by John Riches, 147–63. Edinburgh: T&T Clark, 1986.

———. *St John Damascene: Tradition and Originality in Byzantine Theology*. Oxford: Oxford University Press, 2005.

Lowe, Walter. "Christ and Salvation." In *The Cambridge Companion to Postmodern Theology*, edited by Kevin Vanhoozer, 235–51. Cambridge: Cambridge University Press, 2003.

Luther, Martin. *Career of the Reformer I*. In *Luther's Works*, vol. 31, edited by Harold J. Grimm and Helmut T. Lehmann. Philadelphia: Fortress Press, 1957.

———. *Lectures on Galatians 1535: Chapters 1–4*. Vol. 26 of *Luther's Works*. Edited by Jaroslav Pelikan and Walter Hansen. St. Louis: Concordia, 1963.

Luy, David. "The Aesthetic Collision: Hans Urs von Balthasar on the Trinity and the Cross." *International Journal of Systematic Theology* 13, no. 2 (2011): 154–69.

MacIntyre, Alasdair. *Whose Justice? Which Rationality?* Notre Dame, IN: University of Notre Dame Press, 1988.

MacKinnon, Donald. "Atonement and Tragedy." In *Borderlands of Theology and Other Essays*, edited by George W. Roberts and Donovan E. Smucker, 97–104. Eugene, OR: Wipf and Stock, 2011.

———. "Some Reflections on Hans Urs von Balthasar's Christology with Special Reference to Theodramatik II/2, III and IV." In *The Analogy of Beauty: The Theology of Hans Urs von Balthasar*, edited by John Riches, 164–79. Edinburgh: T&T Clark, 1986.

Macleod, Donald. *The Person of Christ*. Downers Grove, IL: InterVarsity Press, 1998.

Malevez, L. "L'Eglise dans le Christ: Etude de theologie historique et theorique." *Recherches de Science Religieuse* 25 (1935): 257–91, 418–40.

Mannermaa, Tuomo. *Christ Present in Faith: Luther's View of Justification*. Minneapolis: Fortress Press, 2005.

Mansini, Guy. "Balthasar and the Theodramatic Enrichment of the Trinity." *Thomist* 64, no. 4 (2000): 499–519.

Marcel, Gabriel. *The Mystery of Being*. Vols. 1 and 2. Chicago: Charles Regnery, 1951.

Marshall, Bruce D. *Trinity and Truth*. Cambridge: Cambridge University Press, 2000.

———. "The Unity of the Triune God: Reviving an Ancient Question." *Thomist* 74, no. 1 (2010): 1–32.

Marshall, Christopher D. *Beyond Retribution: A New Testament Vision for Justice, Crime, and Punishment*. Grand Rapids, MI: Eerdmans, 2001.

Marshall, I. Howard. *Aspects of the Atonement: Cross and Resurrection in the Reconciling of God and Humanity*. Colorado Springs, CO: Paternoster, 2007.

Martin, Jennifer Newsome. "The Consubstantial Otherness of God: Divine Simplicity and the Trinity in Hans Urs von Balthasar." *Modern Theology* 35, no. 3 (2019): 542–57.

———. *Hans Urs von Balthasar and the Critical Appropriation of Russian Religious Thought*. Notre Dame, IN: University of Notre Dame Press, 2015.
Mascall, E. L. *Existence and Analogy*. London: Longmans, Green and Co., 1949.
Maximus the Confessor. *Ambiguum* 5. In *Maximus the Confessor*, edited and translated by Andrew Louth, 169–79. London: Routledge, 1996.
———. *Opuscule* 3. In *Maximus the Confessor*, edited and translated by Andrew Louth, 191–96. London: Routledge, 1996.
———. *Opusculum* 64. In *On the Cosmic Mystery of Christ: Selected Writings from St. Maximus the Confessor*, translated by Paul M. Blowers and Robert Louis Wilken, 173–76. Popular Patristic Series 25. Crestwood, NY: St. Vladimir's Seminary Press, 2003.
McCormack, Bruce L. "Atonement and Human Suffering." In *Locating Atonement: Explorations in Constructive Dogmatics*, edited by Oliver D. Crisp and Fred Sanders, 189–208. Grand Rapids, MI: Zondervan, 2015.
———. "*Justa Aliena*: Karl Barth in Conversation with the Evangelical Doctrine of Imputed Righteousness." In *Justification in Perspective: Historical Developments and Contemporary Challenges*, edited by Bruce L. McCormack, 167–96. Grand Rapids, MI: Baker, 2006.
———. "Karl Barth's Version of 'Analogy of Being.'" In *The Analogy of Being: Invention of the Antichrist or the Wisdom of God*, edited by Thomas Joseph White, 88–144. Grand Rapids, MI: Eerdmans, 2011.
———. "Processions and Missions: A Point of Convergence between Thomas Aquinas and Karl Barth." In *Thomas Aquinas and Karl Barth: An Unofficial Catholic–Protestant Dialogue*, edited by Bruce L. McCormack and Thomas Joseph White, 99–126. Grand Rapids, MI: Eerdmans, 2013.
McDonald, H. D. *The Atonement of the Death of Christ*. Grand Rapids, MI: Baker, 1985.
McDougall, Joy Ann. "The Return of Trinitarian Praxis? Moltmann on the Trinity and the Christian Life." *Journal of Religion* 83, no. 2 (2003): 177–203.
McFarland, Ian. "Fallen or Unfallen? Christ's Human Nature and the Ontology of Human Sinfulness." *International Journal of Systematic Theology* 10, no. 4 (2008): 399–415.
———. "Present in Love: Rethinking Barth on the Divine Perfections." *Modern Theology* 33, no. 2 (2017): 243–58.
McFarlane, Graham. *Christ and the Spirit: The Doctrine of the Incarnation according to Edward Irving*. Carlisle, UK: Paternoster, 1996.
McGrath, Alister E. *Luther's Theology of the Cross*. Oxford: Blackwell, 1980.
McIntosh, Mark A. *Christology from Within: Spirituality and the Incarnation in Hans Urs von Balthasar*. Notre Dame, IN: University of Notre Dame Press, 2000.

McIntyre, John. *The Shape of Soteriology*. Edinburgh: T&T Clark, 1992.
McKinlay, Brian. "Ludwig Wittgenstein in Rowan Williams's Theological Account of Language." *New Blackfriars* 98 (2017): 327–41.
McKnight, Scot. *Jesus and His Death: Historiography, the Historical Jesus, and Atonement Theory*. Waco, TX: Baylor University Press, 2005.
Menke, Karl-Heinz. *Stellvertretung: Schlüsselbegriff christlichen Lebens und theologische Grundkategorie*. Freiburg: Johannes Verlag Einsiedeln, 1991.
Moltmann, Jürgen. *The Crucified God: The Cross of Christ as the Foundation and Criticism of Christian Theology*. Translated by Margaret Kohl. Minneapolis: Fortress, 1993.
———. *The Trinity and the Kingdom: The Doctrine of God*. Translated by Margaret Kohl. Minneapolis: Fortress, 1993.
Mongrain, Kevin. *The Systematic Thought of Hans Urs von Balthasar: An Irenaean Retrieval*. New York: Crossroad, 2002.
Moss, David, and Lucy Gardner. "Difference—The Immaculate Concept? The Laws of Sexual Difference in the Theology of Hans Urs von Balthasar." *Modern Theology* 14, no. 3 (1998): 376–401.
Murphy, Francesca. Review of *The Beauty of the Infinite*, by David Bentley Hart. *Scottish Journal of Theology* 60, no. 1 (2007): 80–89.
Newkirk, Terrye. *The Mantle of Elijah: The Martyrs of Compiègne as Prophets of the Modern Age*. Washington, DC: Institute of Carmelite Studies Publications, 1995.
Nichols, Aidan. "Adrienne von Speyr and the Mystery of the Atonement." *New Blackfriars* 73 (1992): 542–53.
———. *Divine Fruitfulness: A Guide through Balthasar's Theology beyond the Trilogy*. London: T&T Clark, 2007.
———. *No Bloodless Myth: A Guide through Balthasar's Dramatics*. Edinburgh: T&T Clark, 2000.
———. *Say It Is Pentecost: A Guide through Balthasar's Logic*. Edinburgh: T&T Clark, 2001.
———. "St Thomas Aquinas on the Passion of Christ: A Reading of *Summa theologiae* IIIa., q. 46." *Scottish Journal of Theology* 43, no. 4 (1990): 447–59.
———. *The Word Has Been Abroad: A Guide through Balthasar's Aesthetics*. Edinburgh: T&T Clark, 1998.
Noble, T. A. "The Hallowing of the Flesh in Biblical and Patristic Christology." In *Whistling in the Dark: Of the Theology of Craig Keen*, edited by Janice McRandal and Stephen John Wright. Eugene, OR: Cascade Books, forthcoming.

Nuss, David W. "Jesus the Christ as Stellvertreter: Aspects of Dramatic Soteriology in Selected Writings of Hans Urs von Balthasar." Licentiate in Sacred Theology, Catholic University of America, 2000.

Oakes, Edward T. "*Descensus* and Development: A Response to Recent Rejoinders." *International Journal of Systematic Theology* 13, no. 1 (2001): 3–24.

———. "The Internal Logic of Holy Saturday in the Theology of Hans Urs von Balthasar." *International Journal of Systematic Theology* 9, no. 2 (2007): 184–99.

———. *Pattern of Redemption: The Theology of Hans Urs von Balthasar*. New York: Continuum, 1997.

Oakes, Edward T., and David Moss, eds. *The Cambridge Companion to Hans Urs von Balthasar*. Cambridge: Cambridge University Press, 2004.

Oakes, Kenneth. "The Cross and the *Analogia Entis* in Erich Przywara." In *The Analogy of Being: Invention of the Antichrist or the Wisdom of God*, edited by Thomas Joseph White, 147–71. Grand Rapids, MI: Eerdmans, 2011.

O'Collins, Gerald. *Jesus Our Redeemer: A Christian Approach to Salvation*. Oxford: Oxford University Press, 2007.

O'Donnell, John. "Man and Woman as *Imago Dei* in the Theology of Hans Urs von Balthasar." *Clergy Review* 68, no. 4 (1983): 117–28.

O'Hanlon, Gerard F. *The Immutability of God in the Theology of Hans Urs von Balthasar*. Cambridge: Cambridge University Press, 1990.

Olsen, Glenn W. "Hans Urs von Balthasar and the Rehabilitation of St. Anselm's Doctrine of the Atonement." *Scottish Journal of Theology* 34, no. 1 (1981): 49–61.

Olson, Roger. "Trinity and Eschatology: The Historical Being of God in Jürgen Moltmann and Wolfhart Pannenberg." *Scottish Journal of Theology* 36, no. 2 (1983): 213–27.

O'Meara, Thomas. "Of Arts and Theology: Hans Urs von Balthasar's Systems." *Theological Studies* 42, no. 2 (1981): 272–76.

O'Regan, Cyril. *The Anatomy of Misremembering: Von Balthasar's Response to Philosophical Modernity*. Vol. 1, *Hegel*. New York: Crossroad, 2014.

———. *The Heterodox Hegel*. New York: State University of New York Press, 1994.

———. "Two Forms of Catholic Apocalyptic." *International Journal of Systematic Theology* 20, no. 1 (2019): 31–64.

Oster, Stefan. "Thinking Love at the Heart of Things: The Metaphysics of Being as Love in the Work of Ferdinand Ulrich." *Communio* 37, no. 4 (2010): 660–99.

O'Sullivan, Noel. "An Emerging Christology." In *T&T Clark Companion to Henri De Lubac*, edited by Jordan Hillebert, 327–50. London: Bloomsbury T&T Clark, 2017.

Ouellet, Marc. "The Foundations of Christian Ethics according to Hans Urs von Balthasar." *Communio* 17, no. 3 (1990): 375–401.

Pannenberg, Wolfhart. *Jesus, God and Man*. Translated by Lewis L. Wilkins and Duane A. Priebe. Philadelphia: Westminster, 1977.

———. *Systematic Theology*. 2 vols. Translated by Geoffrey W. Bromiley. Grand Rapids, MI: Eerdmans, 1991–1994.

Pesarchick, Robert A. *The Trinitarian Foundation of Human Sexuality as Revealed by Christ according to Hans Urs von Balthasar: The Revelatory Significance of the Male Christ and the Male Ministerial Priesthood*. Rome: Gregorian University Press, 2000.

Peterson, Brandon R. *Being Salvation: Atonement and Soteriology in the Theology of Karl Rahner*. Minneapolis: Fortress, 2017.

———. "Grace in Our Place? The Concept of Representation in the Theology of Karl Rahner." *Theological Studies* 81, no. 2 (2020): 438–52.

Phan, Peter C. "Mystery of Grace and Salvation: Karl Rahner's Theology of the Trinity." In *The Cambridge Companion to the Trinity*, edited by Peter C. Phan, 192–207. Cambridge: Cambridge University Press, 2011.

Pitstick, Alyssa Lyra. *Light in Darkness: Hans Urs von Balthasar and the Catholic Doctrine of Christ's Descent into Hell*. Grand Rapids, MI: Eerdmans, 2007.

Pitstick, Alyssa Lyra, and Edward T. Oakes. "Balthasar, Hell, and Heresy: An Exchange." *First Things*, December 2006, 25–29.

———. "More on Balthasar, Hell, and Heresy." *First Things*, January 2007, 16–18.

Polkinghorne, John. *The Trinity and an Entangled World: Relationality in Physical Science and Theology*. Grand Rapids, MI: Eerdmans 2010.

Pope Francis. *Maiorem hac dilectionem: On the Offer of Life*. The Holy See, July 11, 2017. https://www.vatican.va/content/francesco/en/motu_proprio/documents/papa-francesco-motu-proprio_20170711_maiorem-hac-dilectionem.html.

Prevot, Andrew. "Dialectic and Analogy in Balthasar's 'The Metaphysics of the Saints.'" *Pro Ecclesia* 26, no. 3 (2017): 261–77.

Przywara, Erich. *Analogia Entis, Metaphysics: Original Structure and Universal Rhythm*. Translated by John R. Betz and David Bentley Hart. Grand Rapids, MI: Eerdmans, 2014.

Quash, Ben. "Drama and the Ends of Modernity." In *Balthasar at the End of Modernity*, edited by Lucy Gardner, David Moss, Ben Quash, and Graham Ward, 139–72. Edinburgh: T&T Clark, 1999.

———. "Four Biblical Characters: In Search of Tragedy." In *Christian Theology and Tragedy*, edited by Kevin Taylor and Giles Waller, 15–34. Burlington, VT: Routledge, 2011.

———. *Theology and the Drama of History*. Cambridge: Cambridge University Press, 2005.

Rahner, Karl. *Foundations of Christian Faith: An Introduction to the Idea of Christianity*. Translated by William V. Dych. New York: Seabury Press, 1978.

———. *Theological Investigations*. 23 vols. Various translators. London: Darton, Longman, & Todd, 1961–1984.

———. *The Trinity*. New York: Seabury, 1974.

Ratzinger, Joseph. *Behold the Pierced One: An Approach to a Spiritual Christology*. Translated by Graham Harrison. San Francisco: Ignatius, 1986.

———. "Stellvertretung." In *Handbuch theologischer Grundbegriffe*, edited by Heinrich Fries, 2:566–76. München: Kösel, 1962–63.

Rauser, Randal. "Rahner's Rule: An Emperor without Clothes." *International Journal of Systematic Theology* 7, no. 1 (2005): 91–94.

Riches, Aaron. *Ecce Homo: On the Divine Unity of Christ*. Grand Rapids, MI: Eerdmans, 2016.

Roche, Mark R. "The Greatness and Limits of Hegel's Theory of Tragedy." In *A Companion to Tragedy*, edited by Rebecca Bushnell, 51–67. Oxford: Blackwell, 2005.

Rogers, Eugene F., Jr. *After the Spirit: A Constructive Pneumatology from Resources outside the Modern West*. Grand Rapids, MI: Eerdmans, 2005.

Rosen, Michael. *Hegel's Dialectic and Its Criticism*. Cambridge: Cambridge University Press, 1982.

Rosenberg, Randall Stephen. "Theory and Drama in Balthasar's and Lonergan's Theology of Christ's Consciousness and Knowledge." PhD diss., Boston College, 2008.

Rosenzweig, Franz. *The Star of Redemption*. Translated by William W. Hallo. New York: Holt, Rinehart and Winston, 1971.

Ruddy, Christopher. "'For the Many': The Vicarious-Representative Heart of Joseph Ratzinger's Theology." *Theological Studies* 75, no. 3 (2014): 564–84.

Sara, Juan M. "Secular Institutes according to Hans Urs von Balthasar." *Communio* 29, no. 2 (2002): 309–36.

Schaede, Stephan. *Stellvertretung: Begriffsgeschichtliche Studien zur Soteriologie*. Tübingen: Mohr Siebeck, 2004.

Scheeben, Matthias Joseph. *The Mysteries of Christianity*. Translated by Cyril Vollert. St. Louis: Herder, 1951.

Schindler, D. C. *Hans Urs von Balthasar and the Dramatic Structure of Truth: A Philosophical Investigation*. New York: Fordham University Press, 2004.

———. "A Very Critical Response to Karen Kilby: On Failing to See the Form." *Radical Orthodoxy* 3, no. 1 (2015): 68–87.

Schindler, David L. "The Embodied Person as Gift and the Cultural Task in America: *Status Quaestionis*." *Communio* 35, no. 3 (2008): 397–431.

———, ed. *Hans Urs von Balthasar: His Life and Work*. San Francisco: Ignatius, 1991.

———. *Heart of the World, Center of the Church: Communio Ecclesiology, Liberalism and Liberation*. Grand Rapids, MI: Eerdmans, 2003.

———. "Norris Clarke on Person, Being, and St. Thomas." *Communio* 20, no. 3 (1993): 580–92.

———. "The Person: Philosophy, Theology, and Receptivity." *Communio* 21, no. 1 (1994): 172–90.

Schmemann, Alexander. *For the Life of the World: Sacraments and Orthodoxy*. Crestwood, NY: St. Vladimir's Seminary Press, 1998.

Schmiechen, Peter. *Saving Power: Theories of Atonement and Forms of the Church*. Grand Rapids, MI: Eerdmans, 2005.

Schroeder, C. Paul. Introduction to *On Social Justice*, by Basil the Great. Translated by C. Paul Schroeder. Popular Patristic Series 38. Crestwood, NY: St. Vladimir's Seminary Press, 2009.

Schumacher, Michele, "The Concept of Representation in the Theology of Hans Urs von Balthasar." *Theological Studies* 60, no. 1 (1999): 53–56.

———. *A Trinitarian Anthropology: Adrienne von Speyr and Hans Urs von Balthasar in Dialogue with Thomas Aquinas*. Washington, DC: Catholic University of America Press, 2014.

Schutt, Russell K., Larry J. Seidman, and Matcheri Keshavan, eds. *Social Neuroscience: Brain, Mind, and Society*. Cambridge, MA: Harvard University Press, 2015.

Schwager, Raymund. *Must There Be Scapegoats? Violence and Redemption in the Bible*. San Francisco: Harper and Row, 1989.

Scola, Angelo. *Hans Urs von Balthasar: A Theological Style*. Grand Rapids, MI: Eerdmans, 1991.

Semeniuk, Gregory J. "Salvation through the Father's Representative: Sacrifice in the Biblical Theology of Hans Urs von Balthasar." PhD diss., Boston College, 2014.

Sherman, Robert. *King, Priest, and Prophet: A Trinitarian Theology of Atonement*. New York: T&T Clark, 2004.

Shults, F. LeRon. "A Dubious Christological Formula: From Leontius of Byzantium to Karl Barth." *Theological Studies* 57, no. 3 (1996): 431–46.

Siegel, Daniel J. *The Developing Mind: How Relationships and the Brain Interact to Shape Who We Are*. New York: Guilford Press, 2015.

Simmons, Ernest L. *The Entangled Trinity: Quantum Physics and Theology*. Minneapolis: Fortress Press, 2014.
Sölle, Dorothee. *Christ the Representative: An Essay in Theology after the "Death of God."* Translated by David Lewis. Philadelphia: Fortress, 1967.
Sonderegger, Katherine. *Systematic Theology*. Vol. 1, *The Doctrine of God*. Minneapolis: Fortress Press, 2015.
Soosten, Joachim von. Editor's afterword to *Sanctorum Communio: A Theological Study on the Sociology of the Church*, by Dietrich Bonhoeffer. Vol. 1 of *Dietrich Bonhoeffer Works*. Edited by Clifford J. Green and Joachim von Soosten. Translated by Reinhard Krauss and Nancy Lukens. Minneapolis: Fortress, 1998.
Sykes, S. W., ed. *Sacrifice and Redemption: Durham Essays in Theology*. Cambridge: Cambridge University Press, 1991.
Tanner, Norman P., ed. *Decrees of the Ecumenical Councils*. 2 vols. Washington, DC: Georgetown University Press, 1990.
Taylor, Charles. *The Language Animal: The Full Shape of the Human Linguistic Capacity*. Cambridge, MA: The Belknap Press of Harvard University Press, 2016.
Taylor, Kevin. "Hans Urs von Balthasar and Christ the Tragic Hero." In *Christian Theology and Tragedy*, edited by Kevin Taylor and Giles Waller, 133–48. Burlington, VT: Ashgate, 2011.
Taylor, Kevin, and Giles Waller, eds. *Christian Theology and Tragedy*. Burlington, VT: Ashgate, 2011.
Tidball, Derek, David Hilborn, and Justin Thacker. *The Atonement Debate: Papers from the London Symposium on the Theology of Atonement*. Grand Rapids, MI: Zondervan, 2008.
Tonstad, Linn Marie. *God and Difference: The Trinity, Sexuality, and the Transformation of Finitude*. New York: Routledge, 2016.
Torrance, Alan. "Trinity." In *The Cambridge Companion to Karl Barth*, edited by John Webster, 72–91. Cambridge: Cambridge University Press, 2000.
Torrance, J. B. "The Vicarious Humanity of Christ." In *The Incarnation*, edited by T. F. Torrance, 127–47. Edinburgh: Handsel Press, 1981.
Torrance, Thomas F. *Atonement*. Downers Grove, IL: InterVarsity Press, 2009.
———. *Incarnation: The Person and Life of Christ*. Edited by Robert T. Walker. Downers Grove, IL: InterVarsity Press, 2008.
———. *Trinitarian Perspectives: Toward Doctrinal Agreement*. Edinburgh: T&T Clark, 1994.
Turek, Margaret M. "Towards a Theology of God the Father: Hans Urs von Balthasar's TheoDramatic Approach." PhD diss., University of Fribourg, 1999.

Ulrich, Ferdinand. *Homo Abyssus: The Drama of the Question of Being*. Translated by D. C. Schindler. Washington, DC: Humanum Academic Press, 2018.

———. *Leben in Der Einheit von Leben und Tod*. Einsiedeln: Johannes Verlag, 1999.

Vanhoozer, Kevin J. "The Atonement in Postmodernity: Guilt, Goats, and Gifts." In *The Glory of the Atonement*, edited by Charles Hill and Frank James III, 367–404. Downers Grove, IL: InterVarsity Press, 2004.

———. *The Drama of Doctrine: A Canonical Linguistic Approach to Christian Theology*. Louisville, KY: Westminster John Knox Press, 2005.

———. *Remythologizing Theology: Divine Action, Passion, and Authorship*. Cambridge: Cambridge University Press, 2010.

Van Kuiken, E. Jerome. *Christ's Humanity in Current and Ancient Controversy: Fallen or Not?* London: Bloomsbury T&T Clark, 2017.

Vasko, Elisabeth T. "Suffering and the Search for Wholeness: Beauty and the Cross in Hans Urs von Balthasar and Contemporary Feminist Theologies." PhD diss., Loyola University Chicago, 2009.

Walatka, Todd. "The Church as Sacrament: Gustavo Gutierrez and John Sobrino as Interpreters of *Lumen Gentium*." *Horizons* 42, no. 1 (2015): 70–95.

———. *Von Balthasar and the Option for the Poor: Theodramatics in the Light of Liberation Theology*. Washington, DC: Catholic University of America Press, 2017.

Walker, Adrian J. "Personal Singularity and the *Communio Personarum*: A Creative Development of Thomas Aquinas' Doctrine of *Esse Commune*." *Communio* 31, no. 3 (2004): 457–79.

Wallace, Jennifer. "Tragic Sacrifice and Faith: Abraham and Agamemnon Again." In *Christian Theology and Tragedy*, edited by Kevin Taylor and Giles Waller, 35–52. Burlington, VT: Ashgate, 2011.

Ward, Graham. "Kenosis: Death, Discourse, and Resurrection." In *Balthasar at the End of Modernity*, edited by Lucy Gardner, David Moss, Ben Quash, and Graham Ward, 16–68. Edinburgh: T&T Clark, 1999.

Weaver, Denny J. *The Nonviolent Atonement*. Grand Rapids, IN: Eerdmans, 2001.

Weinandy, Thomas. *Does God Suffer?* Notre Dame, IN: University of Notre Dame, 2000.

———. *The Father's Spirit of Sonship: Reconceiving the Trinity*. Edinburgh: T&T Clark, 1995.

———. *In the Likeness of Sinful Flesh: An Essay on the Humanity of Christ*. Edinburgh: T&T Clark, 1993.

Weinandy, Thomas, and Daniel A. Keating, eds. *The Theology of St. Cyril of Alexandria*. London: T&T Clark, 2003.

White, Thomas Joseph, ed. *The Analogy of Being: Invention of the Antichrist or the Wisdom of God?* Grand Rapids, MI: Eerdmans, 2011.

Wigley, Stephen. *Karl Barth and Hans Urs Von Balthasar: A Critical Engagement.* Edinburgh: T&T Clark, 2007.

Williams, A. N. *The Ground of Union: Deification in Aquinas and Palamas.* Oxford: Oxford University Press, 1999.

Williams, Delores. "Black Women's Surrogacy Experience and the Christian Notion of Redemption." In *After Patriarchy: Feminist Transformations of the World Religions*, edited by Paul M. Cooey, William R. Eakin, and Jay B. McDaniel, 1–14. Maryknoll, NY: Orbis, 1991.

Williams, Robert R. *Tragedy, Recognition, and the Death of God: Studies in Hegel and Nietzsche.* Oxford: Oxford University Press, 2012.

Williams, Rowan. "Balthasar and Rahner." In *The Analogy of Beauty: The Theology of Hans Urs von Balthasar*, edited by John Riches, 11–34. Edinburgh: T&T Clark, 1986.

———. "Balthasar and the Trinity." In Oakes and Moss, eds., *The Cambridge Companion to Hans Urs von Balthasar*, 37–50.

———. *Christ the Heart of Creation.* London: Bloomsbury Continuum, 2018.

———. "Dialectic and Analogy: A Theological Legacy." In *Religion*, edited by Nicholas Boyle and Liz Disley, vol. 4, *The Impact of Idealism: The Legacy of Post-Kantian German Thought*, edited by Nicholas Adams, 274–92. Cambridge: Cambridge University Press, 2013.

———. *The Edge of Words: God and the Habits of Language.* London: Bloomsbury, 2014.

———. *Eucharistic Sacrifice: The Roots of a Metaphor.* Grove Liturgical Studies 31. Cambridge: Grove Books, 1982.

———. *On Augustine.* London: Bloomsbury, 2016.

———. *On Christian Theology.* Oxford: Blackwell, 2000.

———. *Sergii Bulgakov: Towards a Russian Political Theology.* Edinburgh: T&T Clark, 1999.

———. *The Tragic Imagination.* Oxford: Oxford University Press, 2016.

———. "Trinity and Ontology." In *Christ, Ethics, and Tragedy: Essays in Honour of Donald MacKinnon*, edited by Kenneth Surin, 71–92. Cambridge: Cambridge University Press, 1989.

———. *Wrestling with Angels: Conversations in Modern Theology.* Edited by Mike Higton. Grand Rapids, MI: Eerdmans, 2007.

Wright, N. T. *The Day the Revolution Began: Reconsidering the Meaning of Jesus's Crucifixion.* San Francisco: HarperOne, 2016.

Wynn, Mark R. *Faith and Place: An Essay in Embodied Religious Epistemology.* Oxford: Oxford University Press, 2009.

Yenson, Mark L. *Existence as Prayer.* Oxford: Peter Lang, 2013.

Young, Frances. *God's Presence: A Contemporary Recapitulation of Early Christianity.* Cambridge: Cambridge University Press, 2013.

Young, Frances M., and Andrew Teal. *From Nicaea to Chalcedon: A Guide to the Literature and Its Background.* Grand Rapid, MI: Baker, 2010.

Zeitz, James V. "Przywara and von Balthasar on Analogy." *Thomist* 52, no. 3 (1998): 473–98.

INDEX

absolute relation, 32
Adams, Nicholas, 55–56, 94, 193n19, 195n52, 199n162
admirabile commercium. See exchange formula
analogia entis, 21–32, 49, 56, 62, 68–75, 93, 144, 154, 189n135
Anselm of Canterbury, 9, 45, 93, 99–101, 120
anthropology, 62, 69
apophaticism, 154
Aquinas, Thomas, 23–24, 43, 60–64, 72, 154–55, 188n130
Arianism, 25, 45
Athanasius, 45, 109, 113, 123, 128, 133, 197n107
atheism, 117
Augustine of Hippo, 24, 72, 78, 122, 155, 171

Barth, Karl, 4, 44–45, 53–54, 69–70, 75, 80, 82–83, 109, 111, 134–37
Basil the Great, 136, 140
Begbie, Jeremy, 31
Behr, John, 113, 123, 192n192
being
    finite, 23–25, 41–47, 55, 168
    infinite, 23–25, 34, 43–44, 75, 168, 186n113, 188n130

Belousek, Darrin W. Snyder, 101, 103
Bernanos, 146, 156
Bieler, Martin, 24–25, 32, 43, 153, 185n99
Bonhoeffer, Dietrich, 2, 132, 134–35, 156–62, 179n95
Buber, Martin, 58, 194n31
Bulgakov, Sergius, 25, 183n53

Calvin, John, 101, 134
Carpenter, Anne, 13, 53, 124
Cavanaugh, William, 160
church
    agency, 138, 142–44
    institutional nature of, 132
    marks, 161
    mediation, 148
    political nature of, 148, 157, 160–62
Christ, and Christology
    beatific vision, 66, 116
    Chalcedonian dogma, 55, 57, 69–70, 72, 74–75, 84, 106, 193n19
    Christocentrism, 69–71, 81
    consciousness, 64–68
    enhypostasis, 70–72
    "from above" and "from below," 67, 78, 81, 197n107

Christ, and Christology (*continued*)
  hypostatic union, 65, 70–71, 78, 137
  impassibility, 54, 113, 117–19, 123
  omniscience, 66
  tertium quid, 54–55, 70
  two–will formula, 64–68
Ciraulo, Jonathan Martin, 140, 212n3
Clarke, W. Norris, 45, 188n130
communio sanctorum, 8, 132–33, 135, 139–41, 144–45, 152, 156, 161
concrete *analogia entis*, 69, 72–75, 103, 154
covenant, 95–96, 99, 101–2, 104, 106–7, 128
creaturely being. *See* being: finite
Cyril of Alexandria, 70, 109, 138, 141, 197n95

Day, Dorothy, 160, 220n176
death on behalf of others, 146–47
deification, 10, 13, 18, 48–49, 82, 90, 111–12, 132–39, 141, 208n177, 212n3
de Lubac, Henri, 1–2, 12, 46, 91
de Régnon, Theodore, 181n17
Deus semper maior, 23, 93
dialectic, 42, 54–57, 67–68, 73–75, 84–86, 95, 101, 106, 127, 148
dialogical philosophy, 58, 74, 194n32
difference. *See* distance
discipleship, 132
distance, 19–40, 47–49, 71–73, 96–99, 111–14, 124–27, 186n113
divine being. *See* being: infinite
divine freedom. *See* freedom: infinite
divinization. *See* deification
Dostoevsky, Fyodor, 121

epic, 8, 53, 94, 102, 118, 148–51, 155
eternal blessedness, 126
eternal *eucharistia*, 38, 104, 126–28, 138
ethics, 2, 156–61
exchange formula, 8, 18–19, 47–50, 78–79, 109–11, 192n192
expiation, 99, 102–4, 204n102

feminism, 2 189n138
flesh, 45–46, 72, 78–79, 109–113, 123, 197n107, 207n175, 208n177
Ford, David, 123
forensic logic, 44–46, 82, 107, 134, 137, 166
forsakenness, 26, 34, 49, 103, 110, 114–18, 124–29, 163
freedom
  finite, 42, 45, 57, 66–67, 82, 96–97, 119, 125, 127–28
  infinite, 20, 26, 45, 58, 65, 96–97, 127, 186n108
fruitfulness, 132, 139, 147, 189n138
fugue, 31, 34

Gallaher, Brandon, 56, 72, 186n108
German idealism, 42, 58
Girard, René, 105
Gregory of Nazianzus, 109–10, 185n86
Gregory of Nyssa, 24, 27, 73, 93, 109–10, 135, 139, 152, 154, 190n141, 208n177
Grillmeier, Aloys, 197n107

Hart, David Bentley, 120–22, 207n175
Healy, Nicholas, 28
Hegel, 21–22, 35, 42, 55–56, 61, 120, 149–50, 182n23, 193n15, 193n19
Hengel, Martin, 204n97
hermeneutics, 91–95, 107, 111
Heschel, Abraham, 102, 204n99
Hoffmann, Norbert, 12, 36–38, 187n116, 187n120
Holy Saturday, 115–16
Horner, Robyn, 26–27, 34
human freedom. *See* freedom: finite
human responsibility, 46–47, 83, 157, 159, 170

Ignatius of Loyola, 58, 132, 140
imago Trinitatis, 41
imparted righteousness, 134, 160
imputed righteousness, 134
in-Christ formula, 76, 82, 134
infinite gratitude. *See* eternal *eucharistia*
Irenaeus, 78, 107, 192n192
Irving, Edward, 109

Jenson, Robert, 31, 157
John of Damascus, 70–73, 110
Johnson, Junius, 8–9
judgment, 100, 103, 118, 209n221
justice, 99–103, 204n99

kenosis, *see* Trinity: self-emptying
Kierkegaard, Søren, 120
Kilby, Karen, 28, 61, 94, 153, 155
King, Martin Luther, Jr., 160

Lactantius, 102
Levering, Matthew, 27–28, 56, 184n70
liberation, 119, 125, 140, 160–61, 209n221
Logos-sarx Christology, 70, 72–73, 197n95, 197n107
Luther, Martin, 9, 47, 49, 110–11, 134
lyric, 149

Mackinnon, Donald, 61, 120, 123
maior dissimilitudo, 30, 43, 69, 73, 106
Martin, Jennifer Newsome, 11, 35, 53, 155, 185n98
martyr, 125, 146–49, 161–63
Maximus the Confessor, 56, 64–68, 73–75, 196n69
mediator, 117, 135
modes of being, 65
Moltmann, Jürgen, 21–22, 35, 186n113, 209n203, 209n221
monophysitism, 54–55, 69–72, 74, 197n95
monothelitism, 70, 72, 74
moral exemplar model of atonement, 142, 145
movement of finitization, 24, 25, 29, 104
Murphy, Francesca, 120–22

Nestorianism, 54–55, 60, 68, 70, 74
Nichols, Aidan, 8–9, 50, 61, 169, 186n113, 205n132

O'Regan, Cyril, 11, 32, 67, 82, 117, 119, 185n87

Pannenberg, Wolfhart, 198n113
Péguy, Charles, 4, 219n159
penal substitution, 9–10, 79, 89, 99, 101, 103–7, 117, 203n73
personalism, 53, 74
Pitstick, Alyssa Lyra, 9, 89, 104–5, 208n195
Pope Francis, 160
Prevot, Andrew, 56
procession/mission distinction, 59–64, 67, 74, 127
pro nobis formula, 41–47, 79–80, 103, 111, 132, 146, 187n120, 200n167
propitiation, 103, 204n102
Przywara, Erich, 12, 21–30, 49, 75, 143, 155–66
punishment, 95, 100, 102–6, 110, 118, 123

Quash, Ben, 6, 94, 120–22, 157

Rahner, Karl, 3, 5, 21–22, 46, 79, 83, 99–100, 175n26, 176n48, 181nn17–18, 199n140, 200n167, 203n73
Ratzinger, Joseph, 2, 5, 65
recapitulation, 103, 113
receptivity, 37–40, 43, 46, 59, 62–63, 97–98, 188n130, 189n135, 189n138
replacement, 3, 79–80, 83–84, 135, 170, 176n48
Repräsentation, 3–4, 117, 175n26, 199n140, 200n167, 219n159
restoration, 101–2, 107–8
Rogers, Eugene, 136, 140
Romero, Oscar, 160

sacrament, 138, 159
sacrifice, 9, 25–26, 29, 105, 113, 125
saints, 135–36, 141, 147–48, 153, 160–61. See also *communio sanctorum*
sanctification. See deification
satisfaction, 99, 105, 169
scapegoat, 105, 113
Schindler, D. C., 151, 153
Schumacher, Michele, 3, 9–10, 76
secular institutes, 154
sexual difference, 28, 189n138
Simeon the Stylite, 220n176
simplicity, 20, 24, 27–29, 32–35
solidarity, 4–5, 43, 111–17, 219n159
Sölle, Dorothee, 3, 7, 80, 82–83, 131, 148, 179n95, 216n74, 216n85
Speyr, Adrienne von, 4, 147, 182n28, 189n131
super-action, 108
super-death, 25
supra-personal, 59

Taylor, Charles, 150
Taylor, Kevin, 123–24
theandric energy, 64–65, 144
theological method, 6, 9–11, 91–95, 149–56
theosis. See deification
Tonstad, Linn Marie, 20, 28–29, 39
tradition, 10–12, 35, 151–55, 166–67, 174n13
tragedy, 49, 119–128, 162–63
tragic hero, 121–26
Trinity
    analogy, 23–29, 33–35, 38 60–64, 118, 125, 189n135
    appropriation, 27, 35, 40

begotten, 25, 33, 38, 61
fruitfulness, 40–41, 132
generation, 22, 25–26, 33–41, 61, 122, 128, 188n130
interpersonal, 26–27, 37, 40, 48, 98, 186n113, 189n134
inseparable operations, 20, 27, 33–34, 40, 43, 48
personal distinctions, 27, 33, 40, 112
procession, 36–41, 48, 59–64, 67, 114, 127, 188n130
pro-Nicaea, 20, 23–24, 27, 33
receptivity, 34, 37–40, 43, 46, 49, 59, 62–63, 125, 139, 188n130, 189n135, 189n138
riskiness, 26, 189n135
self-emptying, 22, 25, 28–29, 32, 124
self-giving, 8, 26, 34–35, 38–39, 50, 96, 123–28, 139–40, 162, 186n113

surprise, 33, 40
"trinitarian revival," 20–21
wills, 33

Ulrich, Ferdinand, 12, 24–25, 29, 39, 43, 104, 144, 151, 155, 185n99, 194n35

Vanhoozer, Kevin, 28, 100
Vorstellung, 150

Walatka, Todd, 11–13, 125, 148
Weinandy, Thomas, 118, 133
Williams, Rowan, 3, 75, 90, 94, 100, 118, 124, 132, 135, 143, 148–50, 156, 179n95
Wittgenstein, Ludwig, 150
wrath, 99–104, 107, 118, 162

Young, Frances, 197n95

Zhiming, Wang, 160

JACOB LETT is a lecturer in theology and associate dean at Nazarene Theological College.

www.ingramcontent.com/pod-product-compliance
Lightning Source LLC
Chambersburg PA
CBHW061437300426
44114CB00014B/1720